E. L. DOCTOROW
Essays & Conversations

Ontario Review Press Critical Series

E. L. DOCTOROW
Essays and Conversations

◆————————————————————————

edited by
Richard Trenner

 ONTARIO REVIEW PRESS
Princeton, New Jersey

Library of Congress Cataloging in Publication Data
E. L. Doctorow, essays and conversations.
1. Doctorow, E. L., 1931– —Criticism and interpretation—
Addresses, essays, lectures. 2. Doctorow, E. L., 1931– —
Interviews.   I. Doctorow, E. L., 1931–   II. Trenner,
Richard.   III. Title: E. L. Doctorow, essays and conversations.

PS3554.03Z63   1982   813'.54   82–12569
ISBN 0-86538-023-6
ISBN 0-86538-024-4 (pbk.)

Book design by Larry Zirlin
Photos by Richard Trenner

Distributed by Persea Books, Inc.
225 Lafayette St.
New York, NY 10012

Acknowledgements

I wish to thank Joyce Carol Oates, who suggested a book of essays and interviews devoted to E. L. Doctorow. I am grateful, too, to E. L. Doctorow, who, in meetings in Philadelphia, Princeton, New York, and New Rochelle, and through letters and telephone conversations, freely discussed his work and ideas and made what disinterested editorial suggestions he could.

Grateful acknowledgment is made to Random House, Inc. and E. L. Doctorow for permission to quote from the following works of the author: *Welcome to Hard Times,* © 1960; *The Book of Daniel,* © 1971; *Ragtime,* © 1974, 1975; *Drinks Before Dinner,* © 1979; and *Loon Lake,* © 1979, 1980. All copyright by E. L. Doctorow.

"False Documents" by E. L. Doctorow originally appeared, in slightly different form, in *American Review* No. 26 (November 1977), pp. 215–232. Copyright © 1981 by E. L. Doctorow. Reprinted by permission.

"A Spirit of Transgression" by Larry McCaffery will appear in *Anything Can Happen: Interviews with Contemporary American Novelists,* conducted and edited by Tom LeClair and Larry McCaffery, University of Illinois Press, 1983. Printed by permission.

"Politics and the Mode of Fiction" by Richard Trenner originally appeared in *The Ontario Review,* No. 16 (Spring-Summer 1982), pp. 5–16. Copyright © 1982 by The Ontario Review, Inc. Reprinted by permission.

"The Writer As Independent Witness" by Paul Levine was conducted in March, 1978 for the Canadian Broadcasting Corporation as part of the radio series *Ideas.* Printed by permission.

CONTENTS

Introduction

IN THE CHRONOLOGY of the making of this first book devoted to the study of E. L. Doctorow's writing, the "Introduction" comes last. Having collected as many interesting and useful pieces as I could find or commission—an essay and a speech by Doctorow, three interviews with him, and several critical articles—it is now my job to try to say just what it is I've made. That is a difficult job. This volume presumes to speak with so many voices and to express so many ideas that any attempt to reach the high ground of critical consensus is destined to falter under the weight of qualification. Yet what makes my present task hard is what most makes this collection potentially valuable to the reader of Doctorow's fiction: the multiplicity of critical theories, vocabularies, styles, themes—even prejudices—given free play in it. As if this book recorded an extended and passionate debate on E. L. Doctorow's work, it should unsettle and complicate, as much as confirm and clarify, the reader's sense of the subject. And, I like to think, Doctorow himself would approve of the partly unsettling and complicating force of the critical voices assembled here: After all, one of his chief strategies as a novelist is to assume a dazzling variety of voices in order to state and restate his vision of the order of things. "It was evident to him that the world composed and recomposed itself constantly in an endless process of dissatisfaction." Doctorow writes that of the Little Boy narrator of *Ragtime,* but the words apply equally to his work as a novelist and, in an important sense, to the pieces in this collection, seen as a whole.

In selecting and editing the pieces, then, I have resisted accrediting any one critical method at the expense of another and have tried instead to choose articles that together chart the full spectrum of available opinion. Because it was feasible to commission only a few pieces, I have had to limit most of my choices to previously published articles; and while these indeed offer a rich variety of themes and "approaches," I believe that the coming years will extend that variety considerably, as criticism responds to the growth of Doctorow's canon and the fortunes of his reputation. Although Doctorow's first novel, *Welcome to Hard Times,* was published nearly twenty-five years ago, only in the last seven years, since *Ragtime*'s extraordinary critical and popular success, has his work received sustained, non-journalistic attention.

But to get some sense of the present range of interpretation and the kinds of critical ideas and problems being generated by Doctorow's writing, consider briefly just three of the pieces that appear in this volume: Barbara Foley's "From *U.S.A.* to *Ragtime:* Notes on the Forms of Historical Consciousness in Modern Fiction," John Clayton's "Radical Jewish Humanism: The Vision of E. L. Doctorow," and David S. Gross's "Tales of Obscene Power: Money and Culture, Modernism and History in the Fiction of E. L. Doctorow." Each of the three essayists approaches Doctorow with radically different critical intents, and each succeeds in isolating an interesting aspect of the novelist's work. Barbara Foley sets herself two tasks in her carefully documented, broadly allusive article. First, she describes what she sees as the influence of John Dos Passos, and especially of the *U.S.A.* trilogy, on subject matter and narrative technique in *Ragtime.* And second, she presents her case for a recent, profound shift—a shift symbolized on opposing sides by Dos Passos and Doctorow—in novelists' (intellectuals') collective sense of history's epistemological status. In Dos Passos' work, according to Foley, history has a privileged status because it is seen as fundamentally coherent and verifiable, whereas Doctorow understands history as an artful construct of the willful imagination. History for Professor Foley's Doctorow is, in the end, only another—if brilliant—form of narrative.

And what is the critic's attitude toward the deep shift in historical consciousness that she perceives? Foley writes:

> What I ultimately find disturbing about *Ragtime*—and about many other works of contemporary historical fiction, whether "apocalyptic" or "documentary"—is its underlying postulate that whatever coherence emerges from the represented historical world is attributable to the writer's power as teller of his story, with the result that the process of historical reconstruction itself, rather than what is being represented, comes to the fore.

Conveniently, Doctorow "responds" to Foley's point (to reaffirm for this volume its status as a debate) through his seminal essay "False Documents," in which he makes explicit his view of history's status. Near the close of that piece, Doctorow writes: "I am thus led to the proposition that there is no fiction or nonfiction as we commonly understand the distinction: there is only narrative." But immediately (and with characteristic irony) he complicates his formulation by noting, a little demurely: "But it is a novelist's proposition, I can see that very well." The "debate," of course, is far from closed, but to conclude this brief—and, I hope, enticing—look at Foley's essay, I can simply observe that history's status is a central problem not only in the broad fields of contemporary philosophy and literary theory, but also in so local a matter as reading Doctorow's historical fictions *well*.

Very different critical values inform John Clayton's view of E. L. Doctorow as a "radical Jewish humanist." Where Foley is concerned with Doctorow's view of history and his place in the development of the American historical novel, Clayton is interested in him as both product and expression of a specifically Jewish ethos. The distance from Foley to Clayton—from a dispassionate, text-centered reading, to a deliberately emotional, personality-centered study—is great indeed. Clayton's Doctorow is "radical" in his on-going critique of power in capitalist society, "Jewish" in his heightened responsiveness to human suffering, and "humanist" in his apparently complete rejection of the supernatural. More than any other critic represented here, Professor Clayton offers a reading of Doctorow's fiction as an expression of the artist's unique emotional and intellectual experiences. The humanism that Clayton attributes to Doctorow, if not explicitly defined, seems hardly arguable: In Doctorow's fiction, God is a purely human metaphor, either for power or the longing engendered by a chronically felt absence or loss. I find Clayton's analysis of Doctorow's essentially Jewish values and habits of radical critique both moving and persuasive, and Doctorow himself corroborates Clayton's characterization. Toward the end of a conversation with me ("Politics and the Mode of Fiction"), he observed, "To get back to the idea of a radical Jewish humanist tradition, if I was not in that tradition, I would certainly want to apply for membership." Earlier he described growing up "in a lower-middle-class environment of generally enlightened, socialist sensibility." As Clayton demonstrates, the psychological, political, and religious heritage of that early environment is variously at work in Doctorow's novels—even in *Welcome to Hard Times,* whose Dakota Territory setting is so foreign to the New York City of the thirties and forties that was Doctorow's childhood world. Summarizing his picture of Doctorow's Jewish heritage, Clayton observes:

> . . . caring and doing for other people and a critical attitude to contemporary myths do not belong to Jews. But Jewish culture has always insisted on these qualities; Jewish culture is a deep channel through which such a spirit flows. It is one of the sources of the vision of E. L. Doctorow.

To illustrate the lively and insistent pluralism of critical approaches to Doctorow, consider one final example—"Tales of Obscene Power: Money and Culture, Modernism and History in the Fiction of E. L. Doctorow'' by David S. Gross. Although Professor Gross's theme is radically different from both Foley's and Clayton's, his essay manages to combine the former's allusive rigor with the latter's quite emotional intent. Gross adopts the self-conscious vocabularies of a Marxist hermeneutic and Freudian psychoanalysis to throw into relief the ubiquitous rhetoric of money and money's power in Doctorow's fiction. An awareness of this rhetorical pattern is important to any useful reading of Doctorow. But straining restlessly in the shadows of Gross's extra-literary language and imposing theoretical structure is—a moral passion. One example:

> Time, we are told, is money. And that linear, urgent preoccupation with time is, like money, neurotic and correlative with instinctual repression. Obsessed with time, burdened with an urgent, guilty fear, we retreat into that greedy money/excrement complex, repressing our awareness of what we really need and desire and of the terrible cost of the renunciation we have accepted. To the extent that the money complex rules our culture and our society they are hostile to life and bent on self-destruction.

Here Marx and Freud amalgamated are applied to Doctorow, and these hard insights bear the passionate mark (I intuit) of some experiences keenly lived—or keenly desired—by the author of the passage. Gross thoroughly surveys all four of Doctorow's historical fictions to assemble much evidence of the artist's conscious preoccupation with the deeply economic—and corrupt?—side of life. In Gross's view, what is so extraordinary about Doctorow's fiction is not the mere chronic presence of money's force (probably all novels bear money's imprint), but its explicit, *acknowledged* presence. Gross writes:

> In the four historical novels of E. L. Doctorow both the power of money and our reluctance to acknowledge it are centrally significant. . . . In particular, his historical fictions engage two areas of crucial significance: he makes our distortion and repression of awareness of the heart of the matter—what it means to live in a society where money's power is so complete—a central subject in his works, and he establishes the connections among money, excrement and power with savage irony.

Barbara Foley, John Clayton, David S. Gross—and all the other contributors to this book: each an eager analyst of E. L. Doctorow's fictional world.

Whatever the reader's own theories and habits of analysis, it is easy to take keen, if secret, pleasure in the range of readings (perhaps the strong misreadings?) to which Doctorow, like any sophisticated writer, seems subject in these days of intense and multifarious critical activity. I believe that one of the great pleasures of literature lies, really, in one text's ability to inspire other texts "in an endless process of dissatisfaction." That, in any event, is a proposition to which the essays and conversations in this volume prolifically attest.

Having suggested the breadth and vitality of critical approaches to Doctorow's fiction by considering a random trio of essays, I would like to make a few observations, fundamentally my own, about E. L. Doctorow. I need to be aggressively selective in what I say because of the sheer quantity and complexity of possibilities that haunt phrases like "a writer's development" or "a writer's relation to his culture." As such phrases apply to Doctorow, I might, for instance, consider the various narrative styles he has developed—from the (ostensibly) simple language and linear first-person storytelling of *Welcome to Hard Times* to the willfully difficult syntax, restlessly shifting point-of-view, and shuffled chronology of *Loon Lake*. Or taking up a very different sort of question—one of cultural values and the force of reputation rather than of style and language—I might speculate on Doctorow's quite rare ability to combine serious themes and big audiences. But I want instead to write about what I consider Doctorow's most important quality: his moral vision. I hope that a brief consideration of Doctorow's values will not too much distress the reader who thinks that criticism should confine itself to historical or textual problems. And I know that there is no simple connection to be made between virtuous ideas and good art. But I do believe that Doctorow is so determinedly—and importantly—a moralist that his values are very much worth considering. For me, at least, the essential Doctorow (if I may, for the work of analysis, posit such a quantity) is concerned with the morality of connection and disconnection—of human relatedness and unrelatedness—on various scales, from an entire society to a single family.

Doctorow is both consciously and intuitively committed to an ideal of universal justice, yet he is everywhere confronted by the failure of that ideal.

It is in the tension between aspiration and disillusionment that he finds the themes of his fiction. I once asked Doctorow to characterize his "social ideals." He answered:

> There is a presumption of universality to the ideal of justice—social justice, economic justice. It cannot exist for a part or class of society; it must exist for all. And it's a Platonic ideal, too—that everyone be able to live as he or she is endowed to live; that if a person is in his genes a poet, he be able to practice his poetry. Plato defined justice as the fulfillment of a person's truest self. That's good for starters.

Given so exalted a sense of what life *ought* to offer, it follows that Doctorow concerns himself in his writing with the relentless, often futile, struggle for fulfillment. As a humanist ("All the solutions were to be found right here on earth, and the supernatural was not taken seriously," Doctorow has said of his childhood ethos), he locates the cause of failure and injustice in the social forces that ineffably combine with hearts and minds to *make* individual destinies; chief among them: politics, economics, and class hierarchies. Doctorow repeatedly presents characters struggling for fulfillment against the often destructive or repressive effects of such forces. In good fortune's arbitrary absence, the only counter-force is perception—is understanding and articulating how politics, economics, and social class deeply impinge on individual lives. And frequently, that "counter-force" can be no more than tragic knowledge or, in Doctorow's words, "the solace of shared perceptions."

How does Doctorow bear witness to the human hunger for fulfillment? The chief purely literary way, it seems to me, is through the ironic juxtaposition of contraries—contraries of a remarkable range. That range extends from (and, of course, beyond) passages that violate taboos by ironically uniting ideas or images which the prevailing social order would insist remain apart; to extended patterns of value-laden symbolism; to entire plots that yoke together mutually exclusive social classes or conflicting political philosophies. Let me give an example of each of these three strategies of ironic perception. First, consider one of Joe's raging soliloquies in *Loon Lake*. Doctorow uses a parody of a Hollywood dance sequence and alternates opposing emotions and images to represent the alienated worker's miserable relation to that ingenius instrument and metaphor of modern capitalism, the assembly line:

Then they speed things up and I'm going too slow I drop one of the tin pots on the wrong side of the belt the guy there is throwing tires on wheel rims and giving the tubes a pump or two of air he ignores my shouts he can't take the time. And then the foreman is coming down the line to pay me a call I can't hear him but I don't have to—a red bulging neck of rage.

And then they stop coddling us and throw the throttle to full and this is how I handle it: I am Fred Astaire in top hat and tails tossing up the screws into the holes, bouncing the frames on the floor and catching them in my top hat of tin. I twirl the headlight kick it on the belt with a backward flip of my heel. I never stop moving and when the belt is too slow for me I jump up and stomp it along faster, my arms outstretched. Soon everyone in the plant has picked up on my routine—everyone is dancing! The foreman comes pirouetting along, putting stars next to each name on his clipboard. And descending from the steel rafter by insulated wire to dance backward on the moving parade of car bodies, Mr. Bennett himself in white tie and tails. He's singing with a smile, he's flinging money from his hands like stardust.

Shit, how many more hours of this . . . I thought of Clara I thought of us driving to California in the spring. And then I thought, What if she just left, what if she met someone and said to him, *How do I get out of here?*

And then I resolved not to think at all, if I couldn't think well of Clara, I'd turn my mind from her knowing I was racked, knowing I couldn't physically feel hope in this hammering noise. But I didn't have to try not to think, by the middle of the afternoon my bones were vibrating like tuning forks. And so it had me, Bennett Autobody, just where it wanted me and I was screwed to the machines taking their form a mile away in the big shed, those black cars composed bit by bit from our life and the gift of opposition of thumb and forefinger, those precious vehicles, each one a hearse.

In their direct expression of rage and exhaustion, parts of the passage are hardly ironic, of course. But generally, Doctorow's description of Joe on the assembly line—especially the bitter Fred Astaire fantasy—shows the strategy of ironic juxtaposition in the service of a radical critique brilliantly employed on a small scale.

To see the same sort of linking of contraries at work on a much broader scale, recall the symbolic force of architecture in *The Book of Daniel*. Many buildings, public and private, figure in Doctorow's tragic meditation on the fate of radicals and radicalism in post-World War II America; among them: the state psychiatric hospital to which Susan Isaacson is committed after her suicide attempt ("Designed with the idea that madness might be soothed in a setting of architectural beauty''); the pathetic business establishment of Isaacson Radio, Sales and Repair (''On the bed of the window, resting on old curled crepe paper, bleached grey, are two display radios—a table model and a console with cloth-covered doors and a combination automatic record changer. When you go inside you see that the two window display radios have nothing inside them''); the Lewins' house in Brookline, where for several years Susan and Daniel Isaacson try to live out the illusion that they are normal, middle-class children (''built for two families and designed to look as if it contained only one''); the wretched little house amid ''the obscurity of Bronx architecture'' in which the Isaacson family lives (''He had an odd house. It was the only house on the whole street unattached to any other''); the federal court house in Foley Square, where Paul and Rochelle Isaacson are tried and condemned (''designed to promote the illusion of solemn justice''); the prison in which the Isaacsons die (''We are clients of a new law firm, Voltani, Ampere, and Ohm. If you've seen one prison you've seen them all''); even Disneyland, where Daniel goes to confront his parents' betrayer (''What Disneyland proposes is a technique of abbreviated shorthand culture for the masses, a mindless thrill, like an electric shock, that insists at the same time on the recipient's rich psychic relation to his country's history and language and literature''). Though scarcely complete, this catalogue suggests Doctorow's method of using physical details to symbolize—generally to ironic effect—moral conditions. In *The Book of Daniel,* the narrator's parents end up in the electric chair at Sing Sing while the man who denounced them ends up in Disneyland at Christmastime. On the face of it, these are utterly different fates, but in a novel whose epigraph might well be ''The failure to make connections is complicity,'' they are *not* so different: Doctorow locates Disneyland in ''a town somewhere between Buchenwald and Belsen'' and subjects it to a long and fierce mock-sociological analysis.

Finally, to illustrate what I have called Doctorow's technique of ironic juxtaposing that yokes together in entire plots mutually exclusive social classes or conflicting political philosophies, I can cite his most widely read novel, *Ragtime.* Here he places together social groups that in ''real life'' would almost never directly interact except in rigidly prescribed roles which acknowledge unequal power. These social groups include disfranchised blacks (represented by Coalhouse Walker and his followers); poor immigrants (like Tateh, a Latvian Jew); the white middle class (exemplified by the family from New Rochelle); radicals (like Emma Goldman); and the aristocracy of capital (the chief examples, Henry Ford and Pierpont Morgan). Only an imagination determined to forge together social contraries for moral and analytic purposes would populate one book with ironic representatives of so many different social classes. In the course of *Ragtime,* the various characters act and react in patterns that reveal the fragmenting forces of money, politics, and class—forces often inimical to individual fulfillment. But the social vision of *Ragtime* is less dark (almost genial by comparison) than the tragic meditations of its two predecessors, *Welcome to Hard Times* and *The Book of Daniel,* and Doctorow is able to give it an ending that is "happy," at least for a few of the characters. In a sunny fantasy of social justice, he closes the novel by giving Tateh, that lucky salesman of America's idealized cultural aspirations, the idea for a successful series of movies:

> One morning Tateh looked out the window of his study and saw the three children sitting on the lawn. Behind them on the sidewalk was a tricycle. They were talking and sunning themselves. His daughter, with dark hair, his tow-headed stepson and his legal responsibility, the schwartze child. He suddenly had an idea for a film. A bunch of children who were pals, white black, fat thin, rich poor, all kinds, mischievous little urchins who would have funny adventures in their own neighborhood, a society of ragamuffins, like all of us, a gang, getting into trouble and getting out again. Actually not one movie but several were made of this vision. And by that time the era of Ragtime had run out, with the heavy breath of the machine, as if history were no more than a tune on a player piano.

This vision is a variation of Doctorow's essential moral theme of the ideal of "universal justice." To repeat the definition Doctorow once gave me of his "social ideals":

> There is a presumption of universality to the ideal of justice—social justice, economic justice. It cannot exist for a part or class of society; it must exist for all. And it's a Platonic ideal, too—that everyone ought to be able to live as he or she is endowed to live; that if a person in his genes is a poet, he be able to practice his poetry. Plato defined justice as the fulfillment of a person's truest self. That's good for starters.

RICHARD TRENNER
Princeton, New Jersey

I
E. L. DOCTOROW

For the Artist's Sake

I HAVE ALWAYS DISLIKED the phrase "the arts." It connotes to me furs and black ties and cocktail receptions, the patronage by the wealthy of work that is tangential to their lives, or that fills them not with dread or awe or visionary joy but with self-satisfaction.

"The arts" have nothing to do with the loneliness of writers or painters working in their rooms year after year, or with actors putting together plays in lofts, or with dancers tearing up their bodies to make spatial descriptions of the hope of beauty or transcendent truth.

So as a working writer I distinguish myself from the arts community. I am confirmed in this when I look at the National Endowment for the Arts' board and program structure. In the past, a very small percentage of the arts budget has been given over to literature, to the grants made to young writers or dramatists or poets of promise. In all the time since its founding, the N.E.A. has found only four writers worthy to sit on its immense board. Instead, the heavy emphasis has been on museums, opera companies, symphony orchestras: just those entities that happen to cater to patrons of "the arts."

I suppose I would have to confess, if asked, that I feel about opera, for instance, that it is not a living art in this country, that we do not naturally write and produce operas from ourselves as a matter of course as, for example, Italy did in the nineteenth century, and that, therefore, as wonderful and exciting as opera production may be, it is essentially the work of conservation of European culture; opera companies are conservators of the past, like museums, and their support by the National Endowment reflects the strong bias or belief in the arts as something from the past rather than the present.

The National Endowment programs I value most are just those likely to be proscribed: first, the programs of individual grants to individual artists in whatever medium—the programs endowing directly the work of living artists; and, second, those programs that do not separate the arts from life, from our own life and times but emphasize the connection—the artists-in-education program, the poets who go into schools, for example, and help children to light the spark in themselves. I cannot imagine anything more

Speech before a subcommittee of the House Appropriations Committee, Fall, 1981.

responsible than the work persuading a schoolchild to express his or her anguished or joyful observations—and to be self-rewarded with a poem or a painting. Whole lives ride on moments like that.

Or the inter-arts programs, the folk arts, the expansion arts—all bureaucratic terms for encouraging experiment and risk-taking on the part of artists, and for bringing artists in contact with people everywhere in the country, connecting people with the impulses in themselves. Programs that encourage participation rather than the passive receipt of official art of the past are the ones I think most important: all the programs that suggest to people that they have their own voices, that they can sing and write of their own past—people in their churches, students in their classes or prisoners in their cells. These programs—just the ones branded so vilely in the Heritage Foundation Report as instruments of social policy or public therapy and slated for extinction by our new budgeteers—are the ones I value. And not from any vague idealistic sentiment either: I know as an artist where art comes from. I know there is a ground-song from which every writer lifts his voice, that literature comes out of a common chorus and that our recognition of the genius of a writer—Mark Twain, for example—cannot exclude the people he speaks for.

Art will arise where it is least expected and usually not wanted. You can't generate it with gala entertainments and $200-a-plate dinners. You can, if you're an enlightened legislative body, see to it that you don't ipso facto create an official state art by concentrating your funding on arts establishments. Other people may talk of how many billions of dollars of business is produced from the arts, but to me that is beside the point.

But saying even this, I cannot avoid the feeling that it is senseless for me to testify here today. People everywhere have been put in the position of fighting piecemeal for this or that social program while the assault against all of them proceeds across a broad front. The truth is, if you're going to take away the lunches of schoolchildren, the pensions of miners who've contracted black lung, the storefront legal services of the poor who are otherwise stunned into insensibility by the magnitude of their troubles, you might as well get rid of poets, artists and musicians. If you're planning to scrap medical care for the indigent, scholarships for students, day-care centers for the children of working mothers, transportation for the elderly and handicapped—if you're going to eliminate people's public service training jobs and then reduce their unemployment benefits after you've put them on the unemployment rolls, taking away their food stamps in the bargain, then I say the loss of a few poems or arias cannot matter. If you're going to close down the mental therapy centers for the veterans of Vietnam, what does it matter if our theaters go dark or our libraries close their doors?

And so in my testimony for this small social program I am aware of the larger picture and, really, it stuns me. What I see in this picture is a kind of sovietizing of American life, guns before butter, the plating of this nation with armaments, the sacrifice of everything in our search for ultimate security. We shall become an immense armory. But inside this armory there will be nothing, not a people but an emptiness; we shall be an armory around nothingness, and our true strength and security and the envy of the world— the passion and independent striving of a busy working and dreaming population committed to fair play and the struggle for some sort of real justice and community—will be no more. If this happens, maybe in the vast repository of bombs, deep in the subterranean chambers of our missile fields, someone in that cavernous silence will remember a poem and recite it. Maybe some young soldier will hum a tune, maybe another will be able to speak the language well enough to tell a story, maybe two people will get up and dance to the rhythm of the doomsday clock ticking us all to extinction.

False Documents

FICTION IS A NOT ENTIRELY rational means of discourse. It gives to the reader something more than information. Complex understandings, indirect, intuitive, and nonverbal, arise from the words of the story, and by a ritual transaction between reader and writer, instructive emotion is generated in the reader from the illusion of suffering an experience not his own. A novel is a printed circuit through which flows the force of a reader's own life.

Sartre in his essay "Literature and Existentialism" says: ". . . each book is a recovery of the totality of being . . . For this is quite the final goal of art: to recover this world by giving it to be seen as it is, but as if it had its source in human freedom."

Certainly I know that I would rather read a sentence such as this from Nabokov's *The Gift*—

> As he crossed toward the pharmacy at the corner he involuntarily turned his head because of a burst of light that had ricocheted from his temple, and saw, with that quick smile with which we greet a rainbow or a rose, a blindingly white parallelogram of sky being unloaded from the van—a dresser with mirror, across which, as across a cinema screen, passed a flawlessly clear reflection of boughs, sliding and swaying not arboreally, but with a human vascillation, produced by the nature of those who were carrying this sky, these boughs, this gliding facade.

—whose occasion is in question, whose truth I cannot test, than a sentence such as this from the rational mentality of *The New York Times*—

> The Navy has announced base consolidations and other actions that it said would eliminate 500 civilian jobs and 16 military positions at an annual savings of about five million dollars.

—whose purposes are immediately clear, and with regard to whose truth I am completely credulous.

As a writer of fiction I could make the claim that a sentence spun from the imagination, i.e., a sentence composed as a lie, confers upon the writer a degree of perception or acuity or heightened awareness, but in any event some additional usefulness, that a sentence composed with the most strict reverence for fact does not. In any event, what can surely be distinguished here are two kinds of power in language, the power of the Navy's announcement residing in its manifest reference to the verifiable world—let us call that *the power of the regime*—and the power of Nabokov's description inhering in a private or ideal world that cannot be easily corroborated or verified—let us call that *the power of freedom.*

Immediately I have to wonder if this formulation is too grandiose—the power of the regime and the power of freedom. But it is true that we live in an industrial society which counts its achievements from the discoveries of science and which runs on empirical thinking and precise calculations. In such a society language is conceived primarily as the means by which facts are communicated. Language is seen as a property of facts themselves— their persuasive property. We are taught that facts are to be distinguished from feeling and that feeling is what we are permitted for our rest and relaxation when the facts get us down. This is the bias of scientific method and empiricism by which the world reveals itself and gives itself over to our control insofar as we recognize the primacy of fact-reality. We all kick the rock to refute Berkeley.

So what I suppose I mean by *the power of the regime* is first of all the modern consensus of sensibility that could be called *realism,* which, since there is more than epistemology to this question of knowing the world, may be defined as the business of getting on and producing for ourselves what we construe as the satisfaction of our needs—and doing it with standards of measure, market studies, contracts, tests, polls, training manuals, office memos, press releases, and headlines.

But I shall go further: if we are able to recognize and name any broad consensus of sensibility we are acknowledging its rule. Anything which governs us must by necessity be self-interested and organized to continue itself. Therefore I have to conclude that the regime of facts is not from God but man-made, and, as such, infinitely violable. For instance, it used to be proposed as a biological fact that women were emotionally less stable and intellectually less capable than men. What we proclaim as the discovered factual world can be challenged as the questionable world we ourselves have painted—the cultural museum of our values, dogmas, assumptions, that prescribes for us not only what we may like and dislike, believe and disbelieve, but also what we may be permitted to see and not to see.

And so I am led to an acceptance of my phraseology. There is a regime language that derives its strength from what we are supposed to be and a language of freedom whose power consists in what we threaten to become. And I'm justified in giving a political character to the nonfictive and fictive uses of language because there is conflict between them.

It is possible there was a time in which the designative and evocative functions of language were one and the same. I remember being taught that in school. The sun was Zeus' chariot in fact as well as fiction—the chariot was metaphor and operative science at one and the same time. The gods have very particular names and powers and emotions in Homer. They go about deflecting arrows, bringing on human rages, turning hearts, and controlling history. Nevertheless there really was a Troy and a Trojan war. Alone among the arts, literature confuses fact and fiction. In the Bible the natural and supernatural flow into each other, man and God go hand in hand. Even so, there are visible to our own time volcanoes that are pillars of fire by night and pillars of cloud by day.

I conclude there must have been a world once in which the act of telling a story was in itself a presumption of truth. It was not necessarily a better world than our own, but as a writer of fiction I can see the advantages to my craft of not having a reader question me and ask if what I've written is true—that is, if it really happened. In our society there is no presumption of truth in the act of storytelling except in the minds of children. We have complex understandings of the different functions of language and we can all recognize the esthetic occasion and differentiate it from a "real" one. This means to me that literature is less a tool for survival than it once was. In ancient times, presumably, the storyteller got a spot near the fire because the story he told defined the powers to which the listener was subject and suggested how to live with them. Literature was as valuable as a club or a sharpened bone. It bound the present to the past, the visible with the invisible, and it helped to compose the community necessary for the continuing life of its members.

In Walter Benjamin's brilliant essay "The Story Teller: Reflections on the Works of Nikolai Leskov," I read that storytelling in the Middle Ages was primarily a means of giving counsel. The resident master craftsmen and traveling journeyman worked together in the same room and stories passed between them in the rhythm of their work. Thus each story was honed by time and many tellers. If the story was good the counsel was valuable and therefore the story was true. "The art of story telling is coming to an end," Benjamin says, writing in 1936. "Less and less frequently do we encounter people with the ability to tell a tale properly. . . . one reason for this is obvious: experience has fallen in value . . . we are not richer but poorer in communicable experience."

For our sins, Benjamin implies, we have the novelist, an isolated individual who gives birth to his novel whole, himself uncounseled and without the ability to counsel others. "In the midst of life's fullness, the novel gives evidence of the profound perplexity of the living," he says. "The first great novel, *Don Quixote,* teaches how the spiritual greatness, the boldness, the helpfulness, of one of the noblest of men, Don Quixote, are completely devoid of counsel and do not contain the slightest scintilla of wisdom."

But I am interested in the ways, not peculiar to itself, that *Don Quixote* does its teaching. And of special significance I think is Cervantes' odd claim that he cannot be considered the author of his book. In Chapter 9, Part One, for instance, he introduces the Don's adventures that follow by claiming to have come across an account of them, on parchment, by an Arab historian, in a marketplace in Toledo. "I bought all the parchments for half a *real,*" he confides. "But if the merchant had any sense and known how much I wanted them he might have demanded and got more than six reals from the sale."

I look at another great early fiction, *Robinson Crusoe,* and see that it is treated by its author in much the same way. There is a Robinson Crusoe and this is his memoir, and Daniel Defoe has only edited this book for him. As editor, Defoe can assure us, with all the integrity naturally falling to his profession, that the story is true. "The editor believes the thing to be a just history of fact," he says. "Neither is there any appearance of fiction in it."

So both of these classic practitioners dissociate themselves from the work apparently as a means of gaining authority for the narrative. They use other voices than their own in the composition and present themselves not as authors but as literary executors. In the excellent phrase of Kenneth Rexroth, they adopt the device of the "false document."

I'm not familiar enough with their publishing histories to know the degree of gullibility with which these false documents were originally received by their readers. Certainly the parodic intentions of *Don Quixote* were explicit. But the romances of chivalry and pastoral love that punctuate the narrative stand in contrast to the realistic humiliations of the Don. Cervantes complains at the beginning of Part Two of *Don Quixote* that other writers have, subsequent to the great success of Part One, written their own histories of the same person. In fact, he has Quixote and Sancho Panza review their representations in the piratical works, thus conferring upon themselves an additional falsely documented reality. But let us grant Cervantes' audience, and Defoe's as well, a gullibility no greater than ironic appreciation: in order to have its effect, a false document need only be possibly true. The transparency of the pretense does not damage it. A man named Alexander Selkirk who had been a castaway was famous in Defoe's London and all the English readers needed to know to read *Crusoe* and to believe it, was that there were others who could have had Selkirk's experience. . . .

Of course every fiction is a false document in that compositions of words are not life. But I speak specifically of the novelist's act of creative disavowal by which the text he offers takes on some additional authority because he did not write it, or latterly, because he claims it was impossible to write it.

Come back for a moment to *Robinson Crusoe*. As a false document it interests me enormously. It was published at a time when the life adventures of Alexander Selkirk had been well broadcast in London for several years. In fact Selkirk's autobiography had been published and there is reason to believe Defoe actually interviewed him. Selkirk was a clearly unstable, tormented individual. His months alone on an island had so wrecked what equanimity he had that when he was restored to London he immediately built himself a cave in his garden, and he lived in the cave and sulked and raged, an embarrassment to his family and a menace to his neighbors. Defoe turned this disturbed person into the stout, resolute Englishman (Crusoe), a genius at survival by the grace of his belief in God and in the white European race.

And inevitably, Crusoe the composition has obscured Selkirk the man, whose great gift to civilization, we see now, was in providing Daniel Defoe the idea for a story. The story tells what happens when an urban Englishman is removed from his environment and plunked down in nature. What happens is that he defines the national character.

But the point about this first of the great false documents in English is that at the moment of its publication there was an indwelling of the art in the real life, everyone in London who read *Crusoe* knew about Selkirk, there was intravention, a mixing-up of the historic and the esthetic, the real and the possibly real. And what was recovered was the state of wisdom that existed, for Walter Benjamin, before fact and fiction became ontologically differentiated—that is, when it was possible for fiction to give counsel.

The novelist deals with his isolation by splitting himself in two, creator and documentarian, teller and listener, conspiring to pass on the collective wisdom in its own language, disguised in its own enlightened bias, that of the factual world.

It is not a bad system, but it gets the writer into trouble. To offer facts to the witness of the imagination and pretend they are real is to commit a kind of regressive heresy. The language of politicians, historians, journalists and social scientists always presumes a world of fact discovered, and like a religious tenet the presumption is held more fiercely the more it is seen to be illusory.

Fiction writers are at best inconvenient, like some old relative in mismatching pants and jacket who knocks on our door during a dinner party to remind us from what we come. Society has several ways of dealing with this inconvenience. The writer is given most leeway in the Western democracies which are the most industrially advanced. In these countries, where empiricism works so well as to be virtually unassailable, the writer-nuisance is relegated to the shadow world of modern esthetics or culture, a nonintegral antiuniverse with reflections of power rather than power, with a kind of shamanistic potence at best, subject to the whims of gods and spirits, an imitation with words of the tangible real world of act and event and thunder.

In those countries which are not advanced industrial democracies the writer is treated with more respect. In Uganda or Iran or Chile or Indonesia or the Soviet Union, a writer using the common coin of the political speech or the press release or the newspaper editorial to compose facts in play is accorded the power to do harm. He is recognized to have discovered the secret the politician is born knowing: that good and evil are construed, that there is no outrage, no monstrousness that cannot be made reasonable and logical and virtuous, and no shining act that cannot be turned to disgrace— with language.

Thus the American Center of PEN, the organization of novelists, poets, essayists, editors, and publishers, finds it necessary to distribute each year a poster entitled WRITERS IN PRISON. This poster, which is very large, simply lists the writers who are currently locked in cells or insane asylums or torture chambers in various countries around the world—who are by their being and profession threats to the security of political regimes. The imprisonment of writers is common in countries of the right and of the left, it doesn't seem to matter what the ideology. I know from the novelist Alexander Solzhenitsyn about the Gulag Archipelago, the network of Soviet prison camps and secret police in Siberia, but I know too from Reza Baraheni, the Iranian novelist and poet now living in this country, about the Iranian secret police, SAVAK, and the hideous torture of artists and intellectuals in Iranian prisons. Wherever citizens are seen routinely as enemies of their own government, writers are routinely seen to be the most dangerous enemies.

So that in most countries of the world literature is politics. All writers are by definition *engagé*. Even if they are timid gentle souls who write pastoral verses on remote farms, the searchlight will seek them out.

In this country we are embarrassed or angered by the excesses of repression of foreign petty tyrants and murderous bureaucracies. But forgetting the excesses the point of view is hardly unprecedented. Elizabethan writers lived in the shadow of the Tower and when Plato proposed his ideal republic he decreed that poets were to be outlawed. Part of our problem, as Americans, in failing to apprehend the relationship of art and politics is, of course, our national good fortune. . . . Our primary control of writers in the United States does not have to be violent—it operates on the assumption that esthetics is a limited arena where according to the rules we may be shocked or threatened, but only in fun. The novelist need not be taken seriously because his work is a taste of young people, women, intellectuals, and other pampered minorities, and, lacking any real currency, is not part of the relevant business of the nation.

If these thoughts were a story the story would tell of a real tangible world and the writer's witness of that world in which some writers occasionally, by the grace of God, cause the real world to compose itself according to the witness, as our faces compose themselves in our mirrors.

However I detect a faint presumption of romance in my attitude, and I have to wonder why I suspect myself of being less than hospitable to the forms of nonfictive discourse, as if they were a team from another city.

Nonfiction enjoys the sort of authority that has not easily been granted fiction since Walter Benjamin's storytellers traded their last tales. On the other hand it does give up something for the privilege, it is dulled by the obligation to be factual. This is acknowledged by the same people who would not pick up a novel, but who say of a particularly good biography or history that it reads like one.

Perhaps I feel that the nonfictive premise of a discoverable factual world is in itself a convention no less hoary that Cervantes' Arab historian.

Consider those occasions—criminal trials in courts of law—when society arranges with all its investigative apparatus to apprehend factual reality. Using the tested rules of evidence and the accrued wisdom of our system of laws we determine the guilt or innocence of defendants and come to judgment. Yet the most important trials in our history, those which reverberate in our lives and have most meaning for our future, are those in which the judgment is called into question: Scopes, Sacco and Vanzetti, the Rosenbergs. Facts are buried, exhumed, deposed, contradicted, recanted. There is a decision by the jury and, when the historical and prejudicial context of the decision is examined, a subsequent judgment by history. And the trial shimmers forever with just that perplexing ambiguity characteristic of a true novel. . . .

"There are no facts in themselves," said Nietzsche. "For a fact to exist we must first introduce meaning." When a physicist invents an incredibly sophisticated instrument to investigate subatomic phenomena, he must wonder to what degree the instrument changes or creates the phenomena it reports. This problem was elucidated by Werner Heisenberg as the Principle of Uncertainty. At the highest level of scruple and reportorial disinterest there is the intrusive factor of an organized consciousness. At lower levels, in law, in political history, the intrusion is not instrumental but moral: meaning must be introduced, and no judgment does not carry the passion of the judge.

We all know examples of history that doesn't exist. We used to laugh at the Russians who in their encyclopedias attributed every major industrial invention to themselves. We knew how their great leaders who had fallen out of favor were erased from their history texts. We were innocent then: our own school and university historians had done just the same thing to whole peoples who lived and died in this country but were seriously absent from our texts: black people, Indians, Chinese. There is no history except as it is composed. There are no failed revolutions, only lawless conspiracies. All history is contemporary history, says Croce in *History as the Story of Liberty:* "However remote in time events may seem to be, every historical judgment refers to present needs and situations." That is why history has to be written and rewritten from one generation to another. The act of composition can never end.

What is an historical fact? A spent shell? A bombed-out building? A pile of shoes? A victory parade? A long march? Once it has been suffered it maintains itself in the mind of witness or victim, and if it is to reach anyone else it is transmitted in words or on film and it becomes an image, which, with other images, constitutes a judgment. I am well aware that some facts, for instance the Nazi extermination of the Jews, are so indisputably monstrous as to seem to stand alone. But history shares with fiction a mode of mediating the world for the purpose of introducing meaning, and it is the cultural authority from which they both derive that illuminates those facts so that they can be perceived.

✓ Facts are the images of history, just as images are the data of fiction.

Of course it happens that the people most skeptical of history as a nonfictive discipline are the historians themselves. E. H. Carr, in his famous essay, "The Historian and His Facts," speaks of history "as a continuous process of interaction" between the writer of history and his facts. Carr also quotes the American historian Carl Becker, who said: "The facts of history do not exist for any historian until he has created them." Neither man would be surprised by the tentative conclusions of the structuralist critic Roland Barthes who, in an essay entitled "Historical Discourse," attempts to find the specific linguistic features that differentiate factual and imaginary narrative. "By structures alone," Barthes concludes, "historical discourse is essentially a product of ideology, or rather of imagination." In other words a visitor from another planet could not by study of the techniques of discourse distinguish composed fiction from composed history. The important stylistic device of composed history, the chaste or objective voice, one that gives no clues to the personality of the narrator, Barthes says, "turns out to be a particular form of fiction." (Teachers of English know that form well: they call it Realism.)

So that as a novelist considering this particular non-fictive discipline I could claim that history is a kind of fiction in which we live and hope to survive, and fiction is a kind of speculative history, perhaps a superhistory, by which the available data for the composition is seen to be greater and more various in its sources than the historian supposes.

At issue is the human mind, which has to be shocked, seduced, or otherwise provoked out of its habitual stupor. Even the Biblical prophets knew they had to make it new. They shouted and pointed their fingers to heaven, but they were poets too, and dramatists. Isaiah walked abroad naked and Jeremiah wore a yoke around his neck to prophesy deportation and slavery, respectively, to their soon to be deported and enslaved countrymen. Moral values are inescapably esthetic. In the modern world it is the moral regime of factual reality that impinges on the provinces of art. News magazines present the events of the world as an ongoing weekly serial. Weather reports are constructed on television with exact attention to conflict (high pressure areas clashing with lows), suspense (the climax of tomorrow's weather prediction coming after the commercial), and other basic elements of narrative. The creating, advertising, packaging, and marketing of factual products is unquestionably a fictional enterprise. The novelist looking around him has inevitably to wonder why he is isolated by a profession when everywhere the factualists have appropriated his techniques and even brought a kind of exhaustion to the dramatic modes by the incessant exploitation of them.

Nevertheless, there is something we honor in the character of a journalist—whatever it is that makes him value reportorial objectivity and assure us at the same time that it is an unattainable ideal. We recognize and trust that combination of passion and humility. It is the religious temperament. ✓

The virtues of the social sciences are even more appealing to us. Sociologists and social psychologists not only make communion with facts but in addition display the scientific method of dealing with them. The tale told by the social scientists, the counsel given, is nonspecific, collated, and subject to verification. Because they revise each other's work constantly and monitor themselves as novelists do not, and are like a democracy in that the rule of this or that elevated theorist is subject to new elections every few years, we find them ingenuous and trustworthy. Today we read the empirical fictions of Konrad Lorenz or Oscar Lewis, B. F. Skinner or Eric Erikson, as we used to read Dickens and Balzac, for pleasure and instruction. The psychologists' and sociologists' compositions of facts seem less individualistic and thus more dependable than any random stubborn vision of which the novelist is capable. They propose to understand human character or to define it as a function of ethnic background, sexuality, age, economic class, and they produce composite portraits like those done in a police station—bad art, but we think we see someone we recognize. It is at least a possiblity that the idea of human beings as demographic collections of traits, or as loci of cultural and racial and economic events, is exactly what is needed in our industrial society to keep the machines going. We have in such concepts as "complex," "sublimation," "repression," "identity crisis," "object relations," "borderline," and so on, the interchangeable parts of all of us. In this sense modern psychology is the industrialization of storytelling.

I am thus led to the proposition that there is no fiction or nonfiction as we commonly understand the distinction: there is only narrative.

But it is a novelist's proposition, I can see that very well. It is in my interest to claim that there is no difference between what I do and what everyone else does. I claim as I pull everyone else over to my side of the mirror that there is nothing between the given universe and our attempt to mediate it, there is no real power, only some hope that we might deny our own contingency.

And I am led to an even more pugnacious view—that the development of civilizations is essentially a progression of metaphors.

The novelist's opportunity to do his work today is increased by the power of the regime to which he finds himself in opposition. As clowns in the circus imitate the aerialists and tightrope walkers, first for laughs and then so that it can be seen that they do it better, we have it in us to compose false documents more valid, more real, more truthful than the "true" documents of the politicians or the journalists or the psychologists. Novelists know explicitly that the world in which we live is still to be formed and that reality is amenable to any construction that is placed upon it. It is a world made for liars and we are born liars. But we are to be trusted because ours is the only profession forced to admit that it lies—and that bestows upon us the mantle of honesty. "In a writer's eyes," said Emerson, "anything which can be thought can be written; the writer is the faculty of reporting and the universe is the possibility of being reported.'' By our independence of all institutions, from the family to the government, and with no responsibility to defend them from their own hypocrisy and murderousness, we are a valuable resource and an instrument of survival. There is no nonfictive discipline that does not rule out some element of the human psyche, that does not restrict some human energy and imprison it, that does not exclude some monstrous phantom of human existence. Unlike the politicians we take office first and then create our constituencies and that is to be a shade more arrogant than the politicians. But our right and our justification and redemption is in emulating the false documents that we universally call our dreams. For dreams are the first false documents, of course: they are never real, they are never factual; nevertheless they control us, purge us, mediate our baser natures, and prophesy our fate.

II
CONVERSATIONS

A Spirit of Transgression
Larry McCaffery

◆

ON APRIL 3, 1980, *as* I drove up the hill on Broadview Avenue in New Rochelle, New York, towards E. L. Doctorow's beautiful turn-of-the-century house, I sensed that something about the drive seemed familiar. But it was only after Doctorow had greeted me and was making us some coffee that I realized I was sitting in the house described in the opening lines of *Ragtime:*

> In 1902 Father built a house at the crest of the Broadview Avenue hill in New Rochelle, New York. It was a three-story brown shingle with dormers, bay windows and a screened porch. Striped awnings shaded the windows. The family took possession of this stout manse on a sunny day in June and it seemed for years thereafter that all their days would be warm and fair. . . .

My realization gave me sensations familiar to millions of *Ragtime*'s readers, who are repeatedly asked to examine the thin line which separates fact from fiction, history from storytelling. The street I had driven on is the same street that Harry Houdini cruises along in his black 45-horsepower Pope-Toledo Runabout in one of *Ragtime*'s opening scenes. It is also the street that Coalhouse Walker travels on to see Sarah—before his fancy motorcar is ruined, Sarah is killed, and he sets out to take his tragic revenge. And here I was, sipping coffee and eating breakfast rolls in Father's very own kitchen. . . .

E. L. Doctorow is a handsome man in his early fifties. As we drank coffee (we shifted to beer during the interview) and made small-talk before beginning the interview, he put me at ease with his humor and utter lack of pretentiousness. The telephone rang repeatedly during the several hours I was there: prepublication activities concerning *Loon Lake,* his novel which was to be issued that summer. But Doctorow managed easily to shift several times between his telephone and my tape-recorder.

INTERVIEWER: You spent the first few years of your professional life as an editor, first with the New American Library and then with the Dial Press. What was the background of this involvement with editing?

DOCTOROW: I knew from a very early age that I wanted to write, and the question was, how was I going to support myself? Somehow, I stumbled onto the profession of reader. There was a demand for expert readers on the part of television and film companies in New York during the 1950's. You'd read a novel and write a synopsis of it and tack on a critique in which you said whether you thought this story or novel should be adapted for film or television. I immediately declared myself an expert reader, did a couple of books on a tryout basis to establish my credentials, and I was off and running. I had myself a fairly active career.

INTERVIEWER: How active is "fairly active"?

DOCTOROW: I was reading a book a day, seven days a week, and writing synopses of them. I suppose each synopsis was no less than 1,200 words. I was getting an average of ten or twelve dollars a book, so I was making pretty good money—anywhere between seventy and one hundred dollars a week.

INTERVIEWER: This sounds pretty intense.

DOCTOROW: Yes, it was. No time to do my own work! But then I was offered a staff job as an inside reader for a film company. An inside reader drew a salary, so this job paid me the same amount of money no matter how much work I did.

INTERVIEWER: Did this staff job lead you directly to editing?

DOCTOROW: Well, I hacked away at it for a year, or a year and a half. Then one day we found out about a book that had a good advance word. There's great competition among film companies, you know, to get an early look at these things. What my boss, the story editor, discovered was that there was a set of galleys over at a paperback house called NAL—the New American Library. So I went over there and quickly read the thing. The editor-in-chief, Victor Weybright, had said, "When you're through, come tell me what you think." I did, and eighteen months later he called up and asked if I'd like a job. I began as an associate editor at NAL, became a senior editor, and stayed there for five years. It was a great life, publishing good books in big printings—and, in those days—selling them for pocket change. You could feel good about the way you made your living—reprinting a first novel that nobody knew about, working on everything from Ian Fleming to Shakespeare to books on astronomy and every other damned thing, and seeing those books go out with price tags of fifty or seventy-five cents. I felt very good.

INTERVIEWER: Why did you change houses?

DOCTOROW: Mostly because the owners of this wonderful paperback house sold their company to the Times Mirror Corporation of Los Angeles. Within the year it became quite clear that things were not the same, not as much fun. Publishing is a business of personal enthusiasms, hunches, instincts. The Times Mirror brought in their business consultants and personnel people who had no sympathy for this kind of work. The soul went out of the place. Along about then, a man named Richard Baron, who was part-owner of the Dial Press with Dell Publishing Company, started to talk to me about coming to work at Dial. Eventually I took that job as editor-in-chief, which I held for five years. I got to be vice-president and then publisher before I quit to write full-time.

INTERVIEWER: As an editor, did you find yourself favoring a certain type of book—championing the non-traditional approaches that you yourself were developing during this period, for example?

DOCTOROW: No, not at all. The publishing mentality, ideally, is generous, expansive, catholic in taste. You have to be receptive to lots of things, to know the value of different things. This might mean loving a book because it's highly and seriously accomplished or because it's a good trashy novel with no literary pretensions whatsoever. Or to think up an idea for a book and find just the right writer to do it. The point is that you don't have a set of rules or preconceptions to restrict your availability to what comes along; you just have to be as open to as much as possible and pick and choose from what flows by.

INTERVIEWER: What sort of effect did your experiences as an editor have on your own writing?

DOCTOROW: I don't imagine I would have written *Welcome to Hard Times* if I'd not been working at that film company and reading lousy screenplays week after week. I had no affinity for the genre—I'd never even been west of Ohio. I thought Ohio *was* the West. Oh, as a kid I'd liked Tom Mix radio programs and maybe I went to see a few movies; but, really, I had no feeling for Westerns. But from reading all these screenplays and being forced to think about the use of Western myth, I developed a kind of contrapuntal idea of what the West must really have been like. Finally one day I thought, "*I can lie better than these people.*" So I wrote a story and showed it to the story editor, Albert Johnson, who was by now a friend, and he said, "This is good. Why don't you turn it into a novel?" And so I did.

INTERVIEWER: Was this your first try at a novel?

DOCTOROW: No. I had been trying to write a book about a boy in college. I was actually working on that book when I took up this other project. *Welcome to Hard Times* was crucial for me for a couple of reasons. First, because it showed me my strength, which was *not* autobiographical writing. Somehow I was the kind of writer who had to put myself through prisms to find the right light—I had to filter myself from my imagination in order to write. The second thing I learned was that all writing begins as accident. Eventually it will come around to who you are, it will find some essence, but the *start* of a book is necessarily contingent; you can't plan it. If I had not worked as a reader and gotten angry at what I was reading, I would not have written that particular novel.

INTERVIEWER: You've said somewhere that *Ragtime* began as a set of images that were related to this house we're sitting in. Is this the sort of accident you're talking about that gets you going on a novel?

DOCTOROW: Yes, that's exactly the kind of thing. In the case of *Ragtime*, the creative accident occurred one day as I was staring at the wall. I started to write about the wall. This house was built in 1906. And I was off.

The other element for me in this kind of creative accident is my own desperation. I've learned that, each time around, I have to reach a truly desperate moment. I need to really feel very keenly a crisis of despair in order to find the level of recklessness or freedom that allows me to write the book. This has happened time and again. In the case of *The Book of Daniel*, I knew the subject, it interested me, and I thought I could hang an awful lot on it. I spent about six-months initial work on it—about 150 pages. And those pages were terrible, awful. At this point I thought that if I could ruin a momentous subject like this, then I had no business writing. I threw away the pages and in a state of reckless, irresponsible, almost *manic* despair, I sat down at the typewriter and started writing what turned out to be *The Book of Daniel*. The point is that it had to be done in Daniel's voice, not my own. And I had to really hit bottom to come to this realization. This terrible moment happens with every book, sometimes earlier and sometimes later. In the case of the book I just finished, *Loon Lake,* it happened fairly late, while the book was in its third draft.

INTERVIEWER: You mentioned earlier that you knew very early on that you wanted to be a writer, and yet you studied philosophy at Kenyon College as an undergraduate. How did these two things jibe?

DOCTOROW: I went to Kenyon to study with John Crowe Ransom. He was a wonderful teacher but also an Olympian presence. As much as I learned from him—I studied prosody with him, for instance—somehow I was inclined to a different kind of mental life. And I found it, I thought, in philosophy. I had a mind for philosophy and although I kept taking English courses, it was never with the same excitement I felt for my philosophy work. The philosophy department there was very small and I had some very fine teachers, but the man I responded to most was Philip Blair Rice, a brilliant philosopher and also the associate editor of the *Kenyon Review*— Ransom being the editor. I studied metaphysics and aesthetics with Rice and ethics and logic with his colleague, Virgil Aldridge. I loved it. During that four-year period, I did relatively little writing and had little interest in the established English Department requirements. Instead, I did philosophy and got into theater as a student actor. I had no plan, I just did what interested me. I was erratic, totally without discipline, full of longings, feelings of power, and not knowing what to attach them to. When I graduated, Rice said to me, "Doctorow, you're one of the five best students I've ever had. And of the five, you're the least informed."

INTERVIEWER: What made you turn away from pursuing an academic career in philosophy?

DOCTOROW: I don't think I ever intended to pursue it. On graduation day, Ransom introduced me to Robert Penn Warren, who was getting an honorary degree, and who happened at that time to be teaching playwriting at the Yale Drama School. I had written a play at Kenyon and had acted in several. In my senior year I'd decided that I wanted to be a playwright. Ransom said,

"Red, I think this young man ought to go to Yale," and Warren said, "All right, Pappy." What a beautiful day in June! But this was during the Korean War and my draft board told me I would have only one year for graduate studies before I'd get packed off—and the Yale M.F.A. program was a three-year program. So I ended up going to Columbia for one year, studying English drama and acting and directing, and then I was drafted, just as they had promised. And I never went to Yale. But it's almost as good that Ransom spoke for me on my graduation day.

INTERVIEWER: *Welcome to Hard Times* and *Big As Life* both obviously lie pretty far outside the realm of traditional, realistic fiction. Did you have any sense, when you were starting out as a writer, of reacting against a certain type of fiction, of trying to create your own niche as a writer? I ask this because your early books are so startlingly different from the kinds of books that most other serious writers were producing during that period.

DOCTOROW: I think I've already almost answered that question by suggesting the accident of my involvement with *Welcome to Hard Times*. What happens is that you do something and only then do you figure out what it is. You write to find out what you're writing. It was only after I had written those first two books, for example, that I developed a rationale for the approaches I had taken—that I liked the idea of using disreputable genre materials and doing something serious with them. I liked invention. I liked myth.

INTERVIEWER: I take it, then, that you were hardly under the spell of any particular writers at the time—that you weren't relating, either positively or negatively, to the sort of thing you were seeing every day on your desk as an editor.

DOCTOROW: As an editor, I spent a lot of time taking books and making them work. Structuring them. Cracking them open and putting them back together. Getting their authors to do more—or to do less. I liked doing that and I suppose my own books have gained from the practice. But I've never related to my contemporaries on a competitive basis. Mailer, for instance, was a long-established writer when I started writing; I had read his first book in high school. That whole generation of writers—Mailer, Styron—they're not ten years older than I am, but they've been around a long time. They all flashed pretty early and got the hang of literary combativeness. I think this might have something to do with their going through World War II. When people fight in a war, it takes them a while—and society a while—to wind down afterwards, if at all. The war keeps on after the war is over. Different generations imprint differently, of course. It's the fate of my generation that we've never shared a monumental experience. We think of ourselves as loners.

INTERVIEWER: So you've never seen yourself as part of a literary movement which reacted against the type of fiction being written in the 1940's and '50's?

DOCTOROW: I don't think the real life of a writer has anything to do with literary movements. To the extent that it does, the writer may be in trouble. You're just singing, you're just doing what you can, discovering what you can, living and trying to do something that is sound and good.

INTERVIEWER: One of the criticisms leveled against a lot of fiction written in the past twenty years—but not against yours very often—is that it is "too academic," too directly responsive to the analytic, critical mind. Do you think this type of thinking is actively harmful to the creative process?

DOCTOROW: I did a lot of criticism as an undergraduate. I know what that analytic faculty of mind is. I saw it working in true splendor in Ransom, who had as nice a mind as I've seen. But I think this faculty works against you unless it's in balance with everything else. I like to affect a kind of ignorance about my work that might be a sham, an affectation. On the other hand, I'm really wary of being too critically informed.

INTERVIEWER: It can't be just an accident that *Big As Life* is rarely mentioned on your dust-jacket biographies.

DOCTOROW: Sometimes it's mentioned, sometimes not. Unquestionably, it's the worst I've done. I think about going back and re-doing it some day, but the whole experience was so unhappy, both the writing and the publishing of it, that maybe I never will. It's my *Mardi*—you know, Melville's *Mardi*?

INTERVIEWER: Sure.

DOCTOROW: *Big As Life* is mine.

INTERVIEWER: Except for *Big As Life,* all of your books have used the past to explore not only the past but certain parallel tendencies in the present. In

Welcome to Hard Times, one of your characters expresses this idea as, "We can never start new." In *The Book of Daniel* it goes, "Everything that came before is all the same." Could you discuss this inability of the present to escape from the errors of the past?

DOCTOROW: Those lines came out of those particular books and I'm uncomfortable talking about things in the abstract. I would say that the fact that they're similar and express similar sentiments should not suggest that I started the books because of those ideas. In each case, it came as a discovery to me as I was writing through the personality of the narrative voice I was using.

INTERVIEWER: Obviously, then, you don't begin a work with a specific point to make or a thesis to illustrate. It sounds like you regard your work more as a kind of personal exploration rather than a vehicle consciously devised to develop a theme.

DOCTOROW: I like to quote a remark of Marcel Duchamp. He appeared to have given up painting. Someone said, "Marcel, why have you stopped painting?" He said, "Because too much of it was 'filling in.'" That's a wonderful line. Anybody who finds himself in the situation of writing to a prescribed notion or to illustrate or fill in what he already knows should stop writing. A writer has got to trust the act of writing to scan all his ideas, passions, and convictions for these to emerge *from* the work, be *of* it. I think that's standard wisdom, at least among American writers.

INTERVIEWER: Since all of your works, in one way or another, seem passionately committed to examining major social and political issues, I would assume you would take issue with, say, William Gass's claim about art's "disconnection" from ordinary reality.

DOCTOROW: Yes, I'm opposed to that view. I think art and life make each other. Henry Miller said, "We should give literature back to life." I believe that. I believe more than that.

INTERVIEWER: When you're intensely at work on a project, do you find yourself usually focusing on a specific aspect of writing—the plot movement, the language, the character development, the fleshing out of your own ideas?

DOCTOROW: I think it varies with the book. In *Ragtime* it was the historical imagery and the mock-historical tone which most interested me. And the idea of composition at a fixed narrative distance to the subject, neither as remote as history writing—which is very, very distant from what is being described—nor as close as modern fiction, which is very intimate with the subject. I was aiming for the narrative distance of the historical chronicle that you find, for instance, in Kleist who, of course, was very important in the composition of that book.

In the case of *Daniel,* it was a far different feeling. It was the characters and their complexity that moved me—the historical intersection of social and personal agony, history moving in Daniel, shaping his own pathology— all this had an enormous meaning and interest for me. So did his relationship to his sister and the parents' relationship to each other, and Daniel's relationship to himself as he sits in that library and does these historical essays and descriptions of himself in the third person, breaking down his own voice and transforming his own being to produce this work. Daniel breaks himself down constantly to reconcile himself to what is happening and what has happened to him. This kind of act that the book is—*Daniel's* book—is the central force that I felt in the writing of it.

With *Welcome to Hard Times,* it was just a sense of a place which moved me tremendously. It was the landscape. I loved writing about it, imagining it. I had never been West. Halfway through the book, it occurred to me that maybe I ought to make sure it really was a possible terrain. I went to the library and read a geography book by Walter Prescott Webb—a marvelous book called *The Great Plains*. Webb said what I wanted to hear: no trees out there. Jesus, that was beautiful. I could spin the whole book out of one image. And I did.

INTERVIEWER: What about your new book, *Loon Lake*?

DOCTOROW: It is more like *Daniel* in being a discontinuous narrative, with deferred resolutions, and in the throwing of multiple voices that turn out to be the work of one narrator. So there are similarities with *Daniel,* but the subject is far different and the tone is also different. It takes place in the Depression, a sort of Depression *Bildungsroman*. But not with that form's characteristic accumulation of data. I have a lot of broken-line stuff in it— weighted lines. That's new for me. In *Loon Lake* the sound the words make is important—the sound in the words and their rhythm. I think a good many parts of it are better read aloud.

INTERVIEWER: Was there an accident involved in your getting started with *Loon Lake,* as there was with the others?

DOCTOROW: I was driving through the Adirondacks a couple of years ago. I found myself incredibly responsive to everything I saw and heard and smelled. The Adirondacks are very beautiful—but more than that, a palpably mysterious wilderness, a place full of dark secrets, history rotting in the forests. At least that was my sense of things. I saw a road sign: "Loon Lake." Everything I felt came to a point in those words. I liked their sound. I imagined a private railroad train going through the forest. The train was taking a party of gangsters to the mountain retreat of a powerful man of great wealth. So there it was: a feeling for a place, an image or two, and I was off in pursuit of my book.

INTERVIEWER: You tend to develop rather peculiar narrative structures that several critics have labeled "cinematic." Did the cinema or television affect your notion of structure?

DOCTOROW: I don't know how anyone can write today without accommodating eighty or ninety years of film technology. Films and the perception of films and of television are enormously important factors in the way people read today. Beginning with *Daniel,* I gave up trying to write with the concern for transition characteristic of the nineteenth-century novel. Other writers may be able to, but I can't accept the conventions of realism any more. It doesn't interest me as I write. I'm not speaking now of a manifesto—but of the experience of the writer, or at least this writer. You do what works. Obviously, the rhythms of perception in me, as in most people who read today, have been transformed immensely by films and television.

I don't think, however, that this issue is primarily a matter of writing visually as opposed to not writing visually. I don't know what non-visual writing is. I think all writing puts pictures in people's heads—pictures of different things, but always pictures of the moral state of the characters being written about. Good fiction is interested in the moral fate of its people. Who they are or how they look or what they do or how they live—these are judgments of character, finally. A poem, too, tries to define someone's moral existence. And that comes off the images. Poets are not alone in using imagery. So when someone says my prose is visual, I don't really know what that means. No, what we've learned from film is quite specific. We've learned that we don't have to explain things. We don't have to explain how our man can be in the bedroom one moment and walking in the street the next. How he can be twenty years old one moment and eighty years old a moment later. We've learned that if we just make the book happen, the reader can take care of himself. You remember that television show *Laugh-In*? That was the big hit on television while I was writing *Daniel*. I told people when *Daniel* was published that it was constructed like *Laugh-In*. They thought I was not serious. But the idea of discontinuity and black-outs and running changes on voice and character—it was that kind of nerve energy I was looking for. *Loon Lake*, too, is powered by discontinuity, switches in scene, tense, voice, the mystery of who's talking. Will people be able to understand it? I think they will. Anyone who's ever watched a news broadcast on television knows all about discontinuity.

INTERVIEWER: Daniel says something about life not being as "well plotted" as we would like it to be. Is this one of your problems with the conventions of realism?

DOCTOROW: Life may have been better plotted at one time.

INTERVIEWER: That's an interesting idea. Philip Roth suggested back in the early 1960's that it's more difficult for contemporary writers to create realistic fiction because "reality" is less realistic, more extravagant than any world the writer can hope to create. In fact, your character Harry Houdini in *Ragtime* seems to be an artist-figure who has a difficult time in making his art more wondrous than that of the world. Do you share this sense of a world outstripping your ability as an artist to produce wonders?

DOCTOROW: Certainly the clatter, the accelerated rate of crisis, the sense of diffusion of character, the disintegration of belief or social assumptions are reflected in the novelists who find the novel itself no longer convincing and who write anti-mimetic novels essentially about how it's impossible to write. That view explains a lot of stuff that's been done in the last twenty years, but it doesn't explain Roth, does it? Fortunately, he keeps trying. Whatever the difficulties are, the obstacles, that's the nature of the game.

I enjoy problems and I enjoy adversity, at least professionally, and if life as represented in the headlines of the paper makes the act of writing absurd, I accept that and I'll try to deal with it. That's the condition under which I'll do my work. And I may fail, probably will, probably have, probably always will fail, but that's a kind of occupational hazard—it's built into the trade. I can imagine Cervantes sitting there in jail tearing his hair out while he wrote *Don Quixote*.

INTERVIEWER: When *Ragtime* came out, several critics expressed their surprise about the use of historical figures. Obviously, though, real people and events appear in your earlier book, *Daniel*—sometimes disguised but sometimes not. What do you find so intriguing about the use of real facts and real historical people in your work?

DOCTOROW: As my answer to the last question suggests, if you do this kind of work, you can't finally accept the distinction between reality and books. In fact, no fiction writer has ever stood still for that distinction and that's why Defoe pretended that *Robinson Crusoe* was really written by Crusoe. I don't want to understand that distinction between art and everything else, so I don't. This is not merely an aesthetic position, you understand. I get impatient with people who are moralistic about this issue. Someone said to me, "Don't you think it shows a lack of imagination to use historical characters?" And I said, "Yes, it does. Of course, it was a terrible lack of imagination on Tolstoy's part, too, when he made a character out of Napoleon." In fact, he even made a character out of Napoleon's General Doctorow, an ancestor of mine. Someone said another time, "What would *Daniel* be if there hadn't been a Rosenberg case?" I said, "You're absolutely right. And where would *The Red Badge of Courage* be without the Civil War?" What I think has happened is that people used to know what fiction was and now they've forgotten. It comes as a surprise when they're reading a novel and they find Harry Houdini saying things and carrying on. It could be that there's been such a total disintegration into specialist thinking on the part of all of us in our trades and jargons that no one remembers what the whole life is. What is imagined and what is experienced? The imagination obviously imposes itself on the world, composes a world which, in turn, affects what is imagined. That's true even in science. Indisputable. I suppose this leans towards a kind of philosophical idealist's position, although it isn't really that exactly. I mean, I know that when I kick the rock, I refute Berkeley. But I also know that a book can affect consciousness—affect the way people think and therefore the way they act. Books create constituencies that have their own effect on history, and that's been proven time and again. So I don't see that distinction between facts and art. If you read a good social scientist, an anthropologist, a sociologist, I think you'll find they do everything we fiction writers do. These people who write sociology create composite characters. Anyone who represents a class or a kind of ethnic or economic group is dealing in characterization. That's what I do.

INTERVIEWER: Gass has a line about Plato's soul being one of the greatest literary characters of all time.

DOCTOROW: Well, why not? And if you read the newspapers, you see the creativity involved. Just deciding what to look at and write about is an immensely creative decision. As a newsman, you're deciding what will exist and what won't exist.

INTERVIEWER: I was intrigued by another remark you made once: "When you write about imaginary events in the lives of undisguised people, you are proposing that history has ended and mythology has begun." What were you trying to suggest in your distinction between history and mythology?

DOCTOROW: Just what we've been talking about. All history is composed. A professional historian won't make the claims for the objectivity of his discipline that the lay person grants him. He knows how creative he is. It turned out that American historians had written, for the most part, as an establishment. They had written out of existence the history of black people and women and Indians and Chinese people in this country. What could be more apparent than the creativity of that? That's part of what I meant when I said of the little boy in *Ragtime* that "it was evident to him that the world composed and re-composed itself constantly in an endless process of dissatisfaction."

INTERVIEWER: As you've acknowledged on several occasions, the figure of Coalhouse Walker is based on Kleist's Michael Kohlhaas. What was the background of your decision to use this earlier fictional character in your own book?

DOCTOROW: Several years ago my wife related a true story she'd heard about a housemaid in our neighborhood who bore a child and then buried it in a garden. I knew when I heard this I'd use it someday. I found myself using it in *Ragtime,* where I never knew in advance what was going to happen. Suddenly there was Mother discovering the little brown newborn in the flower bed. There was Sarah coming to live in the house with this baby. Obviously, she would have tried to kill her child only from some overwhelming despair or sense of betrayal. So there had to be a father. I had introduced Houdini driving up Broadview Avenue hill in his car and that was the way I decided to introduce the child's father. He came along in his shining Ford, an older man, and he said, "I'm looking for a young woman of color." Where had he been? I decided he was a musician, a man who lived on the road, going where he found work. Now he was back to make amends. He starts to court Sarah and when she refuses to see him, he plays the piano for the family in their parlor. And that's how I found the central image of the book. Then I began to think about the implications of a black man owning his own car in the early 1900's. I knew Sarah would forgive him and they would be reconciled. But that car: What would happen to that lovely car of his is what happened to Michael Kohlhaas's horses. I had always wanted to rework the circumstances of Kleist's story. I felt the premise was obviously relevant, appropriate—the idea of a man who cannot find justice from a society that claims to be just. So there it was—I'd finally found the use for that legend I'd hoped to find—but not until the moment I needed it.

INTERVIEWER: Both Coalhouse and Younger Brother die in the pursuit of their radical ideas. And, of course, the Isaacsons are framed and eventually electrocuted. You seem to be opting for the view that history is on the side of compromise and cooperation—that idealism is rarely rewarded in our country.

DOCTOROW: I believe it's more complicated than that. The radical ideas of one generation make up the orthodoxy of subsequent generations, so the radical role is to be sacrificial. Certainly in the history of this country, the radical is often sacrificed and his ideas are picked up after he himself has been destroyed. I believe Eugene Debs came up with the idea of social security and he really suffered for that. And among Emma Goldman's outrageous, radical ideas, for which she was deported, was that of a woman's right to her own body, her right to have an abortion if she chooses. Hideous radicalism at the time, yet it's the law of the land, although there is some challenge to it right now.

INTERVIEWER: Tateh is allowed to become a financial success even though he sells out his moral beliefs. Were you tempted to condemn him for abandoning his working-class ideals?

DOCTOROW: No, I love that character, but also understand him. I was making an observation in my treatment of him, that very often a man who begins as a radical somehow—with all his energy and spirit and intelligence and wit—by a slight change of course can use these gifts to succeed under the very system he's criticizing. Very often this happens without his losing his sense of himself as a radical. You can often find among the wealthy a conviction that they are unrestructured radicals. They give a lot of money to political causes of the left, and so forth.

INTERVIEWER: Tateh's presence in *Ragtime* seems to me to undercut some of the criticism your book received for being blindly sympathetic to its leftist characters.

DOCTOROW: Yes, when people claim that I have this sentimental, simplistic approach to the characters on the left, they're not reading carefully. As compassionate as we feel for Tateh and as much as we love him, here's a man who has betrayed his principles and sympathies and gotten ahead that way. After all, he has gotten to enjoy his life by abandoning his commitment to the working class. So that's hardly an uncomplicated, simplistic view of one of the book's leftists. I think I also portray Emma Goldman as a person who stomps all over people's feelings, who just wreaks havoc with people's personal lives wherever she goes. This sort of thing is true of the radical idealist personality, though it's hardly a simplistic portrayal of her.

INTERVIEWER: Do you recall what initially interested you in the Rosenberg case as a possible source for a novel?

DOCTOROW: When I started thinking about the case, the Rosenbergs had been dead fourteen or fifteen years. I think I was in the Army serving in Germany when they were executed, and maybe that's why at the time it was a more remote horror to me than to many others. I was fully sensitive to the

McCarthy period generally. But the case didn't propose itself to me as a subject for a novel until we were all going through Vietnam. Here was the New Left, the anti-war movement, an amplification by a later generation of the torment of the 1950's. At any rate, it seemed to me that I could write about the case, that my imagination could find its corporeal being in those circumstances. I would not write a documentary novel but quite clearly and deliberately use what had happened to the Rosenbergs as *occasion* for the book. I don't mean this as a comparison, only as an example: Defoe knew Alexander Selkirk had been a castaway and that the idea of the castaway was very important and alive in London. And that's all he needed to do *Robinson Crusoe*—the real phenomenon of the castaway.

I felt people would know about the Rosenbergs and that was all I needed to write a book about Paul and Rochelle Isaacson. Although I was perhaps a little older than Daniel, I was of an age where I could respond, symbolically or metaphorically, as a person of his era. So a lot of things came together around this idea. The relationship between radical movements of one generation and another. The idea of a radical family—all the paradoxes and contradictions of that family against whom the entire antagonistic force of society is directed. So I wondered, what is the nature of that experience? What happens to people under such circumstances? How does it feel? I found that I had a proprietary sense of recognition for the subject. Also, I was angry. It seems to me certainly a message of the twentieth century that people have a great deal to fear from their own governments. That's an inescapable world-wide fact. Daniel has a line about every citizen being the enemy of his own country. It is the nature of the governing mind to treat as adversary the people being governed.

INTERVIEWER: Given your personal sympathies, were you ever tempted to make Daniel a thoroughly sympathetic character, rather than giving him sadistic, at times almost monstrous, qualities?

DOCTOROW: Suffering doesn't make people virtuous, at least in my experience. But I see his "sadism," as you call it, in a slightly different way. I see the scene where he abuses his wife, for instance, as the same kind as the scene in which he throws his son up in the air. The act has existential dimensions. Daniel is over-tuned to the world. He doesn't miss a thing. He's a hero—or a criminal—of perception. When he delivers his eulogy of his sister Susan, he says there has been a failure of analysis: Susan could only survive by limiting the amount of reality in the situation insofar as her parents were concerned. She had to come to a very strict, defensive judgment, and eventually it broke her. But Daniel gives himself to the act of perception and opens himself to it—much as all writers must—and he survives that way, survives by however cold and frightening an embrace with the truth. That is perhaps his only strength. Of course, it would take a tremendous act of the will to accept the very idea of a family after this kind of thing has happened to you as a child. Daniel recognizes this, and in acting out the terrible conflicts within himself between giving in and not giving in (his sister chose not to go on and he's trying to go on), he is enduring—by letting in as much truth about himself and his life as he can.

INTERVIEWER: As you've implied, this openness to perception seems to make Daniel an especially interesting example of *any* artist.

DOCTOROW: Maybe the nature of fiction is that, unlike reporting for *The New York Times*, it has to admit everything—all aspects and forms of thought and behavior and feeling, no matter how awful they may be. Fiction has no borders, everything is open. You have a limitless possibility of knowing the truth. But there are always people telling you what you can't do, where you mustn't go. Every time you write a book, someone says, "Oh, you shouldn't have done this or you shouldn't have done that." There's always a commissar who wants to tell you what the rules are. Yet when I'm writing out of a spirit of transgression, I'm probably doing my best work.

Politics and the Mode of Fiction
Richard Trenner

INTERVIEWER: I'd like to talk with you about your political beliefs and activities, both because they interest me and because I think they deeply inform your writing. I see in your work an explicit political rhetoric and an insistent concern with how political and social forces help shape the lives of your characters.

A timely way into this subject might be your recent testimony before a subcommittee of the House Appropriations Committee. As I understand it, P.E.N. asked you to testify against the cuts the Reagan Administration planned for the budget of the National Endowment for the Arts. Your testimony—and the testimony of other advocates of federal funding for the arts—very likely kept the cuts from being as drastic as the President would have liked. And your remarks received a lot of publicity. You spoke memorably and forcefully *for* public support for individual artists and *against* the vast increases in military spending Reagan successfully sought. I think of the almost passionate language and the self-acknowledged sense of futility of your going to Washington to testify. This leads to my first question, which concerns the forms a writer's engagement in the work of political and social change can or should take.

What *should* a writer do who wants to be politically effective in these days of growing militarism and social divisiveness throughout the United States and other parts of the world?

DOCTOROW: That is a question that you struggle with every day. It's an infernal question—the degree of engagement. We're all pretty well educated in the dangers to one's writing of ideological piety, of a fixed political position. Every writer knows how dangerous it can be in terms of doing something good. But I'm rethinking the whole thing. In view of the emergency—I think that it *is* an emergency—is some kind of new aesthetic possible that does not undermine aesthetic rigor? A poetics of engagement.

INTERVIEWER: I'm not sure why you can't have a very powerful political work that is also aesthetically excellent.

DOCTOROW: You can. But it would usually end up acknowledging, by its very nature, the ambiguities of what it's talking about. The works that have been destroyed by ideological commitment are, by and large, obscure today, like a lot of the novels of the Thirties. Political sentimentality is as bad as any other kind.

The failure arises from diction. What very often happens is that the novelist or the poet assumes the diction of politics, which, by its very nature, tends to be incapable of illumination. If you use political diction, you're not reformulating anything. You're telling people what they already know. Your rationale is your own language, and the danger of explicit politics in a book is in giving that up.

INTERVIEWER: Yes, but I see *The Book of Daniel,* for instance, as more than a political book. It's a deeper book, not only in its subject matter but in the sense of the characters' dire spiritual and psychological predicaments. The rhetoric of the novel is political, and yet it's certainly not the sort of sterile and deceptive language that you see in straight political writing. So maybe you have already managed to combine something that is aesthetically good with a strong political statement.

DOCTOROW: Maybe so. But one has to invent each time a way to do that. For instance, when I was in Peru recently, someone asked me an extraordinary question at a lecture I gave. All the questions had been very literary— informed, thoughtful. There were writers there, and academics. It was a civilized audience with elegant manners. And this guy piped up and said, "When are you going to write about the neutron bomb?" Everyone was embarrassed. But it was a good question. "I've been writing about the neutron bomb all my life," I told him. And in one way I have. But what he was talking about was, What are you going to do *now*? How can you feel (and I don't, of course) that anyone's written anything since it's still there? It's your bomb! When are you going to write about it?

I've been thinking about the question ever since it was asked. It's the only one of the evening I remember.

INTERVIEWER: Isn't the novel insufficiently active and direct for the kind of threat that the neutron bomb represents? Maybe what's called for is a lot more direct political action, or at least much more direct rhetoric.

DOCTOROW: I don't know what's called for. I think it was Robert Jay Lifton who discovered that anyone who talks about nuclear bombs has twenty minutes. You can talk about these things for twenty minutes before people numb out. I don't know if it's even *that* long.

INTERVIEWER: On the other hand, what is the alternative to writing about the neutron bomb—about the ever more dominant militarism of our time? What more important subject is there right now?

DOCTOROW: Let me talk about this from the inside of the novelist's mind. In here it's not a subject at all, not to be formulated in moral or ethical terms. In here, as I think about it, the bomb loses its political character entirely. The unsettling experience in writing fiction now may be in finding that the story of any given individual, and I don't care who it is, may not be able to sustain an implication for the collective fate. There's a loss of consequence, that's what I mean. The assumption that makes fiction possible, even Modernist fiction—the moral immensity of the single soul—is under question because of the bomb. To write fiction now as it has been written may be to misperceive or avoid the overriding condition of things, which is that we're in the countdown stages of a post-humanist society. On the other hand, if that's true, I wouldn't mean to imply that the problems of writers of fiction aren't the least of our problems.

INTERVIEWER: Have you been politically active outside of your writing? Or have you used your writing as the main way in which you respond to hard political and social facts?

DOCTOROW: I have generally stayed away from any kind of consistent political activity. I have given benefit readings. I have given my name to various groups and ad hoc committees and causes of one kind or another— peace, trade unionism, civil liberties, getting foreign writers out of prison, and so on. They are all quite specific. And I don't go out and look for them. They are available to me all the time. I'm actually quite selfish. I do relatively little. Going down to Washington to testify on behalf of the National Endowment is, I suppose, an example of direct political action. Or testifying for P.E.N. on the issue of conglomeration in the book industry—the heavy commerce that is coming into the book industry, the effect of that in First Amendment terms. But I'm not a well-organized person and I don't write efficiently. I need a great deal of time in order to get my day's work done— which is a very small number of words—probably between five and six hundred words a day. I have to give myself six or seven hours. It might all happen in fifteen minutes, but not until the end of the sixth hour. You never know. So I'm always very conflicted about doing public things. Sometimes this shows up as bad spirit, a reluctance to be interviewed. Or I will feel I have made a mistake and that in this particular situation I'm being exploited. Or I will think that what I am doing is quixotic and of no real value or consequence at all. I was very much for that writers' congress held recently in New York and lent my name from the beginning to promote and publicize it, but I participated rather marginally on one panel, and then with great reluctance. I'm personally disposed to privacy and a low profile and constantly have to deal with issues of publicity as if I've never dealt with them before. I always feel ill-equipped when someone calls up and says, "Will you do this? Will you speak? Will you give an interview?" I don't learn. It's as if I've never had an experience of this sort before. I can never really adjust to it or think of myself as a forum for any social ideas that I have.

INTERVIEWER: I must say, your interview with Paul Levine has a clear and useful political content. You talk at length about your political views and your sense of history. So sometimes giving an interview works. It's just very hard to predict when one will.

DOCTOROW: I always have the feeling that my mind has no distinction, except possibly in the book I'm writing. In other words, whatever I have to offer only emerges or is realized through the act of writing. My political opinions are quite ordinary. Fiction is really a different mode, an illuminated way of thinking. And every time I give an interview or write or deliver a speech or do anything like that outside of my work, I think I'm hurting myself. I'm not being in myself, I'm being out of myself. And this shows up in the conflicted feelings I have. It's so easy to become an expert in this country. There's such a sucking thirst for expertise and authority. So if you sit down and think for a couple of days and write something about the National Endowment, then you get dozens of requests because you're an expert, you're a voice of authority on money to artists. But whatever you knew, you've said. And you've only been able to say it because you could sit quietly in your room and work it out.

INTERVIEWER: I appreciate that your truest work, politically, is as a writer. I believe that. I've seen it in your books.

DOCTOROW: And yet, if you asked me, "What *are* your politics?"—I'd have a tough time.

INTERVIEWER: Well, let's start with the obvious. You're on the left.

DOCTOROW: I would say I'm a leftist. But of the pragmatic, social democratic left—the humanist left that's wary of ideological fervor. It's a very exhausting place to be. I think the clear, definitive ideologies have all discredited themselves by their adherents.

INTERVIEWER: What is the genealogy of your politics? Are your political values largely the result of personal experience, or what you've seen in the streets, or of your reading over the years? A combination of all three?

DOCTOROW: Victor Navasky wrote about me that I have a kind of primitive politics, almost a primitive sense of what's fair and what's not fair, what justice is and what injustice is. There's something true about that. So to go on to answer your question, in one sense I don't think of my ideas as political because they're so basic, the perceptions so fundamental and indisputable—like the most glaring sort of prophecy. It's at the level of "Don't do this. This is wrong. God is going to punish you." It's that simple-minded. All the analysis is built on it: Stealing is wrong. Therefore tax laws which favor the wealthy are wrong. Murder and torture are wrong. Therefore the foreign policy which funds and supplies murderous torturing dictators is insupportable. I've been called an idealist and naive and a pseudo-Marxist. But in this country the reference has to be the Constitution; and the political analysis, Marxist or otherwise, will have to develop from just such elemental biblical perception, from what we are in our mythic being, not from what Europe is.

INTERVIEWER: As a preface to my next question, let me tell you something about myself. I grew up in a prosperous Republican family in a prosperous Republican town, but my politics, which are not very articulate, are strongly different from the politics of most of the members of my family and the people of my hometown. Why? Difficult to say, but I like to think they are different because I've had glimpses into the lives of both the rich and the poor, and I've had a couple of years during which I was supporting myself and making a bad job of it. And I think I began to connect with what it means not to be protected and supported by money, class, and school affiliations. I wonder, what are the personal antecedents of your political philosophy, however unevolved, in a beautiful theoretical sense, that philosophy may be?

DOCTOROW: I immediately think of my grandfather and my father. Mine was not an experience like yours. I grew up in a lower-middle-class environment of generally enlightened, socialist sensibility. My grandfather was a printer, an intellectual, a chess player, an atheist, and a socialist. His was a kind of socialism that represented progress, the coming into the light from centuries of darkness. He had emigrated from Russia as a very young man. He learned the English language and read Ingersoll and Spencer and Jack London. It was a very Jewish thing, somehow. Humanist, radical, Jewish. The sense of possibility. All the solutions were to be found right here on earth, and the supernatural was not taken seriously. I remember my grandfather giving me Tom Paine's critique of fundamentalism, *The Age of Reason,* when I was ten or eleven. And this continued with my father. My father was a romantic, a dreamer. He was born in New York and lived there all his life, but loved best the real downtown, the docks, the import-export firms, the ship chandlers. He liked to bring home exotic foods. He never traveled but I think he must have dreamed about the sea. He was a midshipman in training in World War I. Toward the end of his life, he routinely read every newspaper, magazine, and journal from every corner of the left.

INTERVIEWER: Did your grandfather and father work in politics?

DOCTOROW: No. My grandfather was a printer and, by the time I played chess with him, he was retired and quite elderly. My father owned a record and radio and musical instrument store in the 1930's and lost the store later in the Depression. He then became a salesman for a jobber in the same industry—home appliances and, later on, *tv* sets and stereo equipment. His politics were expressed through the papers he read at the kitchen table, the lectures he attended, and the sentiments he expressed when the news was read over the radio. I think he belonged to some sort of fraternal Jewish socialist organization that had a very good insurance program, burial benefit.

INTERVIEWER: John Clayton's essay is entitled ''Radical Jewish Humanism: The Vision of E. L. Doctorow.'' Is there something deeply Jewish about your political convictions?

DOCTOROW: I suppose so, though I don't think my kind of vision is *only* Jewish. Historically, there's been a kind of tradition among Jews—often very embarrassing to mainline, establishment Jewish thinking. Emma Goldman is a perfect example of that tradition. Her father was a rabbi. Somehow what she did—when she got over her bomber phase, at a relatively early age—had a Jewish-prophet character to it. Think of the terribly unpopular and personally dangerous positions she got into all her life. The connection between one's precarious position in society and the desire for some analysis that would change society is not exclusively Jewish, but it runs all through modern Jewish history. Yet there's more to it than that. In *Prophets Without Honor,* his book about the renaissance of German-speaking Jews in the thirty or forty years before Hitler, Frederic Grunfeld shows this tradition at work. It's in Freud. It's in Kafka, Schoenberg, in some of the poets killed by Hitler, in the critic Walter Benjamin. Whether they were that radical or not, there was some sort of system to thought—a humanist critique, a social or political skepticism, whatever you want to call it—that had to come from their inability to be complacent or self-congratulatory.

INTERVIEWER: Aside from whatever anti-Semitic impulses at work in some people on the far right, there may be the fearful recognition that radical Jewish humanism is very dangerous to their position.

DOCTOROW: The Nazis used that. The Jews they went after—the Jews who most enraged them—were the assimilated Jews, the families who had lived in Germany or Austria for hundreds of years. Einstein, for instance, infuriated the Nazis. Einstein was coming up with a universe in which nothing stayed the same very long. Things kept transforming and there was no space without time, and energy became mass and mass became energy. They saw all this relativism as a great threat to their psychic security and a typically Jewish maneuver to undercut and destroy the Aryan race. It was not the pious, practicing Jews who kept to themselves who so much enraged the Nazis at the beginning. It was the Jewish professors and composers (like Mahler) and scientists, all of whom had assimilated to one degree or another. The number of poets, novelists, critics, painters, and musicians whom they destroyed. Migod. That's the other connection you make between art and social criticism.

To get back to the idea of a radical Jewish humanist tradition, if I was not in that tradition, I would certainly want to apply for membership. Years ago in New Rochelle, I gave a talk at a Conservative synagogue. This was at a breakfast meeting of a men's club or something like that. The title of my talk was "Other Jews." And it was just this I was talking about: the expression of Jewish rectitude in humanist political terms. I mentioned Emma Goldman. And I mentioned Allen Ginsberg, this Buddhist, homosexual, Beat poet. Ginsberg is right smack in the middle of that tradition. I thought a suburban synagogue was a good place to talk about it.

INTERVIEWER: To move away from the especially Jewish quality of your vision, how would you summarize abstractly your social ideals?

DOCTOROW: There is a presumption of universality to the ideal of justice—social justice, economic justice. It cannot exist for a part or class of society; it must exist for all. And it's a Platonic ideal, too—that everyone be able to live as he or she is endowed to live; that if a person is in his genes a poet, he be able to practice his poetry. Plato defined justice as the fulfillment of a person's truest self. That's good for starters.

INTERVIEWER: To bring that about would, of course, require a tremendous reorganization of the social and economic structure of our society. Would you say that we'd have to have a socialist reorganization to make possible the kind of justice you describe?

DOCTOROW: Probably, yes. But it would come up out of us, our best illusions about ourselves. It would be pragmatic and honest and plain-spoken. We would build on what we already have, we would go out in the barn (which is the Constitution) and tinker. And it's the failure to recognize *that* which has always brought programmatic radicals up short in this country. You want to achieve some degree of genuine enlightened social control of production and services—but without creating a bureaucracy that turns oppressive, and without relinquishing any of the political freedoms that exist now.

INTERVIEWER: Do you think the shift in the opposite direction that Reagan represents is a temporary aberration? Or is it (coming from some deep impulse in the American political character) likely to endure?

DOCTOROW: The great political contests in this country since Franklin Roosevelt have been between the center and the right. So in that sense

Reagan is not an aberration. On the other hand, there is something new about him: the abandonment of the liberal rhetoric by which we've always disguised our grubby actions from ourselves. This president is saying the conflict between our democratic ideals and our real political self-interest is over; that the conflict between our constitutional obligations and the expediencies of economic capital reality is over; the crackling contradiction between our national ideals and our repeated historical abuse of those ideals is over. It turns out after all we were not supposed to be a just nation, but a confederacy of stupid murderous gluttons. So there's a terrible loss of the energy you get from self-contradiction, from the battle with yourself. If there was a way of taking a national EEG, you'd find that the brain waves have gone flat. That's new. The religious fundamentalists and the political right have made explosive contact, and in the light of their conjunction it says Armageddon.

The Writer As Independent Witness
Paul Levine

INTERVIEWER: In your novel *Ragtime,* Freud says to his disciple Jones at one point that "America is a mistake, a gigantic mistake." Do you agree with Freud's judgment?

DOCTOROW: Freud actually said that, and I think in the context of the passage, it becomes very funny. I think it's funny to speak of anything that gigantic as "a mistake." And, of course, considering the sort of cosmic pratfalls of our history, in that sense, yes, we've done everything wrong. To someone of refined taste and culture, we must have appeared in those days really as monstrous. We probably still do appear that way. But I don't agree, of course, any more than I agree that any other nation is a mistake. They're all mistakes. Human life is a mistake.

INTERVIEWER: There are a number of American writers who have treated America in various eras as a gigantic mistake. One thinks of Melville's *Moby Dick,* of the Pequod as a ship of state on an errand which is a gigantic mistake. One thinks of Twain—*Pudd'nhead Wilson*—who writes: "October 12. It was wonderful to discover America. It would have been even more wonderful to have missed it." There's a kind of unrequited love affair in American literature between writers and the country. Do you feel this is a particularly American tradition. Is it a tradition you've been conscious of as you've been writing your particularly *American* novels?

DOCTOROW: I don't know. It seems to me we are, at least on paper, supposed to be different from, or better than, we are. And that kind of irritation confronts us all the time and has from the very beginning. The Constitution was a precipitate of all the best Enlightenment thinking of Europe, and it's really quite a remarkable document. That we don't manage to live up to it is the source of all our self-analysis. But I think that all writers and all nations operate as children do of families whom they love and hate and try to distinguish themselves from and somehow reform at the same time. And I would put a nation's artists in that category—as loving and tortured children.

INTERVIEWER: And yet there is something curious about this relationship between American writers and American society or American culture. It's a problem of definition. There is a sense in which American writers are constantly writing about American identity, as if it were something that was yet to be discovered. In Europe, for instance, the national identity of a Dane or a German or a Russian or a Frenchman is a given. It's not something to discover, it's *there*. And the literature, therefore, seems to begin at a different point (if you understand what I mean) from American literature.

DOCTOROW: Well, of course, this is a very young country, and it is a polyglot mixture that is still forming itself through waves of immigration, most recently Hispanic, and now, it seems, a small Vietnamese immigration. This is a constant of American history. And nothing has really disappeared yet into the mists of ancient history. We're very derivative. We derive enormously, of course, from Europe, and that's part of what *Ragtime* is about: the means by which we began literally, physically to lift European art and architecture and bring it over here. So that we had architects like Stanford White who could copy (to take an uncharitable view) any European style whatsoever on command. That's sort of our curse and our blessing at the same time. Not having fixed, narrowed or focused into a real, true national identity, we can have the illusion about ourselves that we are still in the process of becoming. It's a kind of fascinating suspense to see the ways in which all these strains—ethnic, social strains—clash with technology and industrialism and the effect of one on another, and the effect of both on the simple possibility of surviving. We don't have much of a history—that's the simple, statistical fact of it.

INTERVIEWER: In the last ten or fifteen years, history seems to have become a major subject in American fiction. In the 1960's, one had a series of novels that revisioned history, such as John Barth's *The Sotweed Factor*. Thomas Berger wrote a novel called *Little Big Man* about the only survivor of Little Big Horn, General Custer's massacre. He invented a character. This was the beginning of an attempt to take history as it had been portrayed by the historians and to revise it—not simply to give us a new history but to transform it into something else, perhaps into myth—I don't know. What do you think caused this movement back to—to coin a phrase—"roots"?

DOCTOROW: Well, first of all, history as written by historians is clearly insufficient. And the historians are the first to express skepticism over this "objectivity" of the discipline. A lot of people discovered after World War II and in the fifties that much of what was taken by the younger generations as history was highly interpreted history. And just as through the guidance and wisdom of magazines like *Time,* we were able to laugh at the Russians' manipulation of their own history—in which they claimed credit for technological advances that had clearly originated in other countries, and in which leaders who had fallen out of favor were suddenly absent from their texts—just around that time, we began to wonder about our own history texts and our own school books. And it turned out that there were not only individuals but whole peoples whom we had simply written out of our history—black people, Chinese people, Indians. At the same time, there is so little a country this size has in the way of cohesive, identifying marks that we can all refer to and recognize each other from. It turns out that history, as insufficient and poorly accommodated as it may be, is one of the few things we have in common here. I happen to think that there's enormous pressure on us all to become as faceless and peculiarly indistinct and compliant as possible. In that case, you see, the need to find color or definition becomes very, very strong. For all of us to read about what happened to us fifty or a hundred years ago suddenly becomes an act of community. And the person who represented what happened fifty or a hundred years ago has a chance to begin to say things about us now. I think that has something to do with the discovery of writers that this is possible. At the same time this has been going on, I think there has been the drop in what used to be known as the "regional" novel. It seems to me that books published by Southerners aren't quite the "Southern" novels they were some generations ago. And there doesn't seem to be any other region in the country that finds itself in contemporary ways with strong cultural marks that everyone can relate to. So it's almost as if we're finding in *time* the sort of identification we've been losing in other ways—in space, in ethnic coloration, and so on.

INTERVIEWER: When those novels began to appear (and I'm thinking of novels like *The Sotweed Factor* and *Little Big Man*), and shortly after, we began to get a series of novels that dealt with contemporary reality that was somewhere between journalism and fiction (I'm thinking of a book such as *In Cold Blood* by Truman Capote, which he called a "nonfiction novel"). The early works that I'm referring to here seemed not to have any overt political content. But in more recent works, such as Norman Mailer's *The Armies of the Night*—which is divided into two sections, "The Novel as History" and "History as the Novel"—in Thomas Pynchon's work, and particularly in your own work, there seems to be a very conscious attempt to revise history in such a way that we can begin to understand American society politically. Do you think that this movement that I'm trying to describe has been some kind of conscious effort to come to grips with American society on the part of writers?

DOCTOROW: Well, I think that's the great chore, task, or challenge our fiction writers have always dealt with. It's such an immense place and almost—in all its great, whirling, self-destruction—impossible to make a metaphor of. In fact, I think it's getting more and more impossible to do that. But this is the challenge, and our writers have always been extremely political. I think Dreiser is a political writer. Jack London. All through our history, our writers have been extremely political. I think their treatment in the universities has been anti-political. It's only recently that I've come to realize there's an enormous Marxist interpretation possible, or critical literature, about *Moby Dick*. I don't see this as anything new at all. I think it's impossible to do a book and not be political. If you do a book about a boy and his dog, you're making a political statement. I think the politics of novels become visible when they happen to differ from the prevailing political complacencies around them. And so books like *Daniel* or *Ragtime* would strike some people as being essentially political efforts. It's hard to think of a writer who cannot be given a very rigorous political interpretation. Certainly Henry James. Fitzgerald. Writers of the thirties, of course, were explicitly committed, many of them, to propagandize from a specific political point of view. And that leads to the interesting question of to what degree a writer can understand or know that he is political in order to get his work done. There's some kind of death that creeps into prose when you're trying to illustrate a principle, no matter how worthy. And this is quickly recognized by all critics in this country. But on the basis of that, of course, to declare that art should not have political intent—or can't afford to—that's not justified. One thinks of the intentions of writers, like Dostoyevsky, who simply and modestly wanted to change the world. That didn't seem, somehow, to limit his capacity to express truth. So I guess my answer is, I don't think this is anything new at all. If I were a better literary historian, I could come up with a lot of impressive names and citations, but certainly the careers of Dreiser and Jack London should stand for the novelist who is political.

INTERVIEWER: And yet Dreiser and London (and I think you are right about the universities) stand outside what one would think of as the mainstream. But even a writer who *is* overtly political, like John Dos Passos, is also, in a sense, outside of the mainstream. One can see a shelfful of books on Faulkner or Fitzgerald or Hemingway, and there really isn't a comprehensive critical analysis of Dos Passos' work. And yet one could say there is a whole group of novelists who could be interpreted in a political way, but that's different from someone who chooses an explicitly political theme. Let's talk about one of your novels for a minute—*The Book of Daniel*.

The Book of Daniel begins, or so it seems to me, with one of the major political events of the post-war period, and that was the execution of Julius and Ethel Rosenberg. Now it would be very difficult to begin a novel at that point and not have its overt, rather than its latent, content as political. This is rather different from Capote's *Other Voices, Other Rooms* or Salinger's *Catcher in the Rye*. This is a novel that begins in the bowels of American politics and seems in fact to deal with what Christopher Lasch calls "the agony of the American left." How did you come to write this novel?

DOCTOROW: I don't really know. In the late sixties I found myself thinking about the Rosenberg case, and it seemed to me that the more I found myself thinking about it, I saw that it was something I could write. And not knowing why or how or what conclusions I was going to come to, I started to write that book and discovered I could hang an awful lot on it—not only the explicit and particular story of two people who were trapped in this way, but also the story of the American left in general and the generally sacrificial role it has played in our history. The specific dramatic interest I had was solely in terms of what happens when all the antagonistic force of a society is brought to bear and focused on one or possibly two individuals. What kind of anthropological ritual is that? It is an explicitly political novel in that it deals with politics and political people, but, peculiarly enough, I have never thought of myself as a terribly political person. In fact, it was only after *Ragtime* was published that I was informed (not having realized it) that

I tended to write about historical subjects. That hadn't occurred to me either. There's a certain way in which, in order to get our work done, we really have to be ignorant. We can't know too well what we're doing. If you know too well what you're doing, then writing simply becomes a matter of filling in. At its best, you write to find out what it is you're writing. I suppose this must be a disappointing answer, but my original *conscious* interest in that subject was a technical interest and discovered itself to have some moral basis.

INTERVIEWER: Was your original interest with the children of the Isaacsons (as you call them in the novel), the children that you made up—or with the parents that you found? That is, it seems to me it's a book about an inheritance.

DOCTOROW: It's hard for me to isolate my own motives and feelings. I can tell you that I started to write the book in the third person, more or less as a standard, past tense, third person novel, very chronologically scrupulous. And after one hundred fifty pages I was terribly bored. That was a moment of great despair in my life, because I thought that if I could really destroy a momentous subject like this, then I had no right to be a writer. That moment, when I threw out those pages and hit bottom, was when I became reckless enough to find the voice of the book, which was Daniel. I sat down and put a piece of paper in the typewriter and started to write with a certain freedom and irresponsibility, and it turned out Daniel was talking, and he was sitting in the library at Columbia, and I had my book. I don't know why that happened or how that happened, but that is the experience I had in composing the book. I don't know if it's possible for a writer really, truthfully to describe as a conscious decision a process that is really mysterious to him and largely irrational.

INTERVIEWER: Did you have to do much research on the Rosenberg case or the history of the Cold War or America in the 1940's and '50's for that book?

DOCTOROW: Once I got going, I found myself looking things up, but not in any systematic way. At a certain point, I think, when your mind is organized and you're attuned to whatever your subconscious is doing, you become a kind of magnet for your own experiences and reading, and things in the air become relevant. On the basis of that, you're led from one thing to another. You see a picture in a newspaper, or you're walking through some stacks in a library and you see a title of a book, and in some peculiar, mystical way, things just happen to come up when you need them. Someone will tell you a story at a dinner party or you'll catch sight of a scene on a street corner, and it will become appropriate to the book. The ongoing book or the creative process, I think, generates a certain kind of energy in the writer which makes him a kind of selective magnet for things in his environment. That's what I would call research.

INTERVIEWER: The book is a remarkable imaginative recreation not simply of an event but, really, of an era. And it was the first novel about the Rosenberg case but not the last. This year Robert Coover has published a book called *The Public Burning,* and we've seen on American television in the last two years a three-hour dramatized documentary about the career of Joseph McCarthy. There seems to be now an attempt to understand what happened to America in the years of the Cold War, between the end of World War II (when we supposedly lost a China that was never ours to lose) and the beginning of *détente.* There seems to be a surfacing of that history now, as if we've now got to come to terms with what was buried so deeply in the age that was supposed to be the age of the *end* of ideology. Do you have any explanation as to why *now* we've become so obsessed with this?

DOCTOROW: No, I don't. I don't know anything that everybody else doesn't know. If I have any specific capabilities as a thinker, they only come out in the context of the work I'm doing.

I think there's a natural lag between a trauma such as a war and the country's ability to deal with it psychically. I think approximately fifteen years passed before there was any flow of literature in this country about the Nazis. As I recall, the first popular book on the Third Reich was William Shirer's, which was published probably around 1960. And then, of course, the gates opened. Perhaps there is already a large literature about Vietnam, and that's an exception to the rule.

INTERVIEWER: Nothing about Korea.

DOCTOROW: Nobody seems to want to hear about it. But it's possible that each of these traumatic experiences and the communal attempt to deal with them lifts up the general perception a degree or two, and so the response can be a little faster next time. That would be the only explanation for the fact that we're already trying to deal with Vietnam. We were trying to deal with it as it was going on, and I think we have a lot more work to do. But it leads to interesting questions. For instance, the general supposition now is that what's happening in the seventies is a general retreat from political and social awareness: children in school all back to their studies and quietly intent on getting good grades so they can get jobs; the well-known abandonment of political language for mystical-religious sensation; the development of the great variety of sensitivity trainings; the appearance of one guru after another; and the defection of some of the political leaders of the students to these movements. The common wisdom is that there has been a retreat from a certain kind of political development or communal education. I'm not sure that's true. If you think of the early Wilhelm Reich, for instance, as a man who tried somehow to accommodate or bridge Freudian insight to Marxist sociology, then this is a very clear part of the process. Reich came to believe that there is no hope for political progress until people can be freed from their neurotic character structures. If you're a Reichian, you could make the claim, shaky as it might be, that people's streaming into various kinds of meditation and degrees of self-awareness are simply preparing themselves for a return to political life without some of the hang-ups they had first time around.

INTERVIEWER: Are you a Reichian?

DOCTOROW: No, I don't think so, although there are things about his early work that really fascinate me. I don't know enough about Reich to be a Reichian.

INTERVIEWER: Certainly that attempt to marry the insights of Freud with the insights of Marx seems to be the main intellectual burden of the late 1960's and the '70's. One thinks of people like Marcuse and Norman O. Brown and some of the people working in Europe now who have been trying to marry those insights.

DOCTOROW: It's extremely important and, of course, a fiercely argued point. Reich himself was excommunicated by both the Marxists and the Freudians as a result of his insights. He was driven right out of Europe because of that direction in his work. But surely the sense we have to have now of twentieth-century political alternatives is the kind of exhaustion of them all. The only one to my mind that stands out clean and shining—because it has never really been tested in any serious way—is a philosophical position of anarchism, which at this point seems to be so totally utopian in character as not to be seriously attainable. But certainly everything else has been totally discredited: capitalism, communism, socialism. None of it seems to work. No system, whether it's religious or anti-religious or economic or materialistic, seems to be invulnerable to human venery and greed and insanity. So it seems to me that anyone who likes to think about these things seriously in an effort to find some mediation between individual psychology and large social movements has to be going in the right direction.

INTERVIEWER: I remember in *The Armies of the Night* that Norman Mailer calls himself a left conservative. He "liked to think in the categories of Marx to achieve some of the ends of Edmund Burke," he said. An interesting attempt to bring together these two aspects that you're talking about.

DOCTOROW: I think that political awareness in this country is very primitive generally. In terms of dealing with the issues and coming to terms with them in a rational way, we're terribly behind everyone else. We're doing things and saying things, the meanings of which we don't even know. Certainly, intellectually speaking, there are very few Marxists who have access to universities in this country, to journals except their own. And certainly the political dialogue in the media is rudimentary, and permissible opinion goes from a little bit to the left of center to very far to the right. And all the great political contests in this country are between the middle right and the far right. There's a lot we have to learn, it seems to me.

INTERVIEWER: How do you account for that? It seems clear that the political dialogue in the United States does not move from right to left, as you say. It moves perhaps from right to center—that is, if one thinks in terms of the Western world. The Conservative Party in England starts roughly where the left wing of the Democratic Party starts—with an acceptance, for instance, of the welfare state as a reality, a non-negotiable reality. Is there another country that's industrialized that does not have socialized medicine? So the political discussion in the country is polarized in a completely different way from the political discussions in other countries, including Canada, where there is a social democratic party called the New Democrats. How does one account for the fact that in the twentieth century America has managed to turn its back on the great political dialogues that are going on in the rest of the world?

DOCTOROW: That's an interesting question. I think essentially it's our pragmatism that either protects us or damages us. We started off from the point of view of property, including slaves, and by means of the use of capital—as it discovered technology and was invested in technology—worked our way into a rather generous, prosperous society that was able to ignore the terrible decimation of working people and of minorities in order for it to achieve what it achieved. A kind of social and political blindness came along.

Whenever we have a problem, we tend to try to solve it technologically. Take pollution. The discussion about poisoning the environment or using up our resources is entirely in terms of how, on a technological basis, we can stop doing that. Discussion doesn't come around to why that is being done and who is profiting from it—in any serious way. So the solution to foul air is not any broad reconstruction of industrial power; it's simply to find an engine that will take those soots and hellish gases and make them harmless. We're tinkerers and pragmatists, and our technology is in the hands of those elements of us who have the money to use it and to exploit it for their own protection. And, of course, the media are owned by privileged members of our group and reflect that kind of faith in technology and the ability of the tinkerers. The interesting thing about pollution, of course, is that while it affects people who work in factories, for instance, vinyl chloride factories or asbestos factories, prominently—and they are members of the lower socioeconomic class—it also affects people who live in suburbs but who breathe the same crap. I'm interested to see the extent to which the middle class in this country, which imagines itself the enormous beneficiary of our system, discovers that it, too, is expendable, just as the lower class is. As resources become less and less available, they will be allocated to fewer and fewer people, and at that point those of us who are in the middle class and feel that our lives can't be improved will wake up. But to get back to the question, I think we're a peculiarly pragmatic country, and so far the technology has made it work.

The other major thought I would have about this is what happened to the working class in this country in the 1930's. The more radical historians and critics feel that the American worker had an enormous opportunity in the 1930's which he blew by settling for a wage contract, at which point the structure of American labor was set and the leadership of the unions became, in effect, watchdogs of management.

INTERVIEWER: The historian Christopher Lasch has also argued that an indigenous socialist movement in this country was, in a sense, sabotaged after the Russian Revolution, when American socialists began to look outside of the country rather than inside, and that the last indigenous movement would have been something like the Wobblies, the I.W.W. I wonder if that was something you thought about in terms of *Ragtime* as well as *The Book of Daniel,* since both books in different ways deal with the history of the American left. Emma Goldman is an important character in *Ragtime.* And it's clear in your version of the Rosenberg case (as one character says at one point in *The Book of Daniel*) that the two victims are victimized both by the F.B.I. and the Communist Party, that they're being set up, in a sense, by both groups, crucified by both. Do you have a sense that there was a golden moment in American history where it *could* have all been different?

DOCTOROW: Oh, no, no, I don't feel that way at all. I think the beginnings and ends and moments are artificial constructions. It's possible to cut and slice history really any way you want to, so that something is seen to be beginning or ending. That's probably why history belongs more to the novelists and the poets than it does to the social scientists. At least we admit that we lie.

INTERVIEWER: You're the only honest liars around?

DOCTOROW: Exactly. But in retrospect, I suppose (speaking of *Ragtime* and *The Book of Daniel*) there is some kind of disposition—and no more than that—to propose that all our radicals (and we've had an astonishing number of them) and our labor leaders and our Wobblies and our anarchists and so on, have really been intimate members of the family—black sheep, as it were, whom no one likes to talk about. And I suppose one could make a case for my disposition to suggest that they are indeed related, that they are part of the family, and that they've had an important effect on the rest of us.

There's one other point to be made—that it's so much easier for the right to command mass support, because it does not attempt to reform. It does not attempt to answer the needs of people, alleviate their miseries and their terrors. All it has to do is confirm them in their fear and their hysteria. And it's therefore much easier in this country for the political right to maintain its position. The hard questions and the difficulties—including the difficulty of communicating with people in a massive way—are the occupational hazards of the left in this country. It's much easier to terrify people and confirm them in their rigidity than to say—look, there are other ways we can do this. And I think that shows up in American history. The left, the radicals, have always been easily isolated and made objects of terror and have often been complicitors in their own destruction in some peculiar way. But what happens, sometimes, is that those proposals that the radical has made in one generation become the liberal or even the conservative dogma of the next. And so the very things the radicals were destroyed for come to pass. A clear example is Emma Goldman's feminist stand on abortion and contraception, which was too monstrous to even think about in 1910 and was strongly part of the reason for her deportation, I think—as much as her anarchism. Or Deb's endorsement of the radical idea of social security, which Roosevelt picked up twenty-five years later. So if that hazard for the left exists—the inability to compete with what is easy and fearful and neurotic—nevertheless, somehow every once in a while, an idea does come through.

INTERVIEWER: If the writers are the only honest liars, and they usurp the traditional position of the historians, it means that, in a sense, a tremendous burden is put on novelists to explain, describe, invent, create the reality, unify the reality, of their time. Is this a problem that you feel as a fiction writer as being an extraordinary burden? Do you feel that writers today suffer under an extraordinary burden because of this role?

DOCTOROW: I think it's very hard to write novels. But I think novelists have always felt that way. I don't feel it as a moral burden, if that's what you mean.

INTERVIEWER: No, I didn't mean it as a moral burden.

DOCTOROW: I don't take a vow to be responsible. I'm under the illusion that all of my inventions are quite true. For instance, in *Ragtime,* I'm satisfied that everything I made up about Morgan and Ford is true, whether it happened or not. Perhaps truer because it didn't happen. And I don't make any distinction any more—and can't even remember—what of the events and circumstances in *Ragtime* are historically verifiable and what are not. But I suppose that if you were to say to me, there's a danger in this sort of thing, I would have to agree. There is absolutely a danger. Except that writers are independent witnesses and, theoretically at least, not connected to the defense of any institution, whether it be the family or the Pentagon or God. If there are enough of us, somehow a common wisdom will come through the community and pick and choose what it needs in order to survive and go on. I certainly would much rather trust as a source of truth the variousness of literature, and its width and its breadth, than, for instance, a press release from a government agency, or even a sermon. It seems to me what must be maintained is the absolute multiplicity of us all, the numbers of us who color the palette from which the society draws its own portrait.

III
ESSAYS

The Stylistic Energy
of E. L. Doctorow
Arthur Saltzman

PERHAPS THE MOST frequently criticized aspect of contemporary avant-garde fiction—that is, by those who find the writings of Barth, Coover, Barthelme, Gass, and other recent composers of "metafiction" grounds for distress rather than for delight—is its tendency to minimalize, if not to ignore, the sociopolitical realities that surround its creation. Indeed, a sense of artistic narcissism pervades even the best (particularly the best?) of the novels these writers have produced; their accomplishments seem largely technical and self-contained, so that the artificial worlds they delineate are only occasionally related to the larger world of "journalistic" reality. Instead of entering realms that reflect profoundly on the problems and complexities of our society—so the argument goes—we are instead trapped in word puzzles obsessed with their own fictional nature. Under such ambiguous, labyrinthian conditions, few but scholars and critics care to function.

The critical theories that attend so-called Postmodern fiction prescribe severely limited goals for the novel form. Roland Barthes goes so far as to surmise that "the whole of literature, from Flaubert to the present day, became the problematics of language," which is to say that the most pertinent subject of serious fiction is its own processes. Alain Robbe-Grillet outlines the domain of contemporary fiction even more starkly, claiming that "the genuine writer has nothing to say. . . . He has only a way of speaking."[1] To be sure, those American novels which have most thoroughly incorporated these precepts (Gore Vidal calls them symptoms of "the French disease" which has occasioned so much of this "Research and Development" fiction) investigate no history so fully as that of their own conception. When evidence of our cultural, social, or political situation does manage to intrude, it is usually to emphasize what Donald Barthelme refers to as the numbing "dreck" of contemporary life. Christopher Lasch likewise detects a disturbing retreat of art from its instructional duties:

> The self-consciousness that mocks all attempts at spontaneous action or enjoyment derives in the last analysis from the waning belief in the reality of the external world, which has lost its immediacy in a society pervaded by "symbolically mediated information." The more man objectifies him-

self in his work, the more reality takes on the appearance of illusion. As the workings of the modern economy and the modern social order become increasingly inaccessible to everyday intelligence, art and philosophy abdicate the task of explaining them to the allegedly objective sciences of society, which themselves have retreated from the effort to master reality into the classification of trivia.[2]

The general subordination of secular concerns to stylistic ones finds its literary precedent in the works of the great Modernists, whose politics tended toward the reactionary (Eliot, Yeats, Pound) or the irresponsible (Joyce, Mann).[3] Their notion of an artistic aristocracy was not so very different in its effect on the sort of writing it produced than, for example, Philip Roth's well-known complaint about the predicament of being a writer today: "The American writer in the middle of the twentieth century has his hands full in trying to understand, describe, and then make *credible* much of American reality. It stupefies, it sickens, it infuriates, and finally it is even a kind of embarrassment to one's own meagre imagination. The actuality is continually outdoing our talents, and the culture tosses up figures almost daily that are the envy of any novelist."[4] The former attitude disdains reality for being shabby; the latter cringes from reality for being horrifying.

Whereas the Modernists concerned themselves with what art should aspire to (the transcendant, the mythical), the Postmodernists resign themselves to what art can manage: in Robbe-Grillet's words, "a way of speaking." Let the camera handle matters of mimesis, for which it is better suited than the novel is anyway. The writer's relation to reality is more oblique, more antagonistic. As Richard Poirier explains in *The Performing Self,* the contemporary novelist is at once reluctant to confront reality and obsessed with the prospect of supplanting it with imaginative alternatives. Writing is more than ever self-consciously exhibitionistic, a "performance" that "is an exercise of power, a very curious one. Curious because it is at first so furiously self-consultive, so even narcissistic, and later so eager for publicity, love, and historical dimension. Out of an accumulation of secretive acts emerges at last a form that presumes to compete with reality itself for control of the minds exposed to it."[5]

According to this position—that the Postmodern novel seeks to become a separate, competitive reality—the degree to which it must rely upon intersections with reality-at-large is the degree to which it has been compromised away from its intentions. It is no wonder, then, that given such a restrictive theoretical basis, the Postmodern novel is so often accused of having betrayed its traditional mimetic functions.

With the publication of *Loon Lake,* however, E. L. Doctorow continues to prove that it is possible to have it both ways: his novels are simultaneously artistically venturesome and socially conscientious. Like the Postmodernists, Doctorow extends the stylistic possibilities of language; like the Naturalists, he employs language in the study of social ills. Each of his novels investigates the validity of the inflated platitudes and personalities that constitute the American Dream; at the same time, each novel displays a concern with devising narrative innovations (or, in some instances, borrowing innovations from past avant-gardists, most notably Dos Passos and Joyce) that are appropriate to narrative consciousness or to specific settings or themes. In other words, just as Doctorow's attention to what it means to live in the world is not obscured by his attention to the technical possibilities of the novel, neither is the age-old question of how form and content interrelate sacrificed in favor of his muckraking impulses. The source of these two distinct—and, very often, mutually resistive—novelistic activities lies in Doctorow's very inclusive concept of reality itself. Thematic questions lead him to aesthetic ones: What is the reality which underlies the deceptive images of America perpetrated by the media, by the ruling élite, and by our penchant for nostalgic misremembrances and patriotic abstractions? And what method of narration is most reliable for conveying the reality of a given situation, or of a given idea? As Doctorow has recently said: "The principle which interests me is that reality isn't something outside. It's something we compose every moment. The presumption of the interpenetration of fact and fiction is that it is what everybody does—lawyers, social scientists, policemen. So why should it be denied to novelists?"[6] Beginning with this radical skepticism about the nature and the availability of reality, Doctorow wants both to demythologize America and to demystify his own craft.

Doctorow's first novel, *Welcome to Hard Times,* was developed partly in response to the many Westerns he came upon as a reader of unsolicited screenplays for a film company. "I found them oppressive. They made me ill. So I thought to myself, *I* know more about the true West than these people do, even though at the time I hadn't been west of Ohio.''[7] His depiction of the ''true West'' seldom resembles the romanticized country of ruggedly self-reliant men, virginal-yet-intrepid women, and utter moral clarity. On the contrary, Doctorow's frontier deflates the unsubstantiated hopes and promises that compelled its inhabitants to move West in the first place.

The novel opens with the destruction of the town by the Bad Man from Bodie, who arrives as a kind of personification of the forces that conspire against the faith that ''people naturally come together.'' In a single hour's worth of murder, brutality, and arson, Clay Turner (a remarkable name for someone with so absolute a capacity for sending folks to their graves) razes most of the town and leaves only a handful of citizens behind to rebuild it. That one man can cause the collapse of an entire community emphasizes the frailty of man's attempts to establish order on the frontier. Even the narrator, the most steadfastly optimistic of the novel's characters, cannot stave off the infection of cynicism and despair:

> When I came West with the wagons, I was a young man with expectations of something, I don't know what, I tar-painted my name on a big rock by the Missouri trailside. But in time my expectations wore away with the weather, like my name had from that rock, and I learned it was enough to stay alive. Bad Men from Bodie weren't ordinary scoundrels, they came with the land, and you could no more cope with them than you could with dust or hailstones.

In short, a relentlessly revisionist spirit informs *Welcome to Hard Times*. Blue chronicles the phoenix-like re-emergence of Hard Times from out of its own ashes, and in doing so makes it evident that nature itself scorns and betrays these puny efforts at every turn: winter is paralyzing and seemingly endless; white ants rot out the very wood in the buildings; vultures and rats are more enterprising than the people who hope to sustain the town against them. And as if the hostility of the elements weren't enough, Hard Times is also at the mercy of the placement of the railroad and the location of gold deposits. Economic realities are as capricious as natural ones, and as potentially devastating; the surest occupations on the frontier are bartending, whoring, and gravedigging. Survival is reserved for strong men and scavengers.

One by one the traditional saving myths of the West are dispelled. The family, for example, a long-established symbol of stability, is represented in the town of Hard Times by Blue's makeshift collective, which includes Molly, a whore burned by the Bad Man's fire and sustained by her hunger for revenge, and Jimmy Fee, a homeless orphan, also thanks to Turner. They huddle silently with their respective animosities "like three creatures in a hole," and the only thing they truly share is their common misfortune. "And if I felt like believing we were growing into a true family," says Blue, "that was alright: if a good sign is so important you can just as soon make one up and fool yourself that way." Every relationship we come across in the novel is based on a series of transactions rather than on emotional ties. (That Blue composes on ledgers is particularly significant, for in such a vicious, Hobbesian environment, only the most tangible system of debits and credits can be trusted.[8]) Zar and his stable of whores do not confuse piddling morality with good business sense, and indeed, every interchange between Mayor Blue and prospective new citizen, between procurer and customer, is a what-can-you-do-for-me proposition. To make it as a man you must be rich, unscrupulous, or handy with a gun: to make it as a woman you must prostitute yourself to powerful men. Even Molly, who puts on airs before Zar's whores, "has sharp nails for a believer," and tries to groom and coddle both Jimmy and the marksman, Jenks, to serve as the instruments of her revenge.

It is ironic, however, that despite the consistent exposure of the frontier ideal as a "poor pinched-out claim," its promises continue largely to hold sway. "I have moved from one side of the West to the other, like a pebble rolling in the pan," confesses Blue, "and if you think this place here is not much country I can tell you none of it is." But this doesn't deter Ezra Maple and others like him from believing that a better destiny than Hard Times awaits them somewhere further west, that the idea of the frontier as a safety valve or as a perpetual second chance still obtains. Unfortunately, the frontier, whether it be a dream of future prosperity or a memory of a home left behind, exists only in the imagination. The government agent who comes to the temporarily revitalized town is clear about the ephemeral nature of human communities in the Territory:

> If a man files a claim that yields, there's a town. If he finds some grass, there's a town. Does he dig a well? Another town. Does he stop somewhere

> to ease his bladder, there's a town. Over this land a thousand times each
> year towns spring up and it appears I have to charter them all. But to what
> purpose? The claim pinches out, the grass dies, the well dries up, and
> everyone will ride off to form up again somewhere else for me to travel.
> Nothing fixes in this damned country, people blow around at the whiff of
> the wind. You can't bring the law to a bunch of rocks, you can't settle the
> coyotes, you can't make a society out of sand.

The inevitable triumph of the wilderness over the tiny towns that are grafted
onto it, and of man's selfishness and violence over his nobler impulses, is
the "true knowledge" smoldering in the gunfighter's eyes. Molly is all
respect and deference to those who share in this knowledge, but for Blue,
who waits for perfection like a fool who "didn't know what life is," she
reserves her sharpest scorn.

The second coming of the Bad Man—whose way is paved by the desertion
of Hard Times by Zar, Isaac Maple, and the others once the mine company
pulls out—is less the cause than the *confirmation* of disaster: "He never left
the town, it was waiting only for the proper light to see him where he's been
all the time." He arrives on the scene of a town already collapsed. Although
the novel ends with the death of the Bad Man, everyone else has been killed
or scattered as well; even Blue's surge of defiance cannot prevent the
completion of the Bad Man's "mission." Jimmy Fee escapes the unenforce-
able pratings of Blue to become another Bad Man. (Turner turns out to be a
truer adoptive father than Blue after all, for he represents a sounder approach
to the reality of the Dakota Territory.) Only the mad (Helga, the Swede's
wife) and the dying (the mortally wounded Blue) remain in Hard Times, and
their tenure is about to expire. To the end Blue rails against his own
vulnerability to the false promises that precede destruction, but he hasn't the
strength to set the street afire, in a blaze of Judgment, to keep the buzzards
away. "And I have to allow, with great shame, I keep thinking someone
will come by sometime who will want to use the wood." Even at the end he
cannot break himself of the stupid habit of hope.

Optimism makes Blue the most appropriate narrator, for optimism is
essential to the desire to write things down. The dying Blue expends his last
energies in documenting the story of Hard Times for a posterity he can only
hope will discover it. In an environment where nothing is certain but
misfortune, it is no wonder that Blue's attempts to relate his story truthfully

and purposefully often sputter; time and again he disclaims, questioning his own meager power to know truth and make it known: "I can't be too clear about that. . . . What I'm trying to do now. . . . It is all I can do to remember it for my purposes. . . . No, maybe I'm not telling it right. . . . What my mind sees now. . . . I have been trying to write what happened but it is hard, wishful work. . . . The form remembrance puts on things is making its own time and guiding my pen in ways I don't trust." Blue admits that his writing derives from weakness—it is as shameful as hope, under such uninspiring circumstances—and he cannot put pen to paper without apology. Molly castigates him for being a "talker" and thus someone unworthy of consideration. Certainly, in this vacuum-like wilderness, where letters are hardly ever delivered and where news travels from town to town by rumor and hearsay with the slowness of the changing seasons, Blue's dying claim to permanence and meaning seems defeated from the start. Instead, writing serves more as a sort of penance, as Blue forces himself to relive his mistakes and steep in recriminations.

Compared to the "true knowledge" of power, the knowledge available to the writer is irrelevant. The well-meaning search for truth offers little other reward than frustration:

> I'm trying to put down what happened but the closer I've come in time the less clear I am in my mind. I'm losing my blood to this rag, but more, I have the cold feeling everything I've written down doesn't tell how it was, no matter how careful I've been to get it all down it still escapes me: like what happened is far below my understanding beyond my sight. In my limits, taking a day for a day, a night for a night, have I showed the sand shifting under our feet, the terrible arrangement of our lives?

Reflecting in his ledgers, which had been left by a lawyer who came West to mine for gold and didn't want to be "encumbered" by them, Blue is limited to sparse, severe language. It is reminiscent of Hemingway, whose style shows similar disenchantment with the grandiose sentiments that more elaborate, more decorative language tends to suggest. Doctorow's narrator adheres to the facts he can best account for, and he presents them without embroidery:

> Then the fire's roar smothered his words, and a gust of smoke hid him from my sight. When it cleared again I saw that Major was not up behind

his horse, but down on the ground under him. I ran over: he had toppled with a stroke, his fist was still rigid, there was froth on his lips and a rattle in his throat. I put my hand on him and his eyes opened and he stared at me and died.

The stable was not roofed before the true cold came, we drove the horses into the enclosure of the four high walls and while they snorted so you could see their breath and turned from one corner to another, we took the corral apart and got some of the shaven logs up for joists. There was no good way of keeping warm except by moving.

What these passages represent is, to borrow David S. Gross's phrase, the "radical distrust of language"[9] which deems "talkers" fools and worships direct, wordless action. The malevolent smile of the Bad Man, the shadowy interactions of Zar, and even the mute patience of John Bear are more defensible responses to reality than Blue's obsession with his ledgers.

His writings are the exception to the stinginess with words that typifies the conversations in the novel. Like the novel's barren Dakota landscape, language is denuded, stripped down to the barest essentials. When, for example, Isaac Maple arrives from his month-long journey to join his brother in Hard Times, this is his response to Ezra's desertion:

He took a big curved pipe from his pocket, filled it and lighted it with a box match. He puffed and frowned and stared at the dusty rubble and shook his head: "It don't seem right at all."
I could understand his feelings. A man doesn't go West for nothing. He'd been traveling four or five weeks by train, by steamer, by stage, thinking all the while to find his brother when he got here. And probably to make a life.
" 'Come along when ye can.' Those were his words to me when he left."
"That so?"
" 'Come along when ye can, there's room out there fer two.' "
"That's true enough."

It is as if words were hopelessly insufficient to express such complex emotions. Talk cheapens the facts of life on the frontier.

Given these circumstances, it is hardly surprising that Blue always arrives at the same impasse: the self-defeating nature of confronting reality with language. "I scorn myself for a fool for all the bookkeeping I've done; as if notations in a ledger can fix life, as if some marks in a book can control things," he grumbles, castigating himself for believing not only in the lies of the American frontier, but also in the illusion that people profit from an awareness of their history. (The first appearance of the Bad Man hardly prepares the town to withstand his second appearance.) Behind Blue, of course, we detect Doctorow himself questioning the legitimacy of his own craft: Does it teach anything? Does it contain truth? "Do you think, mister, with all that settlement around you that you're freer than me to make your fate? Do you click your tongue at my story?" asks Blue, standing in for his creator. The ventriloquist peeks out from behind his puppet/narrator for a moment to include us in his reflections on the value of his labors.

Ultimately, even the smallest demand that Blue makes of his narrative, that it be an honest report, cannot be assured him. The content of the story he relates is difficult to relive; equally burdensome is the feeling that he is not "artist" enough to render that story reliably:

> And now I've put down what happened, everything that happened from one end to the other. And it scares me more than death scares me that it may show the truth. But how can it if I've written as if I knew as I lived them which minutes were important and which not; and spoken as if I knew the exact words everyone spoke? Does the truth come out in such scrawls, so bound by my limits?

By striving to foist coherency upon the multifariousness of real events, Blue invites falsification. If the past has some abiding truth to offer, it is far more elusive than even his uncertain narrative pretends it to be.

It is this theme of the difficulty of deriving truth from experience that enables us to understand the place of Doctorow's science fiction novel, *Big As Life,* among his fictions. The sudden appearance of two giant humanoids in a New York harbor is an event that our scientific, religious, and philosophical systems must strain to accommodate, but its significance is further obscured by a conspiracy of social institutions whose principal aim is to maintain order. Army, police, government, and church combine to form a new corporate entity, NYCRAD, whose mission is to manipulate public morale and thereby foster a desirable public reaction to the crisis. Its most crucial function is not to collect data on the giants, but rather "to promote NYCRAD itself, to build the image of NYCRAD as a protective and confidence-inspiring instrument of the public good." A complex of self-serving bureaucratic maneuvers and secret investigations, fueled by "a sinister rationale . . . an institutional rationale, independent and superhuman," NYCRAD grows into a greater and more immediate threat to the public than are the two looming giants it was created to handle.

Despite the disruption of daily life in New York (a system of evacuation, quarantine, rationing, and curfew is installed to combat potential chaos), utilities, bills, and landlords remain regular; strict city-wide enforcement of prayer and inspection rituals assures an acceptable, routinized response to the giants. An Emergency Advertising Council is mobilized to ensure faith in a government that is represented by a President whose platitudes are barely audible above the television static.

Although the giants present no definite danger to the population—their movements can only be measured in months, and the Practical Systems, Destruction section of NYCRAD is confident of at least seventeen "clean" ways of destroying them—they do catalyze a reassessment of American society that is potentially dangerous to those generals, politicians, and business magnates who profit mightily from society as it normally operates. Under the relentless shadow of the giants, society, stripped of its usual bustle, is shown up for its paltry insufficiencies and its ruling injustices. "The windows of empty stores shone brightly with the gross national product." Having been driven into dereliction, the majority now threatens to view the institutions in which they had always placed their faith with far greater objectivity. Not only do the giants signify a negation of what were presumed to be laws of science, they also serve to lay bare the uncertainty and indeterminacy that underlie our social principles. "Our most basic logic is violated by these creatures, our most basic understanding," cries a physicist, and he speaks for ministers and philosophers as well. The scientific and social absolutes by which American citizens have always conducted their lives are revealed as arbitrary conventions upheld solely by a tradition of acquiescence.

To protect against any radical reassessment, NYCRAD places General Rockelmayer, a decrepit World War II hero, at the head of the Redemption Army, a government/church hybrid designed for the "diversion and dispersion of the religious impulse." Meanwhile, the Justification Lab conducts a propaganda campaign against revelation, be it religious or political, and in praise of order and control:

Cooperate with your local authorities. Keep calm and go about your work and play with confidence in your elected government. I would remind my fellow citizens that panic and hysteria are not the qualities that made this country great.

Patriotism and duty are used to defuse the potential apocalypse that threatens to undermine the structure of American life; it becomes increasingly clear in *Big As Life* that the ideals promulgated by NYCRAD for maintaining calm are less important than keeping NYCRAD itself in existence as an incontestable source of authority, "as if it was the organization that counted rather than what it was supposed to do." In short, NYCRAD's fundamental mission is to militate against any alternative to NYCRAD; the giants are essentially a convenient excuse for those in power to consolidate their forces. Helping to ensure NYCRAD, of course, is the need of the majority to trust in its legitimacy and in its "paternal" care.

To some degree, however, our main characters evade the tyrannical auspices of Doctorow's version of Big Brother. Wallace Creighton, a displaced professor of history, achieves a kind of personal revelation. At first he accepts a position inside the mammoth bureaucracy because it represents to him the remarkable recuperative abilities of American society in a time of crisis: " 'One cannot help being thrilled by the virtually automatic engagement of every self-protective capacity of our civilization,' " he writes, officially documenting his admiration. But once he comes to realize the true nature of NYCRAD (its dependence on secrecy and deceit and its decision to destroy the giants offend the scholar's devotion to knowledge and to the freedom of the individual mind) Creighton dedicates himself to sabotaging it. Dressed in the uniform of General Rockelmayer, he proposes to use the system to subvert the system from within.

Red Bloom, on the other hand, represents rebellion from without. A jazzman and con-man, whose only dealings with NYCRAD are temporary and calculated (such as when he infiltrates a Redemption Army band only to manipulate its music into jazz in order to attract his own quartet), Red hugs the periphery of society, discovering in his outcast state an assertion of the integrity of the individual. "You make believe that there is some order and that what will happen is up to you," he explains to Creighton, who has been drawn to this strangely self-possessed musician by an intuition of their spiritual kinship. Creighton sees Red and his provocative wife, Sugarbush, as inviolable, perpetually apart from the demeaning conditions of American life. In a sense, they are human-sized equivalents of the male and female giants in the harbor: enclosed in private time and personal concerns. If Creighton's rebellion is defined by becoming an effective "agent of history," theirs is a natural aspect of their personalities, their idiosyncratic lifestyle, and their love for one another.

Nevertheless, whatever victory of the human spirit the main characters achieve in *Big As Life* is severely qualified. Effective examples of individual free will are exceptions to the pervasive influence of NYCRAD; moreover, even Creighton, Red, and Sugarbush doubt the results of their own evasion tactics:

> Here she was in the safe obscurity of her own little home, one tiny apartment among millions, her own safe place in the city. But it was an illusion. There were no homes, no safe places, only the imagination which was no home at all.
>
> That was why she was crying.

Like the prolonged cry of the giant male (his reaction to a plane's crashing into his temple), the effects of governmental activity are maddening, inescapable.

The high-level decision to destroy the giants is made to eliminate the main obstacle to the supremacy of those institutions which, prior to the giants' arrival, reigned nearly unchecked. Although we sympathize with the refusal of a few citizens to capitulate, we cannot rely on their capacity for making a meaningful difference in how society will be run hereafter. NYCRAD cannot and will not endure the possibility of another, radically different kind of existence in America. That is the greatest crisis in *Big As Life,* and it is not so much caused as it is verified by the sudden appearance of the giants.

The institutionalization of deceit and obscurity makes the task of the artist, who is already discouraged by the seeming immunity of experience to his organizing talents, that much more difficult. In the manner of *Welcome to Hard Times, The Book of Daniel* also directly complains about the inconsistencies and contradictions that plague the writer-hero's analysis of his own past, and that simultaneously mock his aspirations to objective distance—in this case, toward the Cold War hysteria that killed Paul and Rochelle Isaacson, Daniel's parents and the fictional counterparts of Julius and Ethel

Rosenberg. If for Joyce's Stephen Dedalus history is a nightmare from which he is trying to awake, for Daniel it is "that pig, biting into the heart's secrets." His probe into his personal past, a past inextricably tied to this country's political past, is obstructed at every turn; nevertheless, the knowledge it does provide reinforces Doctorow's principal argument that the myths and images that buttress patriotic faith in America are inadequate to obscure entirely the realities that fail to resemble them.

Under the pressure of social unrest, justice proves irrelevant to national policy. Both the Red Scare in the fifties and the Vietnam War in the sixties are promoted by the American government as excuses for institutional barbarism. The one sure lesson Daniel manages to dredge up from past experience is that "justice" is a myth perpetrated by an ambiguous yet formidable THEM, a ruling élite, whose power pervades not only government and law enforcement, but also advertising, restaurant chains, vending machines, Hollywood—all the tributes to unreality that anesthetize us to the ignominious facts of our heritage. Disneyland serves as the central repository of this "symbolic manipulation." Through "a radical process of reduction," Disneyland both glamorizes and trivializes the historical reality of mercantilism and exploitation into cartoon shadows for mass consumption. More sober institutions follow suit: "Banks and churches and courtrooms all depend on the appurtenances of theater. On illusion. Banks, the illusion of stability and honorable dealings to hide the rot and corruption of capitalist exploitation. Churches the illusion of sacred sanctuary for purposes of pacifying social discontent. Courtrooms of course designed to promote the illusion of solemn justice."

The America which emerges from Daniel's research is one that runs on a ruthless system of victimization. The story of the Isaacsons resolves itself into a series of intrusions into the family circle by the powers that be. Even as a child, Daniel is alert to the forces that disrupt the Isaacsons' security and constrict their lives. Ironically, it is his parents' belief in the myths of America that makes them vulnerable to the diabolical forces beneath those myths. As Artie Sternlicht argues: "They were into the system. They wore ties. They held down jobs. They put people up for President. They thought politics is something you do at a meeting. When they got busted they called it tyranny." Like the settlers in *Welcome to Hard Times,* Paul and Rochelle are seduced into a false faith. Sternlicht goes on to explain how, despite their

Socialist sympathies, they still played by the government's rules at their trial: "Instead of standing up and saying fuck you, do what you want, I can't get an honest trial anyway with you fuckers—they made motions, they pleaded innocent, they spoke only when spoken to, they played the game. All right? The whole frame of reference brought them down because they acted like defendants at a trial." Susan Isaacson, too, whose life-long complaint is "They're still fucking us," suffers from "a failure of analysis." Her nervous breakdown and suicide result from psychiatry's failure to save her and from her own political failure to understand what destroyed her family.

In rebellion against this legacy of victimization, the young Daniel dreams of being insulated from the world as a worker in a subway change booth; eventually his rebellion takes the active form of leading his sister in an escape from the Children's Shelter, where they have been placed after the jailing of their parents. Daniel recognizes the warnings inherent in his grandmother's insanity and the helplessness of the Inertia Kid at the Shelter. Refusing to succumb to a failure of analysis on his own part, Daniel instead becomes a self-proclaimed "little criminal of perception." Daniel's apostasy manifests itself during his adult years in his consistently choosing to be the manipulator rather than the manipulated, in his single-minded exploitation of people for whatever information they may have for his "book." In his investigation of the possibility of organizing a Foundation in support of the radical Left, Daniel exhibits the mixture of aggressiveness and sly maneuverability that characterize the government agents who beseiged his family years before. (His sexual sadism toward his wife suggests, too, that one cannot appropriate the tactics of the government without likewise taking on some of its inhumanity.) *The Book of Daniel* has a double function for its narrator: to symbolize both his attempt to do his parents the justice that the courts failed to do them, and his attempt to exorcise the ghosts that "clung to the roof of your mouth, . . . hovered in your brain like fear, . . . resided in your muscles like nerves."

The title of the novel also holds a double meaning: it puts personal and societal identity crises in the same context. Therefore, while Daniel examines his various "selves" (is he a Lewin or an Isaacson? a radical activist or a doctoral student? a husband or a son?), America endures the several strains of McCarthyism, anti-war demonstrations, the Bay of Pigs, Peaceniks, and so on.[10] This is to say that people's private lives are inseparable from their public identities. The question remains, however, whether or not Daniel can, like his Biblical namesake, be "a Beacon of Faith in a Time of Persecution." Will his visions of the complexities of the past enlighten us, or merely baffle us?

The shifting form of the narrative asks what is the most profitable way of making sense of the facts Daniel acquires. Because history is so difficult to capture objectively, Daniel flirts with a variety of narrative strategies—dissertation, journal, poetic confession, documentary, travelogue, political tract—as he seeks to accommodate and clarify the truth. His "rescue mission" must contend with many false starts and regrets; contrary to the confident tone of the Whitman epigram from *Song of Myself* that opens the text, uncertainty rules here. (The image of a doctoral student drowning in his own data, groping frantically for a controlling thesis, is wonderfully appropriate to the presiding tone of the novel.) The potpourri effect of *The Book of Daniel*, peppered with authorial intrusions and changes of focus between first- and third-person narration, and concluding in multiple-choice endings, convinces us that Daniel's work remains a work-in-progress, unsatisfactorily digested. He joins in Blue's dilemma, doubly obsessed by what Samuel Beckett once described as the need to express coupled with the inability to express. The past continually impinges, yet forever unravels. The result of such a maddening situation is that our narrator is never free of his subject; it contaminates even his most trivial experiences. Casually glancing at *Modern Screen,* for example, Daniel wonders Does Dick Really Love Liz? "I think he loves the fraud of spectacular dimension," he decides. "I think if they were put on trial for their lives, he might come to love her." In a sense, the universal incursion that Daniel had always hoped to flee or to conquer continues long after the deaths of Paul and Rochelle. The adult Daniel frequently plunges into a free fall back through the years; his thoughts are oppressed by images of electricity, which powers American mythology (electronic media, Disneyland) and subdues the potential enemies of that mythology (with the electric chair).[11]

In contrast to the spare language of *Welcome to Hard Times,* which marks Blue's narrative as a natural product of the barren Dakota landscape, *The Book of Daniel* offers a profusion of words, as befits the volumes upon volumes that have been dedicated to the famous Isaacson case (and from which Daniel liberally quotes). Employing this encyclopedic approach, Daniel hopes to surround and overwhelm the truth; his asides, associations, and digressions may be likened to military tactics, by which he means to outflank the truth before it can elude him. Still, despite such dedication, Daniel is never convinced that he is on top of his subject. Driving in the rain with his wife and baby son, he intuits a metaphor for the unavoidable convolutions of the narrative process:

> Daniel's eyes focused on the surface of the windshield, trying to anticipate the small explosions of rain. This was too difficult, so he fixed on one drop and followed its career. The idea was that his attention made it different from the other drops. It arrived, head busted, with one water bead as a nucleus and six or seven clusters in a circle around it. It was like a melted snowflake. Each of the mini-drop clusters combined and became elongated and pulled away in the direction of its own weight. As he accelerated the car, so did they increase their rate of going away from the center.

This drifting "away from the center" seems a natural tendency of the information he gathers. The problem of rendering the past honestly reaches beyond good intentions. How can one move back through the years to discover a portrait of the Isaacsons that is unadulterated by time, publicity, rumor, or propaganda?

> But this isn't the couple in the poster. That couple got away. Well funded, and supplied with false passports, they went either to New Zealand or Australia. Or Heaven. In any event, my mother and father, standing in for them, went to their deaths for crimes they did not commit. Or maybe they did committ them. Or maybe my mother and father got away with false passports for crimes they didn't committ. How do you spell comit? Of one thing we are sure. Everything is elusive. God is elusive. Revolutionary morality is elusive. Human character. Quarters for the cigarette machine. You've got these two people in the poster, Daniel, now how you going to get them out?

There is always the nagging suspicion that "life is never this well plotted," that, in trying to make meaning apply to experience (in the manner, too, of the Biblical Daniel trying to understand his dreams), interpretation crosses over into creation, or perhaps into falsification. As he tries to place his parents in the context of other famous dissidents, so as to bestow upon them a profounder dimension, Daniel can only approximate some scenes, often misremembering, and at times recalling what he could not possibly have witnessed. "Probably none of this is true. There's a lot more I can't remember," he says, admitting to his inadequacies. Underlying his depiction of past events is an apology to Paul, Rochelle, and Susan for not being a more capable writer for their sake. The degree to which he fails is the measure of his betrayal of their memory. And wouldn't it be more worthwhile, more justifiable, he wonders, to join the activists against the war in Vietnam, or perhaps to finish his Ph.D., than to persist in this useless fashion? Like Blue's ledgers, Daniel's book causes him far more shame than satisfaction: "IS IT SO TERRIBLE NOT TO KEEP THE MATTER IN MY HEART, TO GET THE MATTER OUT OF MY HEART, TO EMPTY MY HEART OF THIS MATTER? WHAT IS THE MATTER WITH MY HEART?"

Writing itself, then, is indicted for being merely peripheral to experience. Surely it is not the only response to reality analyzed in the course of the novel. Artie Sternlicht channels *his* rebellion into spectacular public demonstrations. An Abbie Hoffman look-alike, he combats the Establishment by using its own most effective weapons—the national media. His method is to infiltrate the media in order to undermine their proprietors: "We're gonna overthrow the United States with images!" he proclaims. The most dramatic of these images is a televised attempt to levitate the Pentagon by incantation in order to shake out its demons. Since America itself is an aggregate of images, this is fighting fire with fire, so to speak. The outrageousness of Flower Children and Yippies may prove more useful to the struggle than Daniel's self-indulgent "novel as private I."

Daniel also examines the opposite alternative chosen by Linda Mindish, which is to repudiate the implications of the past by *embracing* the mythology of the present. By aligning herself exclusively with the forces of middle-class domesticity and consumerism in the sixties, Linda simply refuses to accept the legacy of being the daughter of the man who traduced the Isaacsons in the fifties. This "ahistorical" attitude is exemplified in the extreme by the doddering Selig Mindish himself, whose senility nullifies everything except a passion for driving the tiny cars donated by the Richfield Corporation for Disneyland's Autopia.

However attractive these alternatives may appear to Daniel, he is nevertheless riveted to his chosen task—even to the point of visualizing the electrocutions of the Isaacsons—by the belief that "the failure to make connections is complicity." He does not flinch from connections that might lead him into trouble with the authorities, or from connections that might threaten the reputations of would-be reformers, compassionate lawyers, or even his father. His examination of the institutions that killed his parents leads him to an indictment of his parents' belief that society can somehow cure itself through the operation of those institutions.[12] *The Book of Daniel* refuses to shy from that understanding. It is a confession that may burn more than it purges, but whatever its shortcomings, it still represents the refusal of an individual to capitulate to those forces that would rob him of his freedom and deprive him (in the way the rest of his family is deprived) of the ability to strike back. Although Daniel's coming to terms with history is compromised by his own doubts, it does have a therapeutic effect on him: analysis brings him into greater maturity. If it seems that Blue's dying complaints about having been duped by the illusions of the American frontier are futile, at least Daniel's efforts to rescue the truth—although he is no more secure in his ability to do so than Blue—seem directed to a more positive, redemptive purpose.

The incorporation of real-life personalities into fiction, which Doctorow inaugurated in *The Book of Daniel,* is the trademark of his most celebrated and financially successful novel, *Ragtime.* Shifting his chronological backdrop again, this time to the opening years of the twentieth century, Doctorow interweaves the story of a nameless family from New Rochelle, New York, with the lives of many of the dominant figures of the age, such as Harry Houdini, J. P. Morgan, Henry Ford, Evelyn Nesbit, Stanford White, Emma Goldman, and Sigmund Freud. While it is this imaginative borrowing from history that first arrests our attention in reading *Ragtime,* Doctorow asserts that "the unusual thing" about the novel "was to have narrative distance. To create something not as intimate as fiction nor as remote as history, but a voice that was mock-historical—pedantic."[13] Although the style he employs for this novel evokes much of the feeling of turn-of-the-century nostalgia we recognize from paintings, movies, and the sentimental misrepresentations of history we read in our schoolbooks, Doctorow exploits our stereotypical conception of the good old days only to break down our complacency. For example, the novel opens with a rather seductive portrait of "simpler times":

> Patriotism was a reliable sentiment in the early 1900's. Teddy Roosevelt was President. The population customarily gathered in great numbers either

out of doors for parades, public concerts, fish fries, political picnics, social outings, or indoors in meeting halls, vaudeville theatres, operas, ballrooms. There seemed to be no entertainment that did not involve great swarms of people. Trains and steamers and trolleys moved them from one place to another. That was the style, that was the way people lived. Women were stouter then. They visited the fleet carrying white parasols. Everyone wore white in summer. Tennis racquets were heavy and the racquet faces elliptical. There was a lot of sexual fainting. There were no Negroes. There were no immigrants.

Our easy appreciation of social outings and parades (we fill in the contours of the scene with long skirts, homemade ice cream, horseshoe pitching) is abruptly undercut by the eradication of Negroes and immigrants from the picture, since their sufferings must be neglected in order to preserve the sentimental facade.

As the novel progresses, of course, nostalgia is shown to be not merely misguided, but outrageous, even criminal. The terse, flat prose, which is so amenable to the nostalgic catalogues that typically accompany our vision of this era, is now used to handle the abundant evidence against these myths:

Millions of men were out of work. Those fortunate enough to have jobs were dared to form unions. Courts enjoined them, police busted their heads, their leaders were jailed and new men took their jobs. A union was an affront to God. The laboring man would be protected and cared for not by the labor agitators, said one wealthy man, but by the Christian men to whom God in His infinite wisdom had given the control of the property interests of this country. If all else failed the troops were called out. . . . On the tobacco farms Negroes stripped tobacco leaves thirteen hours a day and earned six cents an hour, man, woman or child. Children suffered no discriminatory treatment. They were valued everywhere they were employed. They did not complain as adults tended to do. . . . In the canneries and mills these were the hours they were most likely to lose their fingers or have their hands mangled or their legs crushed; they had to be counseled to stay alert. In the mines they worked as sorters of coal and sometimes were smothered in the coal chutes; they were warned to keep their wits about them. One hundred Negroes a year were lynched. One hundred miners were buried alive. One hundred children were mutilated.

It is the interplay between these two conflicting visions of America, the charmingly nostalgic and the bitterly ironic, that creates a complex pattern symbolized by the metaphor of ragtime music.

The notion of different meters played simultaneously is also relevant to the way in which Doctorow's historically verifiable characters interrelate with his wholly "created" characters. Those who are famous for their wealth, their beauty, their power to shape events, carry the symbolic freight of the American Dream; by virtue of their exalted status, they may be considered as mythological characters who ride the crest of history. What is more, their eminence is further assured by the masses themselves, who "buy into" the myths that validate the inequalities in American society. Emma Goldman, the well-known anarchist, who serves as a kind of feisty Tiresias ducking in and out of the narrative, explains this phenomenon to a confused but receptive Evelyn Nesbit:

> I am often asked the question How can the masses permit themselves to be exploited by the few. The answer is by being persuaded to identify with them. Carrying his newspaper with your picture the laborer goes home to his wife, an exhausted workhorse with the veins standing out in her legs, and he dreams not of justice but of being rich.

The very fact of their distinction in society seems to mark people who have it as *worthy* of that distinction. (J. P. Morgan goes so far as to investigate the possibility of his belonging to a genetically superior strain of mankind that reaches back to the Pharaohs.) The media further assert the prominence of such people in "common" minds:

> There was a process of magnification by which news events established certain individuals in the public consciousness as larger than life. These were the individuals who represented one desirable human characteristic to the exclusion of all others. The businessmen wondered if they could create such individuals not from the accidents of new events but from the deliberate manufactures of their own medium.

Meanwhile, the degree to which these privileged individuals are magnified is inversely proportional to the degree to which the majority is reduced. The mass of men are anonymous beneath the superhuman images of those who dominate the history books and newspaper headlines; it is significant that the murder of Stanford White by a jealous Harry Thaw over the affections of Evelyn Nesbit is deemed the Crime of the Century, whereas a thousand less "newsworthy" crimes against factory workers, poor people, coal miners, and the rest occur daily and go unadvertised. The lords of government and of capitalism are shown to be in league for the maintenance of a vicious status quo; its victims suffer bureaucratically enforced prejudice.

In none of Doctorow's earlier novels is the rule of the élite portrayed as so bloodthirsty or so absolute. The immigrants, who *do* exist, cower before those stolid officials whose whims decide their fates: "These officials changed names they couldn't pronounce and tore people from their families, consigning to a return voyage old folks, people with bad eyes, riffraff and also those who looked insolent. Such power was dazzling. The immigrants were reminded of home." Acknowledgement of the existence of the poor by the élite, when it occurs at all, takes the perverse form of poverty balls, where the rich come dressed in rags to palatial houses, decorated to look like mines or dirt farms, and smoke cigar butts served from silver trays. There is no meaningful difference in the eyes of the wealthy between the oppressed poor and the circus freaks who are invited to come divert them at parties; both entertainments are amusing at best, vulgar at worst. Doctorow's upper class in *Ragtime* is heartless, manipulative—they have inculcated into their own bestial personalities the traits of an age that worships machinery, and whose progress is most aptly defined by the "screeching and pounding of metal on metal. . . . a suicide rag."

Ragtime's episodic, free-flowing structure resists simple plot summary. As in his preceding novels, Doctorow here anchors his large themes to an analysis of the tribulations of a single family. Compared to the Blue-Molly-Jimmy Fee unit in *Welcome to Hard Times* and the exploded Isaacson family in *The Book of Daniel,* the suburban household of Father, Mother, Grandfather, Mother's Younger Brother, and Boy appears, at least on the surface, to confirm an idea of family solidarity and intimacy congruent with our other nostalgic images. But this, too, proves to be a deception; the pleasant stereotypes suggested by the "generic" names of the family members—we are reminded of the antiseptic caricatures who populated our grade-school readers—are utterly refuted as the novel unfolds. Sharing a residence is no guarantee of shared lives. Each member of the family is isolated from the others by his own obsessions. Father repudiates his authority as head of the family by joining the Peary expedition to the Pole; when he finally returns home, he can never truly dispel the mutual estrangement between himself and his wife, nor does he ever feel comfortable with "the degrees of turn in the moral planet" signalled by the intrusion of Coalhouse Walker, Sarah, and their illegitimate child into his household. Mother's Younger Brother falls prey to the hypnotic charms of Evelyn Nesbit, and then to a fascination with leftist insurrections; he transforms the fireworks Father employed in support of patriotism into devastating explosives, to be used first in support of the Coalhouse gang's vengeance against firehouses and later in support of Zapata in Mexico. Mother, Grandfather, and the Boy, while less susceptible to the allures of the famous, are still alone with their personal interests: Mother in her peace of mind, Grandfather in his declining health, the Boy in the mysteries of pattern and repetition in his life. The disruption of the Norman Rockwell-style portrayal of the family is in keeping with the demystification of such sentimental figures as volunteer firemen and baseball players in *Ragtime,* as well as those men who seem to J. P. Morgan chosen monarchs "of the invisible, transnational kingdom of capital whose sovereignty was everywhere granted."

The plot line that includes Tateh and his beautiful daughter also illustrates the insubstantiality of the American Dream—specifically, that aspect of the Dream which promotes America in the eyes of immigrants as the Land of Plenty and Promise. Tateh suffers one indignity after another, living from day to day and from meal to meal in the slums of New York. Having lost his wife to the corruptive influences of his environment, he ties his little girl to his wrist with string for fear that she, too, will be stripped from him. That Tateh manages to save himself and his daughter from defeat, and to succeed miraculously in the film industry, does not minimize Doctorow's criticism, for Tateh's luck emphasizes the unpredictability and the infrequency of dreams being realized. In contradiction to J. P. Morgan's faith in divine selection of the prosperous on earth, Tateh makes it primarily by blind luck. Chance brings Evelyn Nesbit to dote upon his daughter when all seems lost; chance likewise brings him to the window of the Franklin Novelty Company in Philadelphia to try to sell his "movie books." The fact is that the only *reliable* manner in which power is reincarnated through the generations has to do with the maintenance and accretion of inheritance; as for Tateh, his elevation to Baron Ashkenazy convinces us only of the fickleness of fate, and reminds us of the millions whose talents *aren't* faddish. In a society where the way democracy is instituted robs the majority of its real freedoms, and where a concentration camp mentality of industrial manufacture renders men disposable and interchangeable as the parts they handle on assembly lines, Tateh wins a superior fate by being an artist who happens to point "his life along the flow of American energy."

But even the possibility of so rare an alternative to defeat is denied Coalhouse Walker. The Negro, no matter how qualified or well-mannered he may become, can only hope to be tolerated as a second-class citizen in White America. In fact, because the system of justice is designed to protect the ruling class, thereby ceasing to function when a Negro seeks to share in its benefits, not even second-class status can be guaranteed him. Ironically, Coalhouse Walker's personal talent and dignity, his stylishness and quiet bearing, mark him as "uppity"; vandalizing his car is not just a joke on the part of the volunteer firemen, it is also a lesson in reality. That Coalhouse must form a Provisional American Government of his own to capture the attention of his persecutors through violent means is hardly surprising, since the conventional institutions of justice prove unserviceable for him; nor is it surprising that his revenge fails to vindicate him, but only dooms him. Frustrated by the organized neglect that leads from his personal disgrace to Sarah's death, Coalhouse is forced to undertake a course of action (blowing up firehouses, occupying the Morgan library) that appears to justify the resentment and distrust of the society that brought him to such desperate measures in the first place.[14] As Emma Goldman explains to dumbfounded police and reporters, Coalhouse's actions are the direct result of oppression. Although his case is unusual because of its prominence in the public eye, it is symptomatic of a widespread disease: "The oppressor is wealth, my friends. Wealth is the oppressor. Coalhouse Walker did not need Red Emma to learn that. He needed only to suffer."

Throughout the massive sweep of time and activity in *Ragtime,* our narrator (revealed at the conclusion of the novel as the Boy grown to adulthood) attempts, in the tradition of Blue and Daniel, to make connections. As it happens, his concern with reliable, "duplicable events" is shared by other members of the *Ragtime* cast, most notably by Henry Ford (in the duplication of automobiles at an efficient clip) and by J. P. Morgan (in the duplication of the individual through reincarnation, and in the endless duplication of dollars). The difference, of course, is that the artist's concern, like that of the social historian, is with investing pattern with meaning, not just with revelling in the appeal of pattern for its own sake. The style of *Ragtime,* comparable to a jumble of newsreel clips superimposed on a single vast screen, questions whether or not such patterning can ever be anything but artificial. What emerges as the most attractive aspect of any nostalgic rendition of the early years of this century is apparent *coherency,* as opposed to the baffling flux of real life. In this context it is valuable to note Barbara Foley's argument that a fundamental difference between *Ragtime* and Dos Passos' *U.S.A.* trilogy (the latter encompasses the chronological boundaries of Doctorow's novel) is that Dos Passos tends to mold his fiction to fit a pattern of history, which he feels is more organized, whereas Doctorow prefers to mold history to fit his fiction, whose conscious fabrication strikes him as being the more reliable.[15]

It is with a sense of wonder at the enormity of his task that our narrator returns to the Ragtime era. His preference for short, building-block sentences implies a strict allegiance to the facts; underlying this style is the conviction that the facts are provocative in themselves, requiring no ornamentation. The fatal wounding of Sarah by Secret Service guards who mistake her attempt to get the Vice President's attention for an attempt on his life, the vile treatment of children who work in factories and mines, and the whole-sale slaughter of wild animals by that noted conservationist, Teddy Roosevelt, are but three examples of incidents that probably tempt the artist to engage in satirical overkill, but he presents them matter-of-factly, in the manner of courtroom testimony. That historically documented fact and imaginatively concocted fiction are equally remarkable and co-exist so readily in this novel further supports Philip Roth's "apology" in "Writing American Fiction." When Doctorow recharges historical events with fantastic possibilities, as we witness in the wonderful scene that climaxes with Freud and Jung riding through Coney Island's Tunnel of Love together, the demarcations between reality and illusion disappear completely. In short, these delightful artistic fusions (or syncopations, given the guiding metaphor of the novel's title) show history to be susceptible to the same rage for order as art, as well as to the same processes of selection, amendment, and manipulation; contrary to their aspirations to objective truth, both are fundamentally subjective, creative mediators between self and society, neither of which is entirely dispensable nor entirely sufficient to guarantee that relationship.

If we are gratified by the connections our narrator makes for us between personal experiences and nationally publicized events, between the lives of the anonymous and the lives of the famous, we are still disheartened by how seemingly fruitless these connections are, in terms of improving the quality of life, when made over a distance of years. There is little evidence in the novel to refute Freud's blanket condemnation: "America is a mistake, a gigantic mistake." By all appearances, society is immune to the probings and criticisms of the artist. Regardless of these discouraging circumstances, the Boy is never deterred in the way Doctorow's previous narrators were; unlike Blue and Daniel, who had the necessary dedication to their narratives, but whose confidence in their own abilities and in the value of their writing waned, the Boy displays a natural talent for narration from the very start. He possesses a true genius for recovery: the accumulated data of an entire generation are immediately present in his mind. His suitability for his narrative function is symbolized by metaphors of enlarged perception: "He saw through things and noted the colors people produced and was never surprised by a coincidence. A blue and green planet rolled through his eyes." Deeply sensitive to nuance and subtlety, he writes an account that includes so many coincidences and reflections that he convinces us to entertain the possibility of some ulterior "plot" to experience: Evelyn Nesbit's bathing of Tateh's daughter is paralleled by her own ritualistic body massage given by Emma Goldman; the persistent wooing of Evelyn by Mother's Younger Brother is recalled by Coalhouse's wooing of Sarah; the Franklin Novelty Company, which first purchases Tateh's movie books, turns out to be the source of Henry Ford's pamphlet on reincarnation; Ford and J. P. Morgan share an obsession with reincarnation across half the continent, and this obsession is likewise shared by Harry Houdini, who frantically engages seers to help him contact his dead mother; the burials from which Houdini escapes in his routines are mimicked by the ceremonies on the beach in Atlantic City conducted by the Boy and Tateh's daughter; people are always passing by or going through buildings designed by Stanford White, whose scandalous death overshadows much of the novel. The cast of characters separates and recombines in new and exciting ways, strengthening our faith in some complex system of contingency and interdependence. Characters and events regularly connect in ways we can only call significant.

But it is not simply the Boy's thoroughness that recommends him for a narrative career; he exhibits a sort of extra-sensory perception that not only enables him to enter the minds of adults, but also appears to give him fleeting insights into the future. (Witness his early admonition to Houdini to "warn the Duke," which will only make sense much later when Houdini meets the Archduke Ferdinand, whose assassination will help set World War I in motion.) Finally, only at the very end of his story does he reveal himself as the narrator of *Ragtime;* only on remembering the death of his father aboard the *Lusitania* does he permit his objective posture to falter, and he surrenders himself to personal rumination:

> Poor Father, I see his final exploration. He arrives at the new place, his hair risen in astonishment, his mouth and eyes dumb. His toe scuffs a soft storm of sand, he kneels and his arms spread in pantomimic celebration, the immigrant, as in every moment of his life, arriving eternally on the shore of his Self.

This brief eulogy on his father recalls several occasions in the course of *Ragtime* on which we detect indirect admissions of the difficulties inherent in composing such a book. When we are told, in reference to Houdini's amazing feats, that "today, nearly fifty years since his death, the audience for escapes is even larger," we should recognize that the Boy is also referring to nostalgia, to how it tends to defeat his purposes by being so much more attractive than reality, which, according to the newspapers, becomes more grotesque every day. It can also be argued that his consistent interest in Houdini's doubts about the validity of his career as "a trickster, an illusionist, a mere magician" betrays misgivings about his own chosen vocation. Being an artist, because it depends to a great extent on a detached relationship with "real life"—"The real-world act was what got into the history books," Houdini broods—demands nearly routine self-justification.

The challenge of "reconstituting the world" extends to other characters whose professions don't automatically suggest it. Both Mother and Father complain (through the medium of their son's intuition) of their inability to withstand the chaos that infects their lives. Father especially gives precedent to the Boy's narrative by composing a journal during his adventures at the Pole. He hoped to achieve clarity and perspective by joining the expedition (his compulsive desire for venturing out into the unknown reminds us of Bulkington's in *Moby Dick*) and then turned to writing to help him make a stand against the barbaric disorder of the Eskimo lifestyle: "Father kept himself under control by writing in his journal. This was a system too, the system of language and conceptualization. It proposed that human beings, by the act of making witness, warranted times and places for their existence other than the time and place they were living through.'' The question of finding a comfortable yet useful perspective also underlies the anecdote about Theodore Dreiser trying to ''find the proper alignment'' for the chair in his writing room, which ends with him turning hopelessly in circles. The ''correct'' posture cannot be so readily attained. This is the very problem that confronts Admiral Peary when he tries to determine exactly where the North Pole is located on the shifting ice cap: ''No one observation satisfied him,'' just as no one position satisfied Dreiser, and by extrapolation, no one version of the Ragtime era should satisfy the conscientious artist or reader. Astonished since childhood by the utter instability of things and people around him, the Boy must begin with the premise that ''the world composed and recomposed itself constantly in an endless process of dissatisfaction.''

Ragtime concludes with two final examples of forces which frustrate narration. One of these is the success of Tateh in the creation of *Our Gang*-style film comedies; such a disinfected vision of society shows art failing to illuminate history, and instead *erasing* it. The second obstacle to truth-seeking is represented by Harry K. Thaw, released from an insane asylum, marching annually in the Armistice Day parade at Newport. Here, too, the patriotic platitudes that have presumably been dismissed by the debunking efforts of the novel continue to hold sway on the national scene, even to the point of absorbing men like Thaw. Little has changed despite all that has occurred in *Ragtime;* the novel opens with Father making a living from patriotism, and the market still exists when the novel's frame is completed years later. Thus, as in every Doctorow novel, the dominant American mythology remains relatively intact. Despite their unsavory portrayal in *Ragtime,* those who succeed mightily in this country are role models for the rest who would like to, while those who create those unheroic portrayals carry the brand ''criminals of perception.'' The censure of his social supe-riors, as well as the bafflement of his family, is the price the artist pays for his vigilance.

The artist's duty is reasserted once again in Doctorow's most recent novel: ''The failure of perception is what did you in.'' It is a slogan which is central not only to competent narration, but also to survival itself in a society that steadily shortchanges the majority of its citizens. *Loon Lake* locates this indictment in the years of the Great Depression, as Doctorow continues his revisionist survey of American history. What was true of the periods investigated in his previous novels proves true of the 1930's: once the facts of life are faithfully exposed, nostalgia cannot withstand the strain of too much reality.

The basic myth informing *Loon Lake,* both in regard to the theme and the plot structure of the novel, is the "get-rich-quick" optimism of Horatio Alger, whose tales of virtuous innocents receiving astounding rewards imagine an America of infinite promise and generosity. While Doctorow's Joe, a mill kid from Paterson, New Jersey, who ends up becoming one of the wealthiest, most influential men in America, ostensibly follows the pattern of *Ragged Dick* and *Mark, the Match-Boy,* the self-conscious attitude he takes toward his adventures—in his estimation, a "picaresque of other men's money and other men's wives"—thoroughly subverts the naive convictions upon which Alger's tales are founded. As Joe contends:

> It was a matter of the distance you took, if you went to the top of the Empire State Building as I liked to do seeing it all was thrilling you had to admire the human race making its encampment like this I could hear the sound of traffic rising like some song to God and love His Genius for shining the sun on it. But down on the docks men slept in the open pulled up like babies on beds of newspapers, hands palm on palm for a pillow. Not their dereliction, that wasn't the point, but their meagerness, for I saw this too as I stood at the piers and watched the ocean liners sail.

As always, Doctorow's method is to refute the conventional assumptions of the American Dream by demonstrating its irrelevance to specific cases. Indeed, were Joe to succumb meekly to such assumptions, his fate would never rise above bare subsistence. Out of necessity Joe is a hustler, a thief, a liar, and a rogue, for these are the "virtues" which best assure him of advancement; his irreverence is matched only by his "keenness" for life, which comprises a series of experiments: "I was interested in the way I instantly knew who the situation called for and became him." For example, Joe is initiated into a world where religion only helps the destitute to believe their suffering is purposeful, and where the only visible saint is Saint Garbage; accordingly, Joe kicks the fat local priest in the groin and empties the poorbox. Joe's "polytropic" nature gives him universal access. He is at ease with the railroad hoboes and joins their arguments over leftist politics (which, relegated to hoboes, are hardly granted the status they receive in *The Book of Daniel* or *Ragtime*); he infiltrates Sim Hearn's carnival, winning the trust and affection of the freaks; and he is just as resourceful in gaining the confidences of a shambling poet, a stunning gangster's moll, and the lofty F. W. Bennett himself.

Joe enjoys the freedom of his adventures in the New York countryside until he is struck one night by a vision that directs him from his peripheral activities into a restricted world of luxurious success. The sight of a beautiful, naked girl in an illuminated private car of a passing train becomes a Grail for him, and our dazzled hero follows it to its destination: Loon Lake, the splendid Adirondack estate of the wealthy industrialist F.W. Bennett. Here Joe first encounters that "mysterious system of legalities and caste and extended brilliant endeavor" by whose dictates a select group of entrepreneurs (the euphemism applies equally well to business magnates and gangsters, who together form a class of their own) plot the course of the nation.

That Joe is nearly killed at Loon Lake by a pack of wild dogs is a fitting introduction to the lesson about life his exploits will teach from this point on: fangs and claws are the way of the world. The consequences of aspiring to an exalted lifestyle can be fatal, and very few survive the struggle to realize a satisfactory share of the American Dream: "Something has leaked out through the stitches and some of the serious intention of the world has leaked in: like the sense of high stakes, the desolate chance of real destiny."

In addition to meeting the mythical Bennett and Clara Lukacs, whose figure so entranced him from the train window, Joe makes the acquaintance of Warren Penfield, the so-called resident poet of Loon Lake, who was likewise drawn to this locus of power several years earlier. Penfield's past, which is remembered in a series of fragments interspersed throughout the novel, provides a number of significant correlations with Joe's. Penfield made *his* pilgrimage to Loon Lake to avenge the death of his father, who had been buried alive in a mining accident in Ludlow, Colorado; as a young, introspective boy, he had witnessed the paltry payoff (given in the same railroad car that would later affect Joe so completely) conducted by an indifferent F.W. Bennett, then Vice President of Engineering for the Colorado Fuel and Iron Company. But Penfield, who also carries evidence on his arm of the dogs' savagery, is easily seduced into a meek acceptance of servitude to Bennett as the kept plaything of Lucinda, the world-famous aviatrix and the great man's wife. A "sweet dupe" who is utterly overwhelmed by the sheer force of more powerful personalities at Loon Lake, Penfield tells Joe the story of his life; it is a litany of suffering that seems to Joe "farcically set in the path of historical and natural disaster it comes to me as entertainment." The sad poet is really no more vital than Lucinda's helpless macrocephalic son, and he receives the same sort of simple maternal care from her. Ultimately it is up to Joe to carry out a mission of betrayal against the Bennett stronghold; he repudiates permanent employment at Loon Lake and, with the aid of Penfield's money and admonitions, steals off in one of Bennett's expensive cars.

Loon Lake soon resolves itself into the dilemma of choosing between symbolic fathers, Penfield and Bennett. Both men make important claims upon Joe throughout the course of the novel. Penfield's claim is advanced by Joe's sense of being detached from real life and by his fondness for the intricacies of language. When he is interrogated by police after the murder of Lyle Red James, a double agent at Bennett Autobody in Jacksontown, Joe instinctively relies upon the artful wordmongering of "Mr. Penfield, yes, the hero of his own narration with life and sun and stars and universe concentrically disposed on the locus of his tongue—pure Penfield." Like the poet, Joe is obsessed with a young woman who tyrannizes his consciousness; indeed, Joe's life copies Penfield's youth with uncanny accuracy. His half-protective, half-dependent relationship with the carnival Fat Lady summons to mind Penfield's worship of the massive Buddha in Japan; for that matter, the carnival provides Joe with escape and rejuvenation in much the same way that the Japanese monastery serves Penfield.

But while it is true that Joe's thoughts turn to the poet when he contemplates affairs of the spirit, he finally responds more profoundly to the teachings of F. W. Bennett in dealing with the world of practical concerns; if Penfield has begged wisdom from a Zen instructor, Joe understands that advice on how to live in the world must come from someone whose credentials in *that* field of endeavor are without peer. Appropriating Bennett's car, his wardrobe, and his favored guest from Loon Lake, Joe acquires the appearance of Bennett's true son. By refusing to be burdened by moral considerations during this operation, Joe reflects the attitude that enabled Bennett himself to reach his social status: "Calculating, heedless, and without gratitude, I accepted every circumstance that had put me there, only gunning my mind to the future, wanting more, expecting more, too intent on what was ahead to sit back and give thanks or to laugh or to feel bad." In contrast to Penfield, who personifies the niggling dictates of conscience (the soul), Bennett stands for the material preoccupations of the body (or, as the name of his factory system suggests, the Autobody). Joe has earlier been exposed to such an uninterrupted will to success in the person of Sim Hearn, the carnival owner who silently presides over the exploitation, even the rape and death, of his prize freak; just as Hearn never acknowledges Joe's affair with his wife, neither does Bennett seem to be aware of Lucinda's relationship with Penfield, as both men are preoccupied with more pressing economic activities.

F.W. Bennett recalls J.P. Morgan from *Ragtime* by virtue of his extraordinary capacity for putting his whims into operation, in accordance with the prerogative of wealth. Morgan dreams of ensuring his permanent memory by building his own pyramid, and Bennett, too, is intrigued by monuments, particularly the Indian memorials that lie buried at his Adirondack "camp." His eminence enters into one of Penfield's Japan poems: "The emperor is lacquered, his sword is set with suns, while / in another room doctors dispute the meaning of his stool." Bennett's reign over people and events bespeaks a "frightening freedom," an indomitable will whose effects are immeasurable. Joe's protracted escape from Loon Lake is no escape at all, for it lands him in the dehumanizing service of Bennett Autobody Number Six. Like God Himself, Bennett is at once isolated and omnipresent, and places that may appear to be God-forsaken are not, after all, Bennett-forsaken.

While trying to carve out some sort of meager existence for himself and Clara in Jacksontown, Joe becomes entangled in a network of deceit. Hostilities between the union and Crapo Industrial Services, a Bennett-supervised strong-arm organization led by the gangster chieftain whom Clara once deserted, lead to the brutal murder of Lyle Red James and to the vicious beating of our hero. The circumstances of Lyle's death and his true allegiance remain in doubt, but the primary concern of the police is not to root out the truth so much as to wrap up the case neatly without jeopardizing their collusion with some very influential people. Operating in the dark, left alone by the opportunistic Clara, and facing the interrogation of strangers, Joe plays the trump card that decides once and for all the question of his loyalties:

"I was livid with rage. Oh Penfield. Oh my soul. I could barely get the words out. 'You stupid son of a bitch,' I said to the chief. 'Tell Mr. Bennett it's his son calling. Tell him it's his son, Joe.' ''

It is at this point that Joe assures the direction his destiny will take. Upon his release from the police station, Joe continues to travel west, now with the widowed Sandy James and her baby son, and he even goes so far as to promise to marry her. For a brief moment, caught up in the exhilaration of escape into a new beginning, he discloses his own susceptibility to the myths of the American Dream:

> We were an establishment with not a little pride in ourselves and the effect we made in the world. I thought of a bungalow under palm trees, something made of stucco with a red tile roof. I thought of the warm sun. I imagined myself driving up to my bungalow in the palm trees, driving up in an open roadster and tooting the horn as I pulled up to the curb.

The train ride that follows is described as something out of a Frank Capra film, with a cross-section of American society revelling in unanimous camaraderie and good will. But Joe leaves Sandy and her baby asleep on the train after all, and instead heads off to Loon Lake. He will become the old man's confidant following Lucinda's disappearance with Penfield, and, finally, his adopted son and heir. Thus does the Horatio Alger pattern of achievement, however devalued by evidence of corruption throughout the novel, complete itself. Joe selects the most profitable road available to him: after grooming himself in the finest schools in the East, marrying twice into moneyed families, and entering a number of high-powered corporations, he will eventually duplicate Bennett's achievement as the next Master of Loon Lake.

The thematic complexities of *Loon Lake* are enhanced by Doctorow's stylistic experimentation. The narrative is laced with run-on sentences, as though the stream of consciousness was churning beyond the narrator's ability to organize. Note for example a portion of Joe's reminiscence of Mechanic Street:

> Only the maniacs were alive, the men and women who lived on the street, there was one we called Saint Garbage who went from ash can to ash can collecting what poor people had no use for—can you imagine?—and whatever he found he put on his cart or on his back, he wore several hats several jackets coats pairs of pants, socks over shoes over slippers, you

couldn't look at his face, it was bearded and red and raw and one of his
eyes ran with some yellow excrescence oh Saint Garbage.

Thought-overload also accounts for shifts between first- and third-person
narration and for digression after digression from the main plot line, all of
which is in keeping with the concept of "data linkage" advanced in the
novel. Data linkage is comparable to Daniel Isaacson's desire to "make
connections" in *The Book of Daniel;* it is an ongoing attempt to piece
experience together so that it "computes," offers sense. Wanting to transform apprehended reality into symbolic packages is Joe's most significant
connection to Penfield, who from boyhood on accumulates data in a "relentless faculty of composition."

Approaching the story with the strategies of prose, verse, library research,
and computer science helps to reveal the text *as* a text and confers upon
Doctorow's fiction the instructive qualities of an object lesson or a fable. We
often come upon lyrical interludes in the novel which unite images of
computing, combusting, composing, and sexual commingling, as if to argue
that mechanical, creative, and sensory aptitudes continually impinge upon
one another in the rush of modern living. Similarly, the prevailing message
of the many poetic passages detailing the history of Warren Penfield is that
individual essence and potency are sharply threatened by mass technology
and routinization. When Penfield responds to an enemy attack during the
First World War by sending a semaphore translation of the opening lines of
Wordsworth's "Ode: Intimations of Immortality," he is instinctively aligning himself with the forces that demand the dignity of the individual spirit;
however, those forces are few and relatively inconsequential in *Loon Lake.*
Society is more aptly defined by the savage realities that plunge the poet into
severe depression; he spends time in an insane asylum after the war, and his
entire life afterwards is devoted to securing other durable shelters from the
outside world.

That forces of brutality overwhelm the defenses of the individual is vividly
attested to by the grisly descriptions of work on the assembly line; it is
likewise inherent in the biographical "print-outs" on each of the main
characters, which reduce them to sheer data and compel us to play the game
of reconstructing three-dimensional personalities out of dispersed, fragment-
ed incidents in the novel. By making diligent reference to these assorted
vitae, we can appreciate some additional ironies that do not surface in the

plot of *Loon Lake:* salient among these are the gangster Thomas Crapo's patronage of Boys Town, the March of Dimes, and the Policeman's Benevolent Society, and the vivid similarities between Bennett's successful past and Joe's successful future. Although Joe's origins are closer to Penfield's— the poet had once been voted Boy of the Year before spending time in a Colorado mental asylum, and Joe was voted by classmates as Best Shape of the Head—he later consciously molds his destiny to accommodate the Bennett title and fortune. Lives overlap, intersect, duplicate one another in support of Joe's "account in helpless linear translation of the unending love of our simultaneous but disynchronous lives."

Perhaps the most telling "linkages" in the novel apply to the symbolic associations of the title. The bright, smooth surface of Loon Lake, reflecting back images of itself to anything that approaches, suggests the many parallel scenes in the novel. Events that may appear gratuitous or out of place when we first read them, such as Joe's scattering a fistful of paper money in the forest, take on meaning when they are repeated later on in their chronological contexts (and we discover that this was an act of retribution for the cruel death of the Fat Lady). Joe's running off with Magda Hern, followed by a desertion, looks forward to his escape with Clara, and subsequently, to his escape with Sandy James. The failed strike in Jacksontown in 1936 repeats the failed general strike in Seattle in 1919, as witnessed by Penfield, one of our narrator's alter egos. The secluded lake itself reminds us of the lake created by the earthquake that swallowed Penfield's Japanese girl, and in a sense prefigures the limitless ocean over which he and Lucinda are lost in flight. The lake is also the most prominent of the images of enclaves: placid and isolated as any monastery or asylum, it quickly resumes its calm appearance after being disrupted by the dives of the loons, who themselves replicate the crazy, often self-destructive activities of Doctorow's characters. As one reviewer declares, marvelling at the versatility of this metaphor: "Contemplative stasis, acquisitive action; Yin and Yang; duality contained within a circle—the implications seem endless."[16]

Equally rich is the image of the loon, whose cry can be interpreted as agony or celebration, and whose cycle of plunge and ascent implies to impressionable human witnesses the imminence of death and the possibility of rebirth. It is compared to Keats's nightingale and to Lucinda's plane, both of which seem to encompass "some great personal ideal." The loon serves as nature's own symbol of the desire to transcend the daily requirements of appetite and survival in a strenuous environment. Art, religion, crime, adventure—all the various roads to achievement above and beyond mundane existence examined in *Loon Lake*—comment upon the universality of this desire, for it is the strongest link connecting all the characters we meet.

Of course, very few people ever attain privileged destinies in Doctorow's fiction, and those who *do,* attain them at the expense of the many they choose to exploit. "The Doctorow Novel" may be fairly categorized as one which confirms our suspicions of the promises of the American Dream— enchanting as the patter of the snake-oil salesman—by presenting a panoramic view of our nation through the ironic sensibilities of a narrator who is party to both camps in the perpetual class war. But Doctorow is not content to solidify his political affinities with the proletarian novelists who flourished in America some fifty years ago. He also creates surprising contracts between fiction and reality, between nostalgia and history, which further his proposition "that there's no more fiction or non-fiction now, there's only narrative. Television news is packaged using devices of drama and suspense and image. Newsmagazines package facts as fiction—in the sense of organizing and composing the material esthetically."[17] Conversely, by participating in the responsibilities of these other competitive contemporary media, Doctorow's novels take on some of their characteristics as well: "There's an immense amount of energy attached to breaking up your narrative and leaping into different voices, times, skins, and making the book happen and then letting the reader take care of himself. It's a kind of narrative akin to television—discontinuous and mind-blowing."[18] Doctorow avoids neither the duties of social consciousness that make a writer relevant nor the intricacies of style which make a writer aesthetically intriguing. Success on both fronts elevates Doctorow to the ranks of our most entertaining and most important writers.

NOTES

1. Quoted in John Barth, "The Literature of Replenishment," *Atlantic,* January 1980, p. 68.
2. Christopher Lasch, *The Culture of Narcissism: American Life in an Age of Diminishing Expectations* (New York: W. W. Norton, 1978), pp. 90-91.

3. Cobbett Steinberg, "History and the Novel: Doctorow's *Ragtime,"* *Denver Quarterly,* 10, No. 4 (Winter 1976), 126.

4. Philip Roth, "Writing American Fiction," in *The Novel Today: Contemporary Writers on American Fiction,* ed. Malcolm Bradbury (Totowa, N. J.: Rowman and Littlefield, 1978), p. 34.

5. Richard Poirier, *The Performing Self* (New York: Oxford University Press, 1971), p. 87.

6. Interview with Victor S. Navasky, "E. L. Doctorow: 'I Saw a Sign,' " *New York Times Book Review,* 28 September 1980, p. 44.

7. Interview with Catherine O'Neill, "The Music in Doctorow's Head," *Books & Arts,* 28 September 1979, p. 5.

8. For a fuller discussion of Doctorow's thematic use of money and money-making, see David S. Gross, "Tales of Obscene Power: Money, Culture, and the Historical Fictions of E. L. Doctorow," *Genre,* 13, No. 1 (Spring 1980), 71-92.

9. Gross, p. 86.

10. Barbara L. Estrin, "Surviving McCarthyism: E. L. Doctorow's *The Book of Daniel,"* *Massachusetts Review,* 16 (1975), 577-87.

11. Gross, pp. 89-90.

12. John Stark, "Alienation and Analysis in Doctorow's *The Book of Daniel,"* *Critique: Studies in Modern Fiction,* 16, No. 3 (1975), 104.

13. Interview with Navasky, p. 44.

14. Barbara Foley, "From *U.S.A.* to *Ragtime:* Notes on the Forms of Historical Consciousness in Modern Fiction," *American Literature,* 50 (1978), 94.

15. Foley, pp. 92-93.

16. Robert Towers, "A Brilliant World of Mirrors," *New York Times Book Review,* 28 September 1980, p. 47.

17. Quoted in Walter Clemons, "Houdini, Meet Ferdinand," *Newsweek,* 14 July 1975, p. 76.

18. Interview with Navasky, p. 45.

Radical Jewish Humanism:
The Vision of E. L. Doctorow
John Clayton

THERE IS NO generalization you can make about Jewish writers to which someone can't object, Do you think only Jews do that? So Peretz elaborates on the irony that human justice must *exceed* divine justice. Doesn't Camus? Aren't French writers, English writers, Swedish writers as expert in suffering? Did Chekhov need to be Jewish? And yet. There's something about the writing of even secular Jews that I am aware of as originating in Jewish culture, in a Jewish way of seeing. I'm thinking of Kafka when I say that— metaphysical quandaries seen through the suffering heart, the comedy of suffering as the contract we live by and try to evade. It is the heritage of Jewish writers to deal with suffering, especially suffering as a result of some essential injustice in the human or divine world, suffering to which they offer a response of compassion and yearning for a life modeled on human kindness. Identifying with the oppressed, the Jewish voice, in a passionate, non-modernist tone, argues in defense; humor or pathos or both come out of the ironic tension between human beings expressing kindness, dignity, hope, and a world expressing injustice. It is also the heritage of Jewish writers to insist on probing, often self-torturing examination of themselves, of institutions, of life itself. Partly, it's a habit of Diaspora perception. The Jew, as Thorstein Veblen saw, is, as outsider, the natural sociologist.

Qualities, then, of heart and of mind.

Is E. L. Doctorow part of this tradition? Is it useful to consider him a *Jewish* writer? "The truth is," Allen Guttman writes, "that there has been for Jews of the Diaspora a negative correlation between Judaism and political radicalism. . . . 'Jewish' radicals have actually been converts to the secular faith in revolution."[1] That Doctorow is a radical, humanist writer is clear. Why see him as Jewish at all?

In opposition to Guttman I would argue that radical, secular Jews are in fact *central* to the Jewish tradition. In *The Book of Daniel* Doctorow writes:

> Ascher [the lawyer defending the Isaacsons] understood how someone could forswear his Jewish heritage and take for his own the perfectionist dream of heaven on earth, and in spite of that, or perhaps because of it, still consider himself a Jew.

Here is the paradox I'm insisting on. In a sense, the code of being Jewish can put so much pressure on one to be universally responsive to human suffering that in the absence of strong pressure to accept the religious doctrine, the code takes one beyond parochialism.

And yet one is taken to a kind of faith.

In the brutal electrocution scene in *The Book of Daniel,* Rochelle Isaacson, like the old woman in Tillie Olsen's "Tell Me a Riddle," refuses the comfort of the rabbi: "Let my son be bar mitzvahed today. Let our death be his bar mitzvah." On one level, of course, her cry expresses her rejection of Judaism. But beyond that rejection, it asserts a counter-ritual to bring her son to manhood, an initiation into the community of the oppressed. At the funeral of his sister, when Daniel hires the flock of shamosim to pray over the grave, he is being bitterly ironic, but he is also calling upon his heritage as a way of releasing himself to weep. We are reading the book of Daniel, the Old Testament prophet who lives in an alien land and whose people, always threatened, frighten the rulers. *The Book of Daniel,* caught between irony and longing, is a Jewish book. Rochelle's bequest is suffering, paranoia, and bitterness, but it is also a kind of faith.

Regardless of the revision of history by conservatives like Louis Feuer,[2] immigrant Jewish culture *was* largely radical—anarchist, socialist, communist, zionist, or some amalgam of these with faith in the labor movement. (See Elazer, Howe, Ruchames, Chametzky, Rischin, et al.)[3] The *Forward,* the Yiddish newspaper which, under the editorship of Abraham Cahan, became such a powerful voice of immigrant Jews, was both a socialist *and* Jewish paper, always struggling to maintain its balance between the two. "Cahan felt ever more strongly," Chametzky writes, "that at its core socialism was essentially the acting out of a spiritual ideal."[4]

In both *Ragtime* and *The Book of Daniel* Jewish socialist immigrant life provides a normative vision. In *Ragtime* it is not just the little girl whom Evelyn Nesbit loves—it is the life of the "Jewish slums." Nesbit begins to see through a film of salt tears—that is, begins to see *truly*. Tateh is working-class Jew, revolutionary Jew. That he becomes a self-made man and self-styled "Baron" is part of the irony of the novel, but it does not affect the truth of his original vision. Doctorow also uses Emma Goldman as a way of expressing the injustice, the oppression, in America at the turn of the century—that part of reality unacknowledged by the family of Father,

Mother, and (until he is converted) Younger Brother. The real Emma Goldman, like the old revolutionary woman in "Tell Me a Riddle," very strongly rejected her Jewish roots. It was, nevertheless, these roots that nurtured her, and it was the people of the Lower East Side to whom she turned for refuge. It is interesting that Doctorow chose her to express so much unacknowledged reality.

Doctorow's own grandparents were themselves Russian Jews, his grandfather and father socialist, atheist, strugglers with ideas. Atheist—and yet Doctorow himself had traditional Jewish training and was bar mitzvahed. It is to the generation of immigrant Jews that Doctorow turns for his image of what Life is about. I'm thinking particularly of the figure of the grandmother in *The Book of Daniel*—Rochelle Isaacson's mother. Her job in the novel is to suffer, to express, through Daniel's words, that suffering, to go mad from suffering, like someone staring unprepared into the face of God. Doctorow has acknowledged this grandmother as biographically his own—a tie to Jewish immigrant suffering.[5] "Grandma goes mad," Rochelle tells Daniel as a child, "when she can no longer consider the torment of her life." Her curses express her "love for those whom I curse for existing at the mercy of life and God and for the dust they will allow themselves to become for having been born." The madness, then, is not from passive suffering but from fury at that suffering, from arguing against God. All of Doctorow's books deal with impotent revenge against injustice and oppression. The figure of Daniel's grandmother represents the *heart* of that revenge.

The *heart:* Daniel speaks of the "progress of madness inherited through the heart." From his grandmother to his mother, Rochelle, to his sister, Susan. Unable to bear the pain of loving those who suffer, they go mad.

In Daniel himself the pain of being unable to assuage suffering leads to torture and self-torture. He enacts the injustice he can't end—by burning his wife's skin with a cigarette lighter, by burning his reader: "Shall I continue? Do you want to know the effect of three concentric circles of heating element . . . upon the tender white girlflesh of my wife's ass? Who are you anyway? Who told you you could read this? Is nothing sacred?" Reader as voyeur, as accomplice. Finally, of course, it is Daniel whom Daniel is burning.

Unlike most modern characters, those of Doctorow act or agonize on behalf of a collective, a community.

"A NOTE TO THE READER," Daniel announces after describing a piece of the destruction, within the Soviet Union, of the Bolshevik dream—the show trials (both like and unlike the trial of the Isaacsons):

> Reader, this is a note to you. If it seems to you elementary. . . . If it *is* elementary and seems to you at this late date to be pathetically elementary, like picking up some torn bits of cloth and tearing them again. . . . If it is that elementary, then reader, I am reading you. And together we may rend our clothes in mourning.

During mourning, Jews symbolically rend their clothes (in fact, a piece of cloth pinned to their clothes). Mourning is transformed into an obligatory ritual so that it can be contained and be kept from becoming the private subjective province of an individual; it is collective, communal. Here, Daniel speaks to us as if we were part of his congregation or family, sitting *shiva* over the agonies of this century. It is, of course, Daniel, not Doctorow, in mourning, Daniel who swallows the suffering, tortures himself with it, Daniel who is clearly a product of Jewish culture. We are not meant to identify with Daniel's sadism, his acting-out of false revolutionary roles. At times, Daniel, splitting off a judging, observing ego, creates his imagined reader into an enemy: "I suppose you think I can't do the electrocution. I know there is a you. There has always been a you. YOU: I will show you that I can do the electrocution." But it seems clear to me that we are meant to *identify* with Daniel's pain and his ironic vision. We as readers are pulled into community with the suffering Daniel.

This relation between the reader and the narrator is intensified by the letter Daniel imagines his grandmother sending to the *Forward*. The letter-to-the-editor page, like Daniel's letter, was entitled *Bintel Brief* (Bundle of Letters), and like Daniel's letter, was a repository of pain or problems. "I am an unhappy lonely orphan," an actual letter begins, "and I appeal to you in my helplessness. . . . My story is a tragic one."[6] The story of Daniel's grandmother is not so unusual for the *Forward*. "My dear Mr. Editor, you who hear the trouble of so many, and share the common misery, permit me to say what I have to if my heart is not to burst." The letter is beautiful, very real and painful—and at the same time verges on pastiche. Daniel has it both ways—as true and as ironic. And behind Daniel, Doctorow gives us the letter as the agony not of the old woman alone but of the writer, Daniel, needing the forms of Jewish culture to enable him to express his pain.

At the same time Daniel—though not Doctorow—rejects the code of *mentschlekhkayt*—the ethical code requiring one to be a *mentsch,* to be fully human—caring and doing for others—which is at the heart of Jewish culture. He refuses to be thought of as a "good boy." He will be the executioner, not the victim. Yet his cruelty is, like his grandmother's curses, his rebellion against a world that makes victims. It is a perverted scream of compassion.

The compassion of the novel itself, its longing for justice, can be felt underneath the self-torture of the narrator. Not only is Jewish culture present specifically in the narrative but in the sensibility underlying the narrative— the sensibility not of Daniel but of Doctorow.

Jewish culture is not in evidence in *Welcome to Hard Times* or *Loon Lake,* but themes of justice and injustice, victimization and revenge, pervade these novels. In all these books we are looking at some of the essential *collective* experience of this century: exploitation, class struggle, and racial oppression. In all a futile compassion for others is central.

In *Welcome to Hard Times* Blue is an odd sort of hero for a "Western." He is a "Jewish" hero in a Clint Eastwood movie. "Probably," he tells Jimmy, "your Pa did only one shameful thing in his life and that was to rush in after Turner." Turner, the Bad Man from Bodie, is not to be fought Clint Eastwood style. Blue tries to fight by loving the survivors of Turner's destruction of the town, by re-creating the town—generating new life and new building—and by recording its history. He is a contemplative man of the Book. He certainly acts—does as much as a person can to turn Hard Times into a town whose spirit will dispel the Man from Bodie. Failing, he gives into the spirit of six-shooter justice, and nearly kills Turner. But then he carries the Bad Man, smashed and dying, off the barbed wire, brings him to the cabin, where Jimmy kills both Turner and—by accident—Molly. At the end Blue, guilt-ridden, dying, writes the history of the empty town.

Blue is motivated by compassion for the community and by a desire to prove—as if to God—that to build a community need not be futile. As Molly grows increasingly sure of coming destruction, Blue tries to prove to her that the law of the West breeds more destruction—that in a sense she is wedded to the destroyer. And indeed she dies in an embrace by Turner, killed by Jimmy with the gun she herself bought him to use to protect her.

If the narrator of *The Book of Daniel* tortures himself, unable to stand the suffering and injustice he is helpless to prevent, so too does the narrator of *Welcome to Hard Times.* Unlike Daniel, Blue does not enact the injustice;

he simply suffers it for Molly and the others—indeed, he seems to accept full responsibility for ending it at the same time that he understands his own powerlessness. At times he seems to love victim *as* victim, needs to take upon himself the role of victim.

A futile, agonized struggle against injustice is at the heart of *Ragtime* and *Loon Lake*. Coalhouse Walker, in *Ragtime,* stands up to injustice at the inevitable cost of martyrdom. Younger Brother becomes unable to keep seeing with the eyes of the official culture of the turn of the century. He takes on Coalhouse's vision, becomes a revolutionary, and dies. The survivor is Tateh, who joins, as popular artist, the ranks of the powerful. In *Loon Lake,* when the retarded Fat Lady has literally been screwed to death by the rubes, Joe, in revolt, screws the wife of the carnival owner and tosses to the winds the money earned from the death of Fanny. The poet Warren Penfield originally goes to Loon Lake to assassinate the man of power, F.W. Bennett, who has murdered and dispossessed workers; Joe, it seems, returns to Loon Lake to take up Penfield's purpose. But the Fat Lady is dead, Penfield becomes Bennett's house pet, and Joe becomes his adopted son—following in his footsteps in industry and as master of Loon Lake, becoming an accomplice of power in the CIA.

An agonized but futile compassion, then. Is this the vocabulary of Jewish culture? Yes and no. The figures of Jewish culture suffer for others, often seem to embrace suffering for its own sake. And, in Josephine Knopp's metaphor, they put life "on trial."[7] On behalf of the powerless, they demand. But there is, finally, as Irving Howe insists, a "sweetness" about the Jewish writer. Peretz, in "Bontsha the Silent," a story about a victim who has *not* cried out and whose silence and the littleness of his demands shame heaven, is as ironic as Doctorow. But there is, I think, less bitterness in Peretz. Doctorow's vision has Jewish roots, but it is a terribly dark vision. It seems impossible to defeat the Bad Man from Bodie, J.P. Morgan, F.W. Bennett, or the powers that need to create the mythos of the Cold War—*and* impossible to live human life in the presence of those powers.

If Doctorow's work reveals a compassion for common suffering, a compassion whose roots lie deep in Jewish culture, it reveals also a critical detachment from ordinary institutions and culturally held truths. Jews, Doctorow has said, "take exception to prevailing mythologies."[8] As Thorstein Veblen argued in "The Intellectual Pre-eminence of Jews," it is "by loss of allegiance, or at best by force of a divided allegiance to the people of his origin that [the intellectual Jew] finds himself in the vanguard of modern inquiry. . . . The first requisite for . . . any work of inquiry . . . is a skeptical frame of mind.'' And the Jew in the Diaspora, the outsider working on the inside, has this frame of mind. ''He is a skeptic by force of circumstances over which he has no control.'' It is the tension between traditional Judaism and modern life that gives the Jew his valuable critical ability.[9] But it is not only this tension; Judaism is *essentially* iconoclastic. ''The acknowledgment of God is, fundamentally, the negation of idols,'' Erich Fromm writes.[10] And by ''idols'' Fromm means any fixed system of authority external to living experience. Fromm believes that the Old Testament itself is susceptible to a radical humanist interpretation. ''Radical humanism,'' he writes, ''considers the goal of man to be that of complete independence, and this implies penetrating through fictions and illusions to a full awareness of reality.''[11]

Doctorow begins from myth, but his work is always an act of demythicizing. *Welcome to Hard Times,* for example, takes traditional figures and situations from ''realistic'' Westerns and enlarges them. The Bad Man from Bodie is the mythic outlaw, appearing, magically, when a town is ready for death. The town itself, Hard Times, is as super-real, as stark, and nearly as self-contained as a Beckett landscape. It is in the hands of an invisible power—the mining interests which determine its fate. The battle—between love, pity, and community and the spirit of destruction—is so absolute as to be metaphysical. And there is a terrifying, insistent, cyclical, inescapable pattern of destruction that seems larger than life.

But the realistic dialogue, the naturalistic voice of the narrator, Blue, and the explicable motivations demythicize the world of *Hard Times.* As hero, furthermore, Blue, while not Jewish, *is* radical humanist—and in harmony with the peaceable, compassionate, guilt-ridden, even masochistic figures of Jewish fiction. Standing outside the dominant ethos, he criticizes six-shooter heroism and the myth of the self-made man, the rugged individual.

Similarly, the job of *Ragtime* is to undercut the vision of an innocent, turn-of-the-century America, an America without economic, social, and racial problems.

> Everyone wore white in summer. Tennis racquets were hefty and the racquet faces elliptical. There was a lot of sexual fainting. There were no Negroes. There were no immigrants.

In *Ragtime* history is flattened into myth only to demolish the myth. And *The Book of Daniel* is a work of brilliant cultural criticism, demolishing the American official myth of the Cold War, the sentimental counter-myth of heroic communist resistance, and even the myth of youth revolt of the sixties. Daniel is a brilliant invention; he is so passionately, bitterly involved that every word of his narrative is drenched in pain—and yet he remains outside of all the paradigms of contemporary history.

But what of *Loon Lake*? Events are wrenched so far out of chronology as to seem to deny chronology. We get computer printouts of the vitae of Penfield, Clara, Crapo, F.W. Bennett, and his wife, but the life of Penfield fuses with Joe's, denying historical time, denying even individuated consciousness. At the end the narrative moves from Joe's awareness to Penfield's fantasies. In fantasy, Penfield enters the giantess in search of Godhead (as Joe in imagination entered the Fat Lady). Then the narrative voice says, "You are thinking it is a dream. It is no dream. It is the account in helpless linear translation of the unending love of our simultaneous but disynchronous lives." Joe *is* Warren Penfield. Like Penfield before him, Joe first rebels against, then accommodates himself to, power. But, of course, if Joe is one with Penfield, in other ways he is one with Bennett. Even the clubs and corporations of which Bennett was a member become Joe's as well. Like Bennett he is tough, shrewd, a winner (whereas Penfield is a loser). The novel projects, then, a closed system, a cyclical pattern, repeated over and over, from which there is no escape.

But then whose is the recording instrument, the ultimate voice, in *Loon Lake*? Who is it who knows Power so well, sees oppression so sensitively, sees the pattern so clearly, stands so far outside the cycle? Bennett and Penfield are dead at the novel's close. Joe is Master of Loon Lake. If the consciousness that has shaped this novel is his, then we see the evolution of a character from ignorance and poverty not only to power but to awareness.

But this is, perhaps, to read the novel too naturalistically. It is the artist who stands outside—Joe as artist, Penfield as artist, Daniel as artist, Blue as artist, in the middle of a dying town completing his record. It is the artist who demythicizes by expressing and exposing cultural myths.

There are a number of artists in *Ragtime*—especially Tateh, revolutionary become movie-maker, and Houdini. They are successful. They please audiences. Tateh pleases partly because his silhouettes that flip to create movement and, later, his motion pictures are like Henry Ford's infinitely reproducible cars—his art reflects his times. At the end of the novel he is to make comedies like the Our Gang series, of "mischievous little urchins . . . a society of ragamuffins, like all of us . . . getting into trouble and getting out again." It is a comforting art. One critic has seen this film series as an analogue to the historical futility implicit in Doctorow's vision.[12] But isn't it in fact a *critique* of an art which offers nothing but comfort—tension and release, like Houdini, in trouble and out again. Houdini feels frustrated with his—literally—escapist art, but when he comes too close to reality, audiences become nervous and flee.

"Rather than making the culture," Doctorow has said, "we seem these days to be in it. American culture suggests an infinitely expanding universe that [as his benefactor imprisons the poet in *Loon Lake*] generously accommodates, or imprisons, us all."[13] Doctorow is surely ambivalent about the possibilities of art in society, fearing that perhaps "the artist, no matter how critical or angry or politically dissenting his work may be, is inevitably a conservator of the regime."[14] And certainly he believes that art assists the work of exploitation: in *Ragtime* Emma Goldman is asked, "How can the masses permit themselves to be exploited by the few?" The answer—a Marcusian answer—"By being persuaded to identify with them." The newspapers carrying Evelyn Nesbitt's picture help the laborer to dream "not of justice but of being rich." In *The Book of Daniel,* two images of art that seem utterly opposed turn out, on second reading, to be ironically similar: Disneyland, which offers a "sentimental compression of something that is already a lie"—the lie being the Disney animated film version of some original cultural artifacts—and Sternlicht's collage of cultural images, from Babe Ruth to F.D.R. to Mickey Mouse to Elvis to (had Susan brought the poster of her parents) a Save-the-Isaacsons poster. And the title of the collage: "EVERYTHING THAT CAME BEFORE IS ALL THE SAME." Both Disney and Sternlicht deny history, deny change, turn history into myth.

Does Doctorow? At least one critic believes so.[15] As I have shown, Doctorow struggles with the possibility. But he also sees the novel as "a major transforming act of the culture."[16] While refusing to place his art at the service of an ideology or party, fearing to destroy it, he also refuses the conception of "literature as an intellectual elitist activity, [denying] art any connection to life whatsoever."[17] In fact, Doctorow is tossed back and forth between the rock and the hard place of his dialectic. His art is committed yet unconvinced. He writes out of a Jewish view that history makes manifest the sacred, that history is redemptive—and also out of Modernist doubt. Blue, writing his record, feels that it will never be read. That sounds hopeless, and yet the record, in the form of the novel, *is being read.* And the voice of quiet courage conveys a vision of life's possibilities that stands as a critique of the bleak cycle contained in Blue's record. Blue's hope, at the very end, that "someone will come by sometime who will want to use the wood," is, literally, the last word.

In his Introduction to *A Treasury of Yiddish Stories,* Irving Howe speaks of the "moral seriousness" in Yiddish writers. "The sense of aesthetic distance, the aristocratic savoring of isolation, which make for an intense concern with formal literary problems, were not available to the Yiddish writer. From birth, so to speak, he was an 'engaged' writer. . . . Art for art's sake, whether as a serious commitment or a shallow slogan, finds little nourishment in the soil of Yiddish literature. . . . But then, how could any theory of pure aestheticism take hold in a culture beset by the primary questions of existence and survival?"[18]

E. L. Doctorow, both in those books dealing with Jewish material and those that ignore Jewish material, is in harmony with this tradition. Such an attitude towards art—an attitude of moral seriousness—is by no means the property of Jews, but it runs deep and strong in Jewish culture. Again, caring and doing for other people and a critical attitude to contemporary myths do not belong to Jews. But Jewish culture has always insisted on these qualities; Jewish culture is a deep channel through which such a spirit flows. It is one of the sources of the vision of E. L. Doctorow.

NOTES

1. Allen Guttman, *The Jewish Writer in America* (New York: Oxford, 1971), p. 136.

2. Louis Feuer, "The Legend of the Socialist East Side," *Midstream,* XXIV (February, 1978), p. 35.

3. Daniel Elazer, "American Political Theory and the Political Notions of American Jews," and Louis Ruchames, "Jewish Radicalism in the United States," in *The Ghetto and Beyond*; Jules Chametzky, *From the Ghetto: The Fiction of Abraham Cahan* (Amherst: University of Massachusetts Press, 1977); Irving Howe, *World of Our Fathers* (New York: Simon & Schuster, 1976).

4. *From the Ghetto,* p. 14.

5. In conversation.

6. See the book of selected letters, *A Bintel Brief* (New York: Ballantine, 1971).

7. Josephine Knopp, *The Trial of Judaism in Contemporary Jewish Writing* (Urbana: University of Illinois Press, 1975).

8. In conversation.

9. In *Essays in Our Changing Order* (New York: Viking, 1954), pp. 226-27.

10. Erich Fromm, *You Shall Be As Gods* (New York: Holt, 1966), p.42.

11. *Ibid.,* p.11.

12. David Emblidge, "Progress As Illusion in Doctorow's Novels," *Southwest Review,* LXI (Autumn, 1977), pp. 397-409.

13. E.L. Doctorow, "Living in the House of Fiction," *The Nation,* CCXXVI (April 22, 1978), p. 459.

14. *Ibid.*

15. Emblidge, "Progress As Illusion."

16. "Living," p. 460.

17. *Ibid.*

18. Irving Howe, *A Treasury of Yiddish Stories* (New York: Schocken, 1973), p. 37.

Tales of Obscene Power:
Money and Culture,
Modernism and History
in the Fiction of E. L. Doctorow

David S. Gross

◆━━━━━━━━━━━━━━━━━━━━━━━━━━━━━━━━━━

As AN INTERPRETIVE CODE or theoretical orientation, the bundle of forces suggested by the subject of money in literature is frightening to me both in immensity and complexity. Especially to one who wishes to assert or defend the validity of a Marxist hermeneutic, the examination of literary production and signification from such a perspective seems to amount to an embarrassment of riches. Faced with that immensity, I choose to start with the embarrassment, following a hunch that I might find in a nervous reluctance to speak on this subject the most profitable way into it.

Fredric Jameson has described Marx's statement that "it is not the consciousness of men that determines their existence, but, on the contrary, their social being that determines their consciousness"[1] as an "ever-scandalous discovery."[2] What I want to propose is that the status of money in literature and in its interpretation, as in life, points us toward equally scandalous truths, truths which it has been the function of most modern approaches to literature to mystify or deny. Marx's discovery is offensive because it challenges some basic intellectual assumptions about the putative independence, integrity and lofty origins of consciousness and its productions of serious intent, from religion and philosophy to literature. It opens the forbidden area of materialist determination, threatening notions of consciousness and culture as a clean, privileged refuge from getting and spending, notions which seem to partake of the sacred for intellectuals in modern society. As Jameson goes on to say:

> This determination makes itself felt in the "deja-donné," which always transcends consciousness as given no matter how exhaustively it is assumed, just as it finds its visual representation in the geological deposits of language as script. Such a dimension might well be seen as the ultimate bedrock of the signified.[3]

I cannot go into the implications of this larger area here; there is not space in this discussion for either a defense or an explication of the thesis that "modes of production'' and the social relations which are specific to them constitute crucially determining historical forces and that a recognition of that fact provides the most useful interpretive code for historical investigations.[4] Instead, I want to turn here to the related but narrower question of the power and significance of money, and of the complex repression of awareness of such meanings, the embarrassment I spoke of earlier. For while the importance of money in literature is obvious, to dwell on it seems somehow distasteful, and is likely to be denounced in the same terms in which Marx's scandalous discovery is so often dismissed: as stupid and/or inconsequential or as narrow, ''vulgar'' determinism.

It is a truism that money and sexual/romantic love constitute the central concerns of realist fiction. As Raymond Williams has pointed out in his discussion of British Restoration drama, the London marriage market for the scions of both old aristocratic and newly wealthy rural families points to a significant linking of the two themes which will persist both in drama and in fiction.[5] But Williams' most interesting observation in that regard comes in his discussion of ethical questions in Jane Austen's novels, where he sees a structure of feeling on this question which links her with George Eliot.

Implicitly in the earlier novelist and explicitly in Eliot, Williams sees as decisive an assertion that money and love are causally linked, with money the determining factor, and that this should not be so.[6] In that view, love and sexuality are seen as crucial aspects of human existence which should not be linked to money or used to manipulate people in aggressive, acquisitive desire. All matters of conduct and morality in such novels center around the question of whether principle (or authentic and generous desire) will prevail over money-greed and its dominance in human relations. Austen and Eliot defend that classic humanist position that humans should be the measure of all things, and it is with real anguish that they come to the conclusion that gold, instead, provides that universal standard.

Thus of the two principal subjects of so much literature, it is much more respectable to assert the value and significance of love than money. Once beyond a certain idealist and archaic belles-lettrist prudishness, most critics do not want to deny the significance and suitability of the love-sex complex as both subject matter and central source for literature. And if we assert that the prominence of such concerns in literature suggests or ''reflects'' its centrality in ''real life,'' only the most purely formalist literary critics would be likely to object. The victory of depth psychology, especially in its discussion of dreams, desire and fantasy, is by now fairly clear in these areas. But, of course, not all reluctance or repugnance to speak of this area has vanished, and the traces that remain lead us to that more forbidden area, the enormous shaping power of money in our world and in its literature.

When money's power and significance are central subject matter in literature they are virtually always presented critically. The most cursory reading of the great nineteenth-century novels shows this to be true. And it is equally obvious that from Aristotle through Christ to twentieth-century social critics the power, prestige and privilege accorded to wealth in money has been consistently denounced. Now some small part of such criticism can be linked to the puritanical renunciations which underlie the pathological and compulsive enterprise of capitalism, a distorted and thinned-out version of Marx's purposeful activity or Nietzschean will. But as I have just been indicating, the repressions with regard to money—and, as I will argue following Freud and Norman O. Brown, the pathological nature of our culture's valuation of money—are far more powerful and persistent than parallel attitudes toward bodily love and its position in literature and life.

When money's power is acknowledged it is always criticized; almost as often, awareness of that power is repressed and denied, while in the fiction of at least the last one hundred and fifty years, sexual and emotional repression is attacked. The two subject matters are complexly interrelated, and upon examination the money complex comes to be seen as guilt and renunciation, aliment becomes excrement, death in life. Thus what we find in love and money, those intertwined dualities at the heart of our literature, turns out to be life-affirming and its life-denying opposite, eros and thanatos.

From this perspective it is not hard to understand why our culture would both affirm and deny the power of money, why all literary assertions of that power are critical of what they assert. And when critics and theorists object so strenuously to Marxist assertions that money's power in literature points to its shaping power in our lives and that an urgent desire to illuminate such matters has been a crucial source of literary production, that objection is rooted in a desire to deny terrible truths and maintain the illusions that intellectual and artistic activity is free and independent of such forces.

I

Aristotle's denunciation of money's power is one of the first. In the *Politics* he contrasts what he calls "household management" wealth, in which effort and purpose is directed toward keeping self and family alive, fed and sheltered, with wealth as an acquisitive drive for accumulation of money for its own sake:

> There are two sorts of wealth-getting, as I have said; one is a part of household management, the other is retail trade: the former necessary and honorable, while that which consists in exchange is justly censured; for it is unnatural, and a mode by which men gain from one another. The most hated sort, and with the greatest reason, is usury, which makes a gain out of money itself, and not from the natural object of it. For money was intended to be used in exchange, but not to increase at interest. And this term interest, which means the birth of money from money, is applied to the breeding of money because the offspring resembles the parent. Wherefore of all modes of getting wealth this is the most unnatural.[7]

This text is the classical basis of the ethical critique of money's power, the source of the aristocratic aversion to vulgar trade and commerce, seen always as soiling and demeaning. And Aristotle's strong denunciation of usury (his sexual metaphor is of special interest in light of the view I will be arguing here) is at one with Christ's in the New Testament. The idea of money making money was emphatically denounced by Christ and the early Christians. But, of course, as money's power grew in medieval Europe, and as the secular power of the Church and its own wealth in money increased, Christ's prohibition was modified and usury was redefined, in a crucial and transparent change, as *excessive* interest.

The clear truth is that the power of money—usury, interest, money's ability to make money—lies at the very heart of the capitalist system. This truth violates all our moral standards, seems to make a mockery of all our ethics and to corrode with cynicism all other values. It is no wonder that we seek to deny this truth even as we recognize it.

Marx's observations on money are scattered throughout his works, as one would expect, but he is most explicit on the subject in "The Power of Money in Bourgeois Society," in the 1844 Manuscripts. His stress in that essay resembles that of Diderot in *Rameau's Nephew* in his insistence that when the cash nexus predominates and money is in the saddle, the rich man's ability to buy everything from horses to talent gives him a power which is nearly absolute, which renders nearly meaningless any other distinctions among men.[8] At almost exactly the same time Balzac gave novelistic expression to that truth in these famous words:

> Everybody puts out his money at interest and turns it over as best he can. You're deluding yourself, dear angel, if you imagine that it's King Louis-Philippe that we're ruled by, and he has no illusions himself on that score. He knows, as we all do, that above the Charter there stands the holy, venerable, solid, the adored, gracious, beautiful, noble, ever young, almighty franc! Now, my fair angel, money calls for interest and is forever gathering it.[9]

The comparison and connection between royal power and that of money is important. It supports Jameson's insistence—basing his work on that of the *Tel Quel* group—on "the basic identity of value systems in general, whether on the economic, psychoanalytical, political, and linguistic levels." Further, he suggests, "the rich analogical content of various local studies of value— Marx's analysis of money and the commodity, Freud's of the libido, Nietzsche's of ethics, Derrida's of the word—is itself a sign of the hidden interrelationships of the categories which govern these various dimensions: gold, the phallus, the father or monarch or God, and the myth of the *parole pleine* or spoken word."[10]

Gold or money has a special status in that group; it is everywhere present but its power is always profoundly objectionable. The authority of a leader, the power of sexual energy or of the spoken word may or may not be illegitimate, objectionable. Such forces have their source in human beings, and can be alive and natural. But money's power over people seems the dominance of dead matter over life, and virtually all literary accounts of it are critical. Lionel Trilling faced the issue head on in *The Liberal Imagination,* where he argued that the novel arose in response to the increasing social dominance of money and that its great central themes of social aspiration and the problematic relationship between appearance and reality are rooted in money's power.[11] But our aversion to money's power is so strong and its implications as to the real nature of power in our society so discomforting that most critics seem intent on denying the shaping influence of money and social class in the realm of social life and culture. As Trilling puts it: "We believe that one of the unpleasant bedrock facts is social class, but we become extremely impatient if ever we are told that social class is indeed so real that it produces actual differences of personality."[12]

Now clearly, as my earlier quotation from Aristotle and the biblical "root of all evil" indicate, critical awareness of the power of money did not begin in the capitalist era. But it is equally clear that money is more centrally powerful in capitalism than ever before, that, in particular, the usurious function denounced by the early moralists is at the heart of that system, constitutes its basis, its real foundations. It is for that reason that it has been more difficult to recognize and denounce it than in a society in which it was more tangential to central economic and social activity. In the twentieth century, during which American and Western European money has ruled most of the world, our aversion to such truths and significances has become pathological. In his profound and far-reaching *Life Against Death*, Norman O. Brown devotes his longest chapter to a discussion of money's power and our need to deny it, the loathing it engenders. The chapter bears the title "Filthy Lucre."[13]

The connection between money and excrement established by the title is not new in the modern world either. Brown supplies many illustrations and examples of it, drawn from distant times and places. Hieronymus Bosch's famous fifteenth-century tryptich, "The Last Judgement," in the Prado clearly shows a naked man squatting and defecating gold coins. But it is in the capitalist era—first, in the work of Luther—that the connection becomes dominant in our culture and disastrous in the character structure to which it gives shape.

In addition to his literary and cultural anthropological sources, Brown bases his argument on Freudian theory and the clinical and analytical findings of depth psychology. It has of course been argued that the extrapolation from "sick" individuals to generalizations about a culture are without validity. But that argument ignores the real sources of what we call character or personality. As Christopher Lasch has argued recently, "the unconscious mind represents the modification of nature by culture, the imposition of civilization on instinct."[14] Further, says Lasch, we are correct in reading individual personality in terms of cultural forces since "every society reproduces its culture—its norms, its underlying assumptions, its modes of organizing experience—in the individual in the form of personality. . . . Each society tries to solve the universal crises of childhood . . . in its own way, and the manner in which it deals with these psychic events produces a characteristic form of psychological deformation, by means of which the individual reconciles himself to instinctual deprivation and submits to the requirements of social existence.''[15]

I find Lasch's argument convincing and important. Many of Brown's basic premises violate common sense, but I believe that such aversion to the truths revealed by his analysis of our money culture has its source in the psychic conflicts he describes. We do not want to acknowledge what at some level we sense to be true—that money rules our lives, that money is excremental and hostile to life, and that money is important in fiction because it is at the source of the most important fictions in our lives. In fact, I would argue that all the attacks on naturalism in fiction by those who want to see ''higher'' things discussed (I am thinking especially of Tennyson's denunciation of ''wallowing in the troughs of Zolaism'') have their source not so much in the (related) fear of sexuality and general aversion to the body, but in a desire that the sources of the money/guilt/excrement complex remain repressed.

I have space here for only the barest outline of Brown's closely argued theory. The basic connection with which he begins is between money and quantifying rationality (p. 235). This is Blake's Urizenic, one-dimensional thought, a desire for possessive mastery over objects, over nature, ''partial impulses in the human being (the human body) which in modern civilization have become tyrant organizers of the whole of human life'' (p. 236). Money, he says, is for our culture the heir to religion, ''an attempt to find God in things'' (p. 240). Money's value is fetishistic, irrational, and sacred. Its intrinsic or use value is zero, and the hidden middle term connecting money to the sacred is power (p. 249). Privilege and prestige, says Brown, depend on renunciation, self-repression in the vast (unprivileged) majority. Thus it has resort to deception and enchantment to maintain itself (p. 252).

The basis for the equation of money and excrement is the former's ''absolute worthlessness'' (p. 254). What typifies modern capitalism is alienated, compulsive labor—not the production of necessities for ''the Mouth,'' but superfluous production of fetishized commodities. The maintenance of such a situation is based on renunciation and sublimation—the rigidities of personality always associated by psychoanalysis with arrest at the anal stage of character development. This psychological principle of non-enjoyment is always part of compulsive, acquisitive enterprise. It is *not* natural or inevitable. As Brown puts it, "The modern psychology of possession is superimposed over a deeper psychology of giving, and is constructed, by the process of denial, out of its archaic opposite" (p. 264). This denial of the validity of the generous and life-affirming aspects of human nature divides us deeply, in ways which cripple us while they provide crucial support for the whole money complex.

"The whole money complex is rooted in guilt" argues Brown (p. 268). That position is brilliantly supported by Nietzsche in his discussion of debt and payment, owe and ought, the cultural semantics of duty and obligation, which reduce a human being to his ability to repay a loan.[16] All currency, says Brown, is neurotic currency (p. 271). And our modern secular economy is an economy of guilt without redemption. As Luther argued, capitalism embodies what Christian mythology calls the Devil. And "the Devil (guilt) is lord of this world" (p. 274).

Time, we are told, is money. And that linear, urgent preoccupation with time is, like money, neurotic and correlative with instinctual repression (p. 274). Obsessed with time, burdened with an urgent, guilty fear, we retreat into that greedy money/excrement complex, repressing our awarenesses of what we really need and desire and of the terrible cost of the renunciation we have accepted. To the extent that the money complex rules our culture and our society they are hostile to life and bent on self-destruction.

II

Now, at some level we know all this is so. Were there no conflict involved in the renunciation required of us, if we really liked to live in or under excrement, we would not feel the inner longing and despair which social critics are always describing. And imaginative literature in our time is always responding to money-power, either by flight, savage parody, or direct presentation and exposure. Modern literary response is more diverse than that in nineteenth-century realist fiction. In some modern novels the question is avoided entirely, as writers have sought to separate their work as much as possible from material reality, concentrating almost entirely on formal innovation, where the medium becomes the message. Elsewhere, as in the fictions of Kafka, the power of money remains crucially significant but is expressed obliquely and indirectly, in a form which combines allegory and fantasy or nightmare. But there are Modernist works in which money is powerfully and immediately present. In such works the resonances of money/gold power are extended to other areas of human action and desire in ways that were still obscure in earlier realist fiction, though the sense of risk and fear all this raises is also strong. Thus the presentation of the deeper meanings of the money complex is often accompanied by a maze of Modernist formal strategies which seem designed to distance and protect the author from responsibility for speaking such unpleasant truths.

In the four historical novels of E. L. Doctorow both the power of money and our reluctance to acknowledge it are centrally significant. His work does display the protective strategies to which I just referred, but the complex mixtures of distancing ironies and direct exposure he creates allow him to reveal the hidden sources of malaise in our culture more clearly than most modern writers. In particular, his historical fictions engage two areas of crucial significance: he makes our distortion and repression of awareness of the heart of the matter—what it means to live in a society where money's power is so complete—a central subject in his works, and he establishes the connections among money, excrement and power with savage irony.

Doctorow's approach to American history is radically ironic. In *Welcome to Hard Times* life on the barren northern prairies at the turn of the century is his subject and it is the traditional Western myths that he wishes to debunk. In *Ragtime* we are in the New York City of the first two decades of this century, and sentimental nostalgia and schoolbook histories of that era are the objects of his irony. *Loon Lake* uses the Great Depression of the thirties to debunk the notion of any commonality of interests between masters and men. *The Book of Daniel* seeks to expose the real source and nature of the Cold War and American life in the fifties and sixties. This historical order is of course not the order of publication; nor will I discuss the novels in that order. Instead I will deal with the novels as they become increasingly Modernist in technique.

All in all, Doctorow's vision of twentieth-century American history is a terrible and negative one, which recalls Nietzsche's discussion of the historical sense in *The Use and Abuse of History*:

> The unrestrained historical sense, pushed to its logical extreme, uproots the future, because it destroys illusions and robs existing things of the only

atmosphere in which they can live. Historical justice, even if practiced conscientiously, with a pure heart, is therefore a dreadful virtue, because it always undermines and ruins the living thing—its judgement always means annihilation. . . . For the historical audit brings so much to light which is false and absurd, violent and inhuman, that the condition of pious illusion falls to pieces.[17]

The illusions which Doctorow's historical vision seeks to uproot and destroy are those which would deny money's power or attempt to see that power as anything but cruel and destructive. Thus in *Ragtime* we get a strange mixture of lyrical evocations of a supposed "simpler era" with a bitter debunking of such illusions, illusions that would ignore the historical realities which decree that time is money. In the opening pages of exposition much of the novel's action is summarized, "giving it away" in a manner very like the placards held up at the beginning of each scene in Brecht's *Mother Courage and Her Children,* for similar purposes of forcing ironic distance and thus forcing thought. The following excerpts illustrate the strange, flat and abrupt style—a disconcerting combination—and the debunking signification which is the aim of both style and subject matter:

> Patriotism was a reliable sentiment in the early 1900's. Teddy Roosevelt was President. . . . There seemed to be no entertainment that did not involve great swarms of people. Trains and steamers and trolleys moved them from one place to another. That was the style, that was the way people lived. Women were stouter then. They visited the fleet carrying white parasols. Everyone wore white in summer. Tennis racquets were hefty and the racquet faces elliptical. There was a lot of sexual fainting. There were no Negroes. There were no immigrants.

Then, after many similar sentences but still in the three-page opening paragraph—including this reference to Winslow Homer: "This was the time when Winslow Homer was doing his painting. A certain light was still available along the Eastern seaboard. Homer painted the light. It gave the sea a heavy dull menace and shone coldly on the rocks and shoals of the New England coast"—Evelyn Nesbit is introduced. She is the first of many actual historical personages who have active roles in the novel:

> She had been a well-known artist's model at the age of fifteen. Her underclothes were white. Her husband habitually whipped her. She happened once to meet Emma Goldman, the revolutionary. Goldman lashed

her with her tongue. Apparently there *were* Negroes. There *were* immigrants.

All is image and ersatz, disconnected. Doctorow is most directly satirizing the non-ironic presentation of the sort of text he is mocking in traditional schoolbook histories, wanting to destroy their easy and mystifying historical generalizations which prevent any accurate historical understanding. He seems almost to question the possibility of accurate linguistic, historical generalization, mocking our views of the past from art history to popular culture. But most centrally and challengingly, this passage, like the novel as a whole, tells us that our sentimental view of the past tells lies in seeking to conceal the realities of class and racial oppression and its support of the money complex; when we see "all people" dressed in white and amusing themselves we are actually seeing the past as if only the ruling class existed, specifically ignoring the very existence of the Negroes and immigrants who provide for its privileged position.

It is significant that Emma Goldman's radical anti-capitalism introduces the demystifying perspective in the novel (the role and fate of such radical vision is the main subject matter of *The Book of Daniel*). She insists on what has been the thesis of this essay—that our culture knows but does not want to know the obscene power of money, capital. Thus, key sections of the novel describe the terrible lives of immigrants in the Bowery, their famous textile strike in Lawrence, Massachusetts and its brutal repression. The main capitalists in the novel are Henry Ford and J. P. Morgan, representing industrial capital and finance capital respectively. In presenting Morgan, Doctorow makes his most explicit statement on the power of money:

> Pierpont Morgan was that classic American hero, a man born to extreme wealth who by dint of hard work and ruthlessness multiplies the family fortune till it is out of sight. He controlled 741 directorships in 112 corporations. . . . Moving about in private railroad cars or yachts he crossed all borders and was at home everywhere in the world. He was a monarch of the invisible, transnational kingdom of capital whose sovereignty was everywhere granted. Commanding resources that beggared royal fortunes, he was a revolutionist who left to presidents and kings their territory while he took control of their railroads and shipping lines, banks and trust companies, industrial plants and public utilities.

Again, the flat tone, the blunt, crude, simplified and summary approach. It is as if to break through the distortions and blindnesses it is necessary to imitate the comic-book style which is usually the vehicle for the mystified vision he is attacking. But there is no denying the truth of his picture of Morgan. And the novel also clearly demonstrates the irrational, sacred power of money. Morgan's insane Orientalism represents such matters perfectly. Egyptian antiquity is Morgan's mode of attempting to establish belief in his own immortality. He plunders the graveyards of European, Classical and Egyptian cultures, illustrating Brown's view that the main architects of the money complex are "guilt, the aggressive fantasy of becoming father of oneself, and death anxiety or separation anxiety" (p. 290).

The second half of *Ragtime* centers around an allegorical contest between money-power as symbolized by Morgan and those who suffer under it and may provide resistance to it, represented not by a historical character but by a fictional one, a black piano player named Coalhouse Walker. Like the money-power he represents, and the electricity which will represent it in *The Book of Daniel,* Morgan is only rarely visibly present in this part of the novel, is out of the country during the final confrontation, during which Coalhouse and his gang occupy by force the huge, monumental Morgan library in New York City. Morgan's absence when his power is so present, exercised by surrogates, his employees and the police, represents fittingly that money-power which it seems to be our culture's determination to deny all the more vehemently the more total and brutal it becomes.

Coalhouse, on the other hand, is very present indeed. He is a wonderful player of piano rags. ("Small clear chords hung in the air like flowers. The melodies were like bouquets. There seemed to be no other possibilities for life than those delineated by the music.") He speaks with grace and charm, and he regards the world with "large dark eyes so intense as to suggest they were about to cross." Most of all, he is a man of absolute devotion to principle; he defends his personal dignity fanatically, refusing to bend at all in the face of money-power and racial prejudice.

All of this novel is a mixture of ironically employed clichés and stereo-types (parodying, as I have argued, our tendency to maintain our illusions by seeing the past that way) and startlingly original moments and movements which together attempt to alter and deepen our sense of real historical significances. And the incident which provokes the long confrontation with Morgan, state power, and all of white society is one of the strangest.

Coalhouse has been driving out from Harlem to New Rochelle on Sundays, courting a woman who is already the mother of his child. His Model T is brightly polished, and he is dressed with style and flair. Some whites come to resent him as an uppity nigger, and on one occasion a group of volunteer firemen block the road in front of their station and demand a toll from Coalhouse. After a fruitless attempt to get help from a policeman, he returns to his car. "It was spattered with mud. There was a six-inch tear in the custom panasote top. And deposited in the back seat was a mound of fresh human excrement."

Now I dare say there are very few other novels where excrement has such a place and significance. Coalhouse's rage is such that all the rest of his life is devoted to a violent quest for redress, a suicidal desperation, which does end in his death. And the startling presence of excrement in this situation points toward those life-denying and irrational roots and ramifications of the money-power complex which are Brown's concern and the central subject of *Welcome to Hard Times*. Upon Coalhouse's occupation of the Morgan library, the police arrest Emma Goldman, for obvious if absurd reasons, and she speaks with reporters:

> . . . as an anarchist, I applaud his appropriation of the Morgan property. Mr. Morgan has done some appropriating of his own. At this the reporters shouted questions. Is he a follower of yours, Emma? Do you know him? Did you have anything to do with this? Goldman smiled and shook her head. The oppressor is wealth, my friends. Wealth is the oppressor. Coalhouse Walker did not need Red Emma to learn that. He needed only to suffer.

At the book's end, Mother's Younger Brother, a member of the narrator's family who has left his job in their fireworks factory to become ordnance man in Coalhouse's band, explains his actions to Father in words which connect the themes of the novel in a striking manner, words which again evoke Brown's view of capitalist power as excremental, unclean, life-denying, feeding on death:

> You are a complacent man with no thought of history. You pay your employees poorly and are insensitive to their needs. I see, Father said. The fact that you think of yourself as a gentleman in all your dealings is the simple self-delusion of all those who oppress humanity. . . . You have travelled everywhere and learned nothing, he said. You think it's a crime

to come into this building belonging to another man and to threaten his property. In fact this is the nest of a vulture. The den of a jackal.

III

If *Ragtime* seeks to debunk the sentimental nostalgias of schoolbook American history, *Welcome to Hard Times* challenges those central American myths of the frontier embodied in our traditional Westerns. Right from the start, the straight Westerns have evoked a counter-assertion. From the time of the earliest Westerns, other authors have felt the need to cast the myth in an ironic mode, to show the feet of clay, deflate idols and ideals which already in Stephen Crane's time were seen as false and mystifying, to suggest the inadequacy of these myths in the face of the actual modern world. In such books false gods are revealed; a pessimistic "realism" constantly reveals new ways in which the traditional version rests on values, assumptions, views of reality which are unreal, false, insubstantial—either as a result of deliberate distortion and deception or of naive wishful thinking, the repressive embarrassment with which I began this essay.

I would argue that from Crane's "Blue Hotel" to Doctorow's *Welcome to Hard Times,* the central concern has been to expose the predominance of money, greed and force on the frontier, to reveal the extent to which the spirit and practice of capitalism, of hucksterism and exploitation, underlie and belie the more noble myths of conflict on the frontier. Crane in 1900 and Doctorow in 1975 both seek to expose the inadequacy and insanity of the ideology of individualism, both as an account of the experience of the West and as an answer to our problems. These writers use epic or mythic elements and conventions to teach us the inner truths of our national traditions, truths concealed rather than revealed by the traditional Western. And the myth which such authors propose as a substitute for the one they are debunking points to a world where the isolated individual—such a positive figure in the familiar Western—is in a hopeless situation, with no real community, no stay against the storm.

In Crane's story the mystifying myths of manly combat in the American West blind the alien Swede to the realities of Scully the hotel keeper's boosterism and hucksterism and to the economic interests which are of real concern to the good citizens of the tavern where he meets his death, with the price he paid for his last drink still showing on the cash register. In Doctorow's reworking of our national mythos of the frontier, a tiny town on the barren flats of the Dakota territory around the time of Crane and of *Ragtime* is the scene of a violent cycle of death and destruction, commercial enterprise, more death and destruction. In *Hard Times* the spirit of the frontier is the sadism of the death instinct, expressed both in arbitrary machismo violence and the alienating manipulations of commercial self-interest.

The world Doctorow shows us is a place where what is needed is real community, but life in *Hard Times* offers only the illusion, the appearance of community; the only real ties among humans there are those of the cash nexus. Such an assemblage—like the strivings of traditional will and virtue—proves terribly inadequate in the face of the related threats of sadistic violence and economic ruin.

Welcome to Hard Times tells the story of two and a half years in the life of its tiny town. It begins with the destruction of the town and the murder of five of its nine citizens by an archetypal "mysterious stranger" of the first order, a man always referred to as "the Bad Man from Bodie."[18] The town is painfully rebuilt from its ashes (from lumber salvaged from nearby "dead towns"), and grows a little as a result of what turn out to be false hopes of economic fortune. The book ends with a scene of complete anarchy and violence, as the Eastern banks pull out their money and the Bad Man from Bodie returns and lays waste once again to the town. Everyone either flees or dies, and the deserted town is left to the buzzards feeding on the corpses, empty, except for one crazy woman and the slowly dying narrator.

There is no escaping this novel's savage debunking of any and all innocent pastoral myths of life on the frontier. It is of course true that money and violence are very common elements in the traditional Western, but there their effect is softened and mystified so that they appear as of only secondary significance, their meaning confined to the "test" they provide to the rugged individual who is the real subject of the tale. In *Hard Times* individualist responses to the catastrophic events are completely inadequate.

The story is told in the first person by a man named Blue, the Mayor of the town, his title having come to him not from an election but from his habit of writing things down, of keeping records, and because he is the prime mover in trying to make a town of that barren place. He writes his account of the town's history in three of the ledger books which have been provided him in his capacity as agent for the stagecoach company, ledgers where he has also recorded the business transactions which have been the only life of the town. As he composes his narrative of the town's terrible history he looks at the earlier entries and remarks that "the pages are full of dealings, of claims and ownings." Thus the centrality of profit-loss economics in Doctorow's account of the West is always being suggested by what is posited of the pages themselves, those ledgers, and the accompanying assumption of the primacy of "the bottom line."

The mystifications of the familiar Western mode form a central subject of Blue's narrative. Near the end he tells us: "Like the West, like my life: the color dazzles us, but when it's too late we see what a fraud it is." And twice he evokes the egalitarian, libertarian aspect of the traditional myth of the West as the lie that brought him and the others out from the East—the idea that out there "if you're half a man you can make your life without too much trouble."

But not only the mystifications of such myths are brought under Blue's critical scrutiny. His narration is highly self-conscious and self-critical, repeatedly calling into question the very possibility of truth in this or any other narrative. Again and again, more frequently as the book progresses, he interrupts the story to repeat his purpose: "to tell the truth about what happened" or "to tell how things were," but always to express his feeling that he has failed to do so, that he can't get it right. He has a radical distrust of language itself—"as if some marks in a book could control things." In separate passages near the end of the novel he wonders, "Does the truth come out in such scrawls, so bound by my limits?" and expresses his fear that his narrative has not shown "the terrible arrangement of our lives."

That radical distrust of language is of course a particularly modern theme, and for Doctorow it is intimately connected to his central concern, the terrible helplessness in a world where humans are connected only by money (the "terrible arrangement" in the phrase I just quoted). In a world where only economic relations really matter, as social critics since the Enlightenment have been telling us, all other values are eroded and distorted, and the real, viable connections of community will not be present. For language not to be deceptive and obscuring, some sort of basis for trust must exist. If the "circuit of speech" is only a vehicle for cynical self-interest, such trust is continually being destroyed. Language does not connect, it deceives, it controls, it manipulates. In a sense it can be said that real speech ceases to exist. This disintegration or superfluity of language is brilliantly symbolized by Doctorow in the Bad Man from Bodie, who never speaks. Twice he destroys the town, smiling all the while as he rapes and murders, burns and destroys. But we never hear him speak a word (some may remember Aldo Ray's great, silent, smiling, evil presence in the movie version). So language is impotent or misleading in this novel.

What Doctorow seeks to show in this novel is a pattern of economic and psychological relationships which are concealed rather than revealed by the traditional accounts of the Western experience, where capitalism's relationships are the basis for an existence and a culture which make a mockery of traditional values and norms of conduct, of the liberal vision of individual purpose or quest. He makes his view the basis for a new de-mystified myth, a myth of sleazy self-interest, fear, and macho violence. Zar, the Russian whore master, tells Blue, "Frand . . . I come West to farm . . . but soon I learn, I see . . . farmers starve . . . only people who sell farmers their land, their seed, their tools . . . only these people are rich. And that is the way with everything." And in fact the town is entirely parasitical; it has no agriculture, no industry. Its residents sell sex, booze and general merchandise to miners who are working a company lode in the nearby hills. Blue is willing to appeal to commercial hopes and motives in his desperate desire to get people to live in town, but he is all too aware that this accumulation of jealous, selfish, frightened men forms no community. Molly, the former prostitute who was terribly treated by the Bad Man from Bodie on his first visit and now lives only on her desire for revenge, tells Blue that his zeal for settlers is only a pathetic desire to be part of a herd. And, in fact, it is of that that Blue dreams: "I dreamed the Man from Bodie was driving a herd across some badland: and riding each head was a wolf or some buzzard with its claws planted. I was in the middle, running with the rest, and I couldn't shake free of the claws." A herd and not a community, what Sartre calls seriality, the illusion or substitute for community in our society, where isolated monads are connected only by the alienating ties and fetters of ownership and marketplace.

A striking feature of this novel is the repeated allusion to excrement. On the first page we are told that the wagon trains on the horizon left "a long dust turd lying on the rim of the earth." On the third page one of the Bad

Man's first victims ends up on his knees in a fresh pile of manure. There are many other examples. Molly frequently refers contemptuously to the men of the town as "filth" or "shit." Now, on one level such language and such themes have the effect of putting an ironic distance between Doctorow's narrative and the traditional "clean" Western pastoral. But I think the shit is there for a deeper reason, to help embody a vision which ties together the themes of the book, quite deliberately pointing to the ideas suggested by Norman O. Brown. "Money is condensed wealth," Brown says; "condensed wealth is condensed guilt. But guilt is essentially unclean. 'Monks eat the world's excrement, that is to say sins,' says Rabelais" (p. 266). Like Brown, Doctorow suggests that compulsive, competitive money-making, the commercial spirit of capitalism, is pathological and destructive, part of a structure of repressed, sublimated and distorted eros which manifests itself as secret, compulsive sexuality, guilt and a connected set of moral and financial debts and obligations, sadism and masculine violence—Thanatos, the death instinct.

"Until the advent of psychoanalysis and its doctrine of the anal character of money," says Brown, "the profoundest insights into the nature of the money complex had to be expressed through the medium of myth—in modern times, the myth of the Devil" (p. 301). In Doctorow's myth the Devil is the Bad Man from Bodie. He brings fire and death to the town; Blue tells us that the embers glowing on the ground after the Bad Man has gone were "like peep holes to hell." And it is this malignant figure which links money and excrement, violent sex and violent death, that Doctorow sees as the embodiment of the nightmare actualities which are concealed or denied by the traditional Western. For Doctorow as for Brown, prudential calculation, the hoarding of wealth, excrement, and violence, these are the pathological traits characteristic of Western society. When the bankers from the East pull their money out of the mine, killing the town, Blue calls them "Those white-faced, black-derbied Eastern sons of Hell!", pulling together the threads, establishing the connections between the Bad Man's violence and the money relations which have sickened the life of the town.

What the town needs against the arbitrary cruelty, the absolute amorality and cynicism represented by the Bad Man from Bodie, would be some real ties among its inhabitants, ties of love and obligation which could fuel some courageous, intelligent opposition. And during the period of the town's growth, when the possibility of increased Eastern banking investment in the mines seems to promise prosperity, Blue even dares to articulate such hopes, that they'd be ready if the Bad Man came back. Molly derides his hopes: "Oh Jesus God, spare me from this man, this talker." She tells him that none of its residents care about the town, that they're all only in it for the money. He replies with the hope that "if business is good" that won't matter.

But when the hopes disappear, when the people flee the town and the Bad Man returns, Blue realizes that she was right, that his visions of brotherhood and sharing in such a situation were ridiculous, absurd. In the final holocaust, Molly and the Bad Man both die, and Blue is mortally wounded. Death, destruction, rotting corpses in the street are the only fruits borne by this awful narrative.

IV

In *The Book of Daniel* Doctorow's concern is with two moments from much more recent history than his turn-of-the-century narratives, the Cold War of the early fifties and the anti-Vietnam war period of the late sixties. He concentrates in that novel on the repressive force of money-power embodied both in the state and the "private" sector, and on the dangers to those who oppose that power, who seek to expose the myths and illusions which allow it to maintain its power. As Doctorow puts it, to see that money-complex for what it really is is to "make the connections," connections we are not supposed to acknowledge, like that between money and excrement. He even tells us that liberalism is "the failure to make connections. The failure to make connections is complicity."

The radical, on the other hand, does make the connections, but he does so at considerable risk. In seeing what he is not supposed to see and saying what he is not supposed to say, the radical writer or intellectual or political activist becomes, in a phrase repeated again and again in the novel, "a criminal of perception." The most explicit statement on the subject is this one by Daniel:

> I have an idea for an article. If I write it maybe I can sell it and see my name in print. The idea is the dynamics of radical thinking. With each cycle of radical thought there is a stage of genuine creative excitement during which the connections are made. The radical discovers connections

between available data and the root responsibility. Finally he connects everything. At this point he loses his following. It is not that he has incorrectly connected anything, it is that he has connected everything. Nothing is left outside the connections. At this point society becomes bored with the radical. Fully connected in his characterization it has achieved the counterinsurgent rationale that allows it to destroy him. The radical is given the occasion for one last discovery—the connection between society and his death. After the radical is dead his early music haunts his persecutors. And the liberals use this to achieve power.

Like the "atom bomb spies," Julius and Ethel Rosenberg, or in the novel the narrator's parents, those who make the connections and are motivated thereby to oppose the money-complex and seek to change it face the real possibility of being destroyed by it. The central metaphor in the novel for both those connections and the hidden power of capital, invisible but deadly, absent when present, is electricity.

Electricity works perfectly as a central metaphorical device in this novel. It represents the hidden, potentially deadly power of those forces which connect all aspects of our lives. The representative power of modern civilization, it pervades our lives, participates in virtually all aspects of production, shapes both the commodities and the artificial appetites that will seek out those products in impossible hopes for fulfillment and meaning. It carries the television messages which, as McLuhan and others have told us, so dominate our consciousness that "the medium is the message." Electricity connects us all into what Buckminster Fuller sees positively as "the global village." But to those who see the real motive force of this society to be maximizing profit, expanding the capital of those in power, the network into which electricity connects us all is likely to appear more like a concentration camp than a village.

Electricity also powers Disneyland, where one of the novel's final scenes is enacted. Electricity allows the Disney conglomerate to take whatever it wants from our literary culture—*Alice in Wonderland, Snow White, Huckleberry Finn*, etc.—and shape it to its ends. "Most of them have passed through a previous process of film or animation and are made to recall the preemptive power of the Disney organization with regard to Western culture." Few children, says Daniel, who ride in the Mad Hatter's Teacup will have read *Alice,* and thus they will know it only through the Disney film, if at all. "And that suggests a separation of at least two ontological degrees between the Disneyland customer and the cultural artifacts he is presumed upon to treasure in his visit. . . . And even to an adult who dimly remembers reading the original *Alice,* and whose complicated response to this powerfully symbolic work has long since been incorporated into the psychic constructs of his life, what is being offered does not suggest the resonances of the original work, but is only a sentimental compression of something that is already a lie.''

Daniel draws out the specific political implications of his view of Disneyland like this: "What Disneyland proposes is a technique of abbreviated shorthand culture for the masses, a mindless thrill, like an electric shock, that insists at the same time on the recipient's rich psychic relation to his country's history and language and literature. In a forthcoming time of highly governed masses in an overpopulated world, this technique may be extremely useful both as a substitute for education and, eventually, for experience.'' Thus Disneyland is shown as a manifestation of the interconnected nature of mass cultural, political, technological and economic forces, and as a tool whereby actual political-private relationships are at once concealed and debased. Mindless, manipulative spectacle is substituted for the sort of experience which might satisfy real needs and lead to an awareness of the existence and significance of mediating connections through the political to the money complex on the part of so many citizens now anesthetized by the Disneyland, McDonald's, Howard Johnson's world.

''And behold, it came to pass, just the kind of world we said it was.'' Thus ends Doctorow's *raga* history of the Cold War. And that points to the importance of *The Book of Daniel.* Like his fictions of our more distant past, this novel directs us back toward the awarenesses of the connections between the public and private, political and personal I discussed earlier, relations for so long obscured rather than illuminated by American fiction, at least as it is conventionally discussed. Doctorow considers and represents the many ways we have been shaped by the powerful forces which direct modern life. He reveals as well those cultural forces which have obscured and mystified the nature and power of those shaping forces.

V

Loon Lake, Doctorow's latest novel, is in many ways his most complex, demanding and ambitious work. It combines the Modernist complexity in the narrative line of *The Book of Daniel* with the ironic use of traditional modes of historical vision of *Welcome to Hard Times* and *Ragtime*. Like all three, its central concern is with money, money's power, and how obscene that power is.

In *Loon Lake* the scene is the Depression of the thirties—thus filling the gap between *Ragtime* and *The Book of Daniel*—and the embodiment of money and its power is Edward Bennett, an industrialist with wide holdings, specializing in autobody manufacture. He is related to the Ford and Morgan of history and of *Ragtime*. He is the proprietor of Loon Lake, a secluded "rustic retreat" of 50,000 acres in the Adirondacks, dominated by a huge mansion/"cottage," with a large servant staff and a pack of wild dogs guarding it. It all seems designed to purchase isolation, to separate and protect Bennett's vast wealth from the Americans of the Depression whose labor produced it. Doctorow even suggests that that is "what wealth is, the desire for isolation, its greatest achievement is isolation, its godliness is in its isolation."

The novel is dominated by Bennett's money-power. The reaction to it is provided by the two narrative voices of the novel (actually, there are four: the two switch frequently without explanation or transition between first- and third-person perspectives): Joe, a poor kid from Paterson, N.J. who stumbles across the estate by accident, while following a private railroad car in which he has seen a beautiful naked girl, on a private line leading to Loon Lake, and Warren Penfield, a privately published poet, "kept" by Bennett at Loon Lake, who arrived in a similar manner many years earlier. Bennett's power is archetypical: He is an allegorical representation of that obscene power of money in capitalism, especially in its imperialist, monopoly stage, concern with which has always dominated Doctorow's fiction. At one point Joe works on the assembly line for a Bennett company in Indiana and observes that it seems as though Bennett could "make the universe punch in." Just before Joe, who has always loathed Bennett, decides to submit to him and become his son, he gives us this portrait:

> The man resisted all approaches he was stone he was steel I hated his grief his luxurious dereliction I hated his thoughts the quality of his voice his walk the way he spent his life proving his importance ritualizing his superiority his exercises of freedom his arrogant knowledge of the human heart I hated the back of his neck he was a killer of poets and explorers, a killer of boys and girls and he killed with as little thought as he gave to

breathing, he killed by breathing he killed by existing he was an emperor, a maniac force in pantaloons and silk slippers and lacquered headdress dispensing like treasure pieces of his stool, making us throw ourselves on our faces to be beheaded one by one with gratitude, the outrageous absurdity of him was his power. . . .

Notable for my purposes here is the pieces of stool Bennett is said to "dispense." *Loon Lake* makes explicit the money/power/excrement connection I have been arguing in this essay. Bennett's strike-breaking, union-busting violence is a central subject in the novel—largely through Joe's involvement in Indiana with Red James, a union leader who turns out to be a spy for Bennett. Bennett's agent for his union-busting is a gangster named Thomas Crapo, a man whom he entertains at Loon Lake and whose girlfriend Clara is the object of the affections of both Bennett and Joe. He runs Crapo Industrial Services, Inc., made up only of spies, goons, finks and the like, men whose loyalty is purchased by Bennett to keep his absolute power intact. Given his centrality to the novel in his direct connection to Bennett's money-based power, Crapo's name is surely of symbolic significance.

In fact, whenever money appears in this novel it seems to be overdetermined. It resonates with obscene power that goes far beyond any empiricist evaluation of its signifying function. Doctorow seems to want to suggest an eerie fetishistic or totemistic sense of money's absolute domination. Thus, in *Loon Lake* Doctorow continually foregrounds money (usually connected to violence, and/or violent sexuality) in a way he had not done earlier. While this book is the most Modernist of Doctorow's novels, distancing us more from its content by techniques which call attention to its "literary" nature, it is also, oddly, the most explicit in its representation of money's power in American history. It is so because, as I have argued, the "representational" power of money creates the same kinds of alienated, distanced, free-floating overdetermination in our lives. The *representation* of money's own representative but distorting power calls for the kinds of Modernist techniques which culminate in *Loon Lake*.[19] It is in this way, then, that Doctorow's historical fiction can be understood as also a movement toward the often ahistorical style of Modernism. Thus Doctorow creates historical contexts for that style in the same way his fictions create historical contexts for the illusory ahistorical "value" of money.

The earliest appearance of money in *Loon Lake* is also one of the most interesting: a series of signifiers presented paratactically, with no attempt to enclose them or account for them in a larger explanatory discourse, to mute or nullify their radical signification. It bears quoting at length to demonstrate the way subjects like money's power and its relation to other forces in society are presented in this novel:

> And then one day I [Joe] am caught breaking the lock on the poorbox, the fat priest in his skirts grabbing my neck with a hand like pincers, not the first time slapping my head with his flat hand and giving me the bum's rush back to the sacristy behind the stone Christs and Marys and the votive candles flickering like a distant jungle encampment and I conceive what a great vaulting stone penitence this is, with its dark light quite deliberate and its hard stone floors and its cathedral carved space intimating the inside of the cross of man the glory of God, the sin of existence, my sin of existence, born with it stuck with it enraging them all with it God the Father the Son and That Other One really pissing them off with my existence I twist turn kick the Father has balls they don't cut off their own balls they don't go that far the son of a bitch—spungo! I aim truly and he's no priest going down now with eyes about to pop out of his head, red apoplectic face I know the feeling Father but you're no father of mine he is on his hands and knees on the stone he is gasping for breath You want your money I scream take your fucking money and rearing back throw it to heaven run under it as it rains down pennies from heaven on the stone floor ringing like chaos loosed on the good stern Father. I run through the money coming down like slants of rain from the black vaults of heaven.

What is most striking in this passage is the juxtaposition of those elements Jameson cites as fundamentally interrelated in their dominance of Western cultural value systems. The passage also introduces the Modernist method of the novel: the predominance of separate images, fragments, events, moments, the privileging of disconnected signifying elements as conveyors of meaning, the implicit criticism of logical connected prose. Money and the Church and Joe's threat to the money/ideology/power complex (the poor box and Joe's theft); sexual perversion and power and violence ("the fat priest in his skirts" and his use of force against Joe); *images* and power ("the stone Christs and Marys, the great vaulting stone penitence, dark light quite deliberate, cathedral carved space intimating" etc.); that power exercised over the hordes displaced by money at that time ("a distant jungle encampment" [here necessarily having its thirties-slang meaning as hobo encampment, though, of course, traces of the original meaning persist, the original root of the metaphor, retaining thereby significant power as protest, indictment]); Joe's guilt, more general guilt in the culture and its significance as source and maintenance of the Church's ideological hegemony (the vaulting penitence referred to earlier and "the sin of existence, the sin of my existence"); male sexuality and power (the priest's balls); violent sexual conflict and rebellion (the kick at those balls); religion and money in popular culture ("pennies from heaven"); money and sexual obscenity ("Take your fucking money"); destructive power of money over earlier, sacred meanings and values ("pennies from heaven on the stone floor ringing like chaos loosed on the good stern Father"); Joe's individualist, nihilistic rebellion ("you're no Father of mine").

It is certainly a striking passage, clearly demonstrating here in the overture Doctorow's recognition of and determination to place before us the workings of those forces I have been discussing in this essay. The only element missing from the money/power/guilt/excrement complex I have been examining in Doctorow's fiction is the last one. But there is no lack of excrement in this novel. A key recurring element in its bewildering montage, presented as vivid childhood memory flashes belonging to *both* principal narrative point-of-view characters, Joe of Paterson and Warren Penfield, is the picture of a beautiful blond young girl, pants pulled down, being held out over the street to piss by her mother. (This connects Joe and Penfield more directly than anything else in the novel.) The second time this image appears it is preceded by a description of a peddler's horse: "golden balls of dung dropping / from the base of its arched tail," evoking "the not unpleasant odor of fresh horse manure," and ends: "And this beautiful little girl / turned a face of such outrage upon me that I immediately recognized you Clara and with then saintly inability to withstand / life you closed your eyes and allowed the thin stream of / golden water to cascade to the tar which was instantly black and / shown clearer than a night sky." Among many resonances to be noted there are the gold in the description of both substances, the shine of the wet tar.

Just before the long passage I discussed above, is the piece, clearly alluding to Joyce's *Portrait* and establishing this section as an overture, a theme-introducing part of the book, and suggesting the similarity in prose strategy between Doctorow's work and Joyce's: "But I was alone in this, I was alone in it all, alone at night in the spread of warmth waking to the warm pool of undeniable satisfaction pissed from my infant cock into the flat world of the sheet and only when it turned cold and chafed my thighs did I admit to being awake, mama, oh mama, the sense of real catastrophe, he wet the bed again—alone in that, alone for years in all of that.'' In all of that indeed.

In addition to the scene in the overture, the most striking sequence in which money is specifically present, foregrounded—as opposed to its implicit presence throughout the novel as an emanation of Bennett's all-encompassing power—is in a strange section, pieces of which are repeated completely out of context elsewhere, underlining its significance and reinforcing the novel's imagistic anti-rationalist form. (In fact, given Doctorow's Modernist presentation, ''sequence'' is probably a mistaken term.) Before Joe of Paterson comes to Loon Lake he is hoboing around the East and hooks up with a sleazy carnival. The freak show is the big draw, and Fanny, the enormous Fat Lady, is the star of the show. Soon Joe realizes that the carnival owner's most important source of revenue is the Fat Lady's prostitution. She is enormous, grotesque, physically sick and terribly retarded, doesn't even know she's doing it for money; yet she is strangely generous and responsive: ''. . . if they came in the folds of her thighs or in the creases in the sides of her which spilled over the structure of her trunk like down quilts, she always screamed as if they had found her true center.''

Night after night the same thing—a long line outside her trailer. At first Joe tries to see it positively: ''I decided that between this retarded whore freak and the riffraff who stood in line to fuck her some really important sacrament was taken, some means of continuing with hope, a ritual oath of life. . . .'' But in a scene presented one hundred pages later, completely out of place chronologically, everything changes. Winter is near, the carney is ready to fold. Fanny is sick, so as a grand finale, with a state trooper standing guard, a huge, obscene crowd gathers in the tent to watch and participate as Fanny is fucked to death. It's a powerful, horrible scene. The tough, streetwise Joe is appalled. ''Some sort of hot shame rose from the roots of my sex into my stomach and chest: it felt like illness.'' ''Maniacally, I felt betrayed by her, by life itself, the human pretense. I became enraged with her! In my nostrils, mixed with the sharp fume of booze, was an organic stench, a bitter foul smell of burning nerves, and shit and scum.''

After the awful scene Joe is led away to a cheap motor court by the carney owner's wife. She has absconded with the season's take and wants to take off for California with Joe. "The room had the shit smell of old untreated wood. She removed from her purse a manila envelope and from the envelope removed a stack of greenbacks which she placed on the cotton towel." This woman is a freak herself, a Hungarian immigrant crippled years earlier in fall from a trapeze. "She pulled the string tie of a small canvas coin sack and spilled a stream of coins on the bed." Then they make love, for hours. Joe fucks her viciously, violently. "I wanted to do to her what had been done to the Fat Lady, I wanted the force of a hundred men in unholy fellowship, I went at her like a murderous drunkard." They go on for hours, "the coins sticking to the wet ass, the wet belly" until she falls asleep in pained exhaustion. Joe quietly dresses, steals the paper money and leaves. Once outside—in the fragment which appears twice in the novel—"With all my might I reared back and threw the bills into the wind. I thought of them as the Fat Lady's ashes."

All the elements are there in that sequence: money, shit, obscenity, violent sexuality, hideous power, deformation and death. The same angry iconography Doctorow has used to represent American experience since *Hard Times*. The difference is that here there is an almost total absence of the traditional realist discursive explanatory devices, whereby such images or elements are explained, an interpretation established within the text of the novel. It seems that Doctorow has become increasingly convinced of the necessity for radically Modernist prose strategies in order to avoid what Walter Benjamin termed "a servile integration into an uncontrollable apparatus."[20]

He refuses here to explain the causal relations which he certainly suggests exist among these elements, lest he explain away their terrible urgency. The same is true when he deals with the obscene power of Bennett's wealth, a force which permeates this novel in the same frightening, paranoia-inducing present-when-absent manner as the electricity in *The Book of Daniel*. This refusal to employ traditional modes of discourse in a "straight," non-ironic manner seems rooted in a conviction that, like money in capitalist society, traditional, "normal" Western uses of language have become so much a part of the same quantifying rationality which money expresses—where all values, from spiritual to aesthetic to sexual, have been debased and reduced to money equivalents—that traditional modes of literary discourse cannot be used by one who wishes to expose, to protest. Whatever the intentions, such modes lead to an imperialist mode which imitates the oppressor and implicitly reinforces his domination.[21]

Doctorow's sense of modern capitalism as a total system, insane and destructive, is so strong in *Loon Lake* that he brings up the question of the need for other modes of understanding and aesthetic representation as a central subject in the novel. His representational strategies are based on images and imagination, resonances and fragments, trying to do without the linear cause-effect grammar of the West—all this within an almost schizophrenic narrative line, switching points of view without reason or warning, refusing to be straight, to explain, to make the connections for us. This is made present as subject from the point of view of Penfield, who searches in Japan through Zen Buddhism for some approach to truth or wisdom which will not bear the stamp of money's obscene power, to him most vivid in his memory of the bullet-perforated bodies of striking coal miners in Ludlow, Colorado.

VI

In all these novels, despite the maze of Modernist distancing strategies—which almost seem designed to protect him from the impact on us of his terrible vision—Doctorow's persona can most definitely be felt. And I think that persona is, like Edgar in Doctorow's play *Drinks Before Dinner,* "inconsolable." And in his violent and vulgar imagery and language he resembles his own description of Edgar in the Introduction to the play: "He is someone who helplessly tells his truth, as visionaries do, without tact." And I believe that the truth he tells, about which he is inconsolable, is, in Everett Knight's fine phrase: "the fact that we have created an economic and political system which, to survive, is obliged to give money precedence over men."[22]

Let me return here at the end to the sort of general, theoretical proposition with which I began this essay, with one final quotation from Marx:

> Money is the jealous god of Israel, beside which no other god may exist. Money abases all the gods of mankind and changes them into commodities. Money is the universal and self-sufficient *value* of all things. It has, therefore, deprived the whole world, both the human world and nature, of

their own proper value. Money is the alienated essence of man's work and existence; this essence dominates him and he worships it.[23]

At some level I think we all know this. But we don't want to know it, often don't know that we know it, don't want to understand what we know. But Doctorow's historical fictions seek constantly to shock, to break down our intellectual defenses, to anger or disturb us into engaging that knowledge, in a sad and angry collage of American myths and realities of this century. He certainly offers no specific answers or solutions. It could be argued that his only positive offering is, in his own words "the solace of shared perceptions" (*Drinks Before Dinner*). And certainly it would be absurd to try to dismiss the despair in a vision which presents as if self-evident "the true dereliction of the planet," and asserts in the same breath "that convictions of friendship, love, the assumptions of culture, the certainty of calendars were fragile constructs of the imagination, and there was no place to live that was truly home . . ." (*Loon Lake*). But the ruthless historical demystification he practices, the terrible power of which is so well described by Nietzsche, can surely be seen in a positive light, as the sort of radical criticism which contributes to the shared understandings which could provide the only realistic basis for that centuries-old, often-interrupted praxis whereby human emancipation might become a reality and not a cruel joke. Doctorow's uncompromising critical vision is surely at one with those praised by Nietzsche when he writes: "I love the great despisers, because they are the great adorers, and arrows of longing for the other shore."[24]

Notes

1. Karl Marx, "Preface" to *A Contribution to the Critique of Political Economy, The Marx-Engels Reader,* ed. Robert C. Tucker, second edition (New York: Norton, 1978), p. 184.

2. Fredric Jameson, *The Prison-House of Language* (Princeton: Princeton University Press, 1972), p. 184.

3. *Ibid.*

4. For a fine recent examination and defense of this position see Fredric Jameson, "Marxism and Historicism," *New Literary History,* 9 (1979), 41-73, esp. pp. 67-72.

5. Raymond Williams, *The Country and the City* (London: Oxford University Press, 1973), pp. 51-54.

6. Williams, pp. 113-17, 167-69.

7. Aristotle, *Politics,* trans. Benjamin Jowett (New York: Modern Library, 1943), p. 71.

8. Karl Marx, "The Power of Money in Bourgeois Society," Tucker, pp. 101-05.

9. Honoré de Balzac, *Cousin Bette,* trans. Marion Ayton Crawford (London: Penguin, 1965), p. 305.

10. Jameson, *Prison-House,* pp. 180-81.

11. Lionel Trilling, "Manners, Morals and the Novel," "Art and Fortune," in *The Liberal Imagination* (New York: Doubleday, 1953), pp. 200-15, 245-67.

12. Trilling, p. 209. This repression of awareness, this refusal to acknowledge what at some level we know, is central to what Marxists call reification or false consciousness. Fredric Jameson speaks to the question in "Reification and Utopia in Mass Culture," *Social Text,* 1 (Winter, 1979), where he argues that the aestheticism and withdrawal of literature professors has a symbolic content and expresses "(generally unconsciously) the anxiety aroused by market competition and the repudiation of the primacy of business pursuits and business values: these are then, to be sure, as thoroughly repressed from academic formalism as culture is from the work of the sociologists of manipulation, a repression which goes a long way towards accounting for the resistance and defensiveness of contemporary literary study towards anything which smacks of the painful reintroduction of just that 'real life'—the socio-economic, the historical context—which it was the function of the aesthetic vocation to deny or to mask out in the first place" (p. 139).

13. Norman O. Brown, *Life Against Death: The Psychoanalytical Meaning of History* (New York: Vintage Books, 1959), pp. 234-304. All subsequent references are to this edition and will be indicated parenthetically in the text.

14. Christopher Lasch, *The Culture of Narcissism: American Life in an Age of Diminishing Expectations* (New York: Warner Books, 1979), p. 77.

15. *Ibid.,* p. 76.

16. Nietzsche, *The Genealogy of Morals,* in *Basic Writings of Nietzsche,* trans. and ed. Walter Kaufmann (New York: Modern Library, 1968), pp. 499-508.

17. Nietzsche, *The Use and Abuse of History,* trans. Adrian Collins (Indianapolis: Library of Liberal Arts, 1977), p. 42.

18. For an illuminating discussion of the power and prevalence of this trope in American literature, see Roy Male, *Enter, Mysterious Stranger* (Norman: Univ. of Oklahoma Press, 1979).

19. For a very interesting discussion of just this subject see Marc Shell, "The Gold Bug," in *Money Talks* (Norman, Okla.: University of Oklahoma Press, 1980), pp. 11-30. Ronald Schleifer's "Foreword" (pp. ix-xiv) also deals with this matter in an interesting way. (An earlier version of the present article also appears in this volume. I would like to take this opportunity to thank Ronald Schleifer for his thoughtful advice at every stage of this article's composition. His stimulating suggestions drew my attention to key areas of the subject, and his editor's eye was unerringly accurate. His aid was invaluable.)

20. Walter Benjamin, "Theses on the Philosophy of History," *Illuminations,* trans. Harry Zohn (New York: Schocken Books, 1969), p. 258.

21. This is much too large an issue to deal with fully here. Derrida and his epigones are clearly dealing with this matter in their criticism of closure or plenitude. A valuable

recent discussion of the question is in Fredric Jameson's *The Political Unconscious: Narrative as a Socially Symbolic Act* (Ithaca: Cornell University Press, 1981), pp. 236-7, p. 287, where he argues that Modernism should be seen both as a symptom of a reified and damaged social order and as the expression of a utopian desire to transcend it, an expression not possible within the strictures of a traditional realism so much a part of that which it seeks to oppose.

22. Everett W. Knight, *The Novel as Structure and Praxis* (Atlantic Highlands, N.J.: Humanities Press, 1980), p. 5.

23. Karl Marx, "On the Jewish Question," Tucker, p. 50.

24. Nietzsche, *Thus Spake Zarathustra,* in *The Philosophy of Nietzsche,* trans. Thomas Common (New York: Modern Library, 1954), p. 9.

The Reds and *Ragtime:* The Soviet Reception of E. L. Doctorow

Ellen Chances

APPROXIMATELY THREE YEARS elapsed between the original publication date of E. L. Doctorow's *Ragtime* (1975) and the introduction of the novel to the Soviet reading public. *Règtaim*—the Russian title is a direct transliteration of the English—appeared in 1978 in *Foreign Literature*,[1] a popular Soviet magazine whose purpose is to translate current literature from around the world. (In fact, a chapter from Joseph Heller's *Something Happened* had been published in the same magazine not too long before.) Vasily Aksenov, one of the Soviet Union's most distinguished writers of contemporary prose,[2] translated Doctorow's novel into Russian; it was his translation that graced the pages of *Foreign Literature*.

One would have expected the publication of *Ragtime,* in Aksenov's translation, to receive attention and discussion in the Soviet press. This, however, was not the case. A search of journal and newspaper articles of the period unearthed very little relevant material. The reason for this state of affairs probably had less to do with any lack of interest in the Doctorow novel than with Vasily Aksenov's personal fate. It is important to recall that it was at about this time that Aksenov fell out of favor with Soviet authorities because of his role in the *Metropol* affair. On January 18, 1979, twenty-three Soviet writers, feeling that greater freedom of expression was now possible in the USSR, asked the Writers' Union to publish an anthology which would include works that had been rejected for publication by the censors. Both well-known establishment figures such as Aksenov (one of *Metropol*'s five editors) and the poet Andrey Voznesensky, as well as young authors just embarking on their careers, joined the group of twenty-three. The Writers' Union rejected their plea, and the "literary almanac," called *Metropol*, was printed in the West.[3]

Some of the *Metropol* contributors, including Voznesensky, have, after a short period of official disgrace, once again found their works in print in the Soviet Union. Aksenov, like certain other writers in the *Metropol* almanac, has not yet been allowed to resume publication of his works in Russia. During the autumn of 1980, Aksenov emigrated to the United States. He now resides in Washington, D.C. We can surmise, therefore, that it was

Aksenov's problems with the authorities that account for the silence of Soviet literary critics on the subject of *Ragtime.*

Silence was certainly not observed when the Doctorow novel first appeared in *Foreign Literature,* nor was there lack of enthusiasm before the Russian version came on the scene. The July, 1977 issue of *Questions of Literature,* a highly respected scholarly journal of literary criticism, contained a discussion of *Ragtime* and other noteworthy foreign novels of the 1970's.[4] The author of the essay, N. A. Anastas'ev, a young literary critic whose accomplishments include a book on Faulkner and articles on twentieth-century American literature, focuses primarily on narrative technique in *Ragtime.* He first points out the wide acclaim enjoyed by Doctorow's book. The accolade, he continues, is deserved. Rarely does one find such command of two artistic forms, literature and music, writes Anastas'ev. The rhythm of Doctorow's words and phrases duplicates the syncopation of ragtime music of the early twentieth century.

Anastas'ev spends a great deal of time on questions of narrative voice in *Ragtime.* Citing Doctorow, he explains that the author wanted to avoid the fetters of the traditional novel in its lack of distance from its characters. History and journalism impart movement and energy to the narration.[5] The Soviet scholar speaks about the tension generated by the dispassionate, "objective" form—one event rapidly follows another with no one character occupying center stage—that alternates with the intrusive single viewpoint of "the little boy." The independence of the events "objectively" described is destroyed. The reader does not merely read about a car coming up the avenue; the little boy sees a car and hears its motor. Thus, there is the sensation of direct personal observation. Events are filtered through the boy's consciousness. Later, Henry Ford is introduced into the novel. His entrance, though, has been foreshadowed in the boy's consciousness, explains Anastas'ev. The young boy serves the function of the traditional simpleton who can see things and people directly, who can "scrape away the husk of words and pretensions and see the kernel of the nut."[6]

In addition to material on narrative voice, the *Questions of Literature* article on *Ragtime* includes a detailed discussion of the role of the document, of fact, in the novel. Anastas'ev begins by sketching in the background. He talks about the increased tendency toward the merging of fact and fiction. He points out this structure in *Ragtime,* where historical figures (such as

Stanford White, Harry Houdini, Emma Goldman, and Pierpont Morgan) stand alongside the fictional characters conjured up by Doctorow's vivid imagination. The Soviet literary critic explains that there is a close connection between the historical figures and the words, actions, and inner world of the boy. In this way, the principle of "movement and energy" reigns. However, Anastas'ev comments, when he looks at the novel as a *whole*, he does not see the emergence of internal harmony or have the sense of an *artistic* whole.

The sense of lack of wholeness is not a negative feature, in Anastas'ev's eyes. He contrasts it to Dos Passos' *U.S.A.* trilogy. There the "chronicle of events" sections on history also alternate with episodes sketching in the fates of fictional characters. The Soviet scholar sees a difference in the overall effect in Doctorow and Dos Passos. In *U.S.A.*, the "camera eye" device, the pure-fact sections, are part of a consecutively ordered epic narration. In *Ragtime*, though, Anastas'ev suggests, the documentary devices make themselves felt as the attempt to "bridle personal experience."[7] The use of fact in fiction can serve to demythologize the past, writes Anastas'ev. Although the Soviet expert on American literature appreciates the contributions made by documentary devices in fiction, he does not go into more detail than this.

Another Soviet perspective on Doctorow's novel emerges from "A Popular Novel and the Music of History," the article that accompanied the Russian translation of *Ragtime* in the magazine *Foreign Literature*.[8] Its author, Yasen Zasursky, whose specialty is the American novel, is professor and Dean of Journalism at Moscow University. Zasursky explains that when the novel first came out, it quickly made the bestseller lists. According to the Soviet critic, some Americans regarded it as a popular book with no redeeming literary qualities, while others claimed for it a permanent place in the history of the American novel. Whatever the critical position, Zasursky continues, *Ragtime* made a big splash. It was read with great interest, and people were forced to rethink problems of America's past and present that have defied resolution.

Throughout his analysis of Doctorow's novel, Zasursky places the work in an historical context. Bound up with the musical motif of the book, claims Zasursky, is the canvas of historical events of the epoch of American history from the Spanish-American War to World War I—the mounting power of monopolies; the transformation of the United States into an "imperialist state''; the growth of the workers' movement and antitrust sentiment; the Lawrence and Paterson strikes; the rise of technology as signaled by the introduction of the telephone, the streetcar, the automobile, the airplane, the first skyscrapers; the insufferable poverty of New York City's Bowery, Harlem and Lower East Side; the terrorist acts of the anarchists; and the initial American forays into cinematography.

Doctorow, remarks Zasursky, is not the first American prose writer to invest an historical age with musical resonances. The Soviet scholar cites F. Scott Fitzgerald, who christened his own era of the 1920's the ''Jazz Age.'' For Doctorow, however, writes Zasursky, ragtime is a symbol of the *past,* an attribute of history. In this respect, then, Doctorow bears little resemblance to his predecessor.

The author of *Ragtime,* Zasursky asserts, does find literary kinship with American writers of his own time. In the words of Zasursky, American literature of the 1970's was marked by a return to the country's past. He explains that the 1976 Bicentennial celebrations encouraged Americans' interest in history and led to a stocktaking of the American people's experience in the last two centuries. Hence, the increase in the number of historical novels written in this period. Furthermore, Zasursky suggests, dissatisfaction with the America of today has forced thoughtful artists to seek—within the mysteries of the country's past—clues to explain the ''spiritual, moral, and political crisis which has hit the greatest capitalist country in the world.''

Tracing recent trends of American literature, Zasursky offers a brief analysis of prose of the 1950's and 1960's. He emphasizes the frequent presence of far-fetched subject matter not dealing with the realities of life, and the later reaction to this trend in the form of documentary prose. He mentions representatives of the latter tendency, including Truman Capote, Norman Mailer, and the ''new journalists'' Tom Wolfe and Jimmy Breslin. In this fashion, says Zasursky, the historical novel of contemporary American literature came to be. Zasursky then goes on to point out that America's present-day historical novel is a ''symptom . . . of the profound ideational searches'' that mark the writing of prose in the United States today.

What concerns Zasursky the most is the way in which Doctorow's examination of the past sheds light on present conditions in the United States. For instance, the scene in *Ragtime* where the reader escorts the characters on their streetcar ride out into the countryside serves, for Zasursky, as a commentary on the pitiful plight of mass transportation now. Zasursky states that while reading that passage, the American reader no doubt thinks nostalgically about the cheap and good mass transport of a bygone era. Such details, found in abundance in Doctorow's novel, claims Zasursky, demonstrate the "diseases of contemporary America."

Coalhouse Walker, too, from Zasursky's perspective, is seen as playing an ideological role in the novel, reminding the reading audience of the great difficulties black Americans face in the present era. In general, Zasursky proclaims, Doctorow accurately portrays the various shapes taken by the struggle against social inequality.

Like Anastas'ev, Zasursky speaks of the relationship binding *Ragtime* to Dos Passos' *U.S.A.*[9] Here, too, he emphasizes the political implications, for he centers on Doctorow's narrow social outlook as opposed to Dos Passos' broader vision.

Finally, Zasursky turns to the ironic mode that he observes in *Ragtime*. Again, he relates irony here, as well as the irony in other modern American works (in black-humor literature, for example), to the political and social structure of the country. "Irony," declares Zasursky, "exposes the spiritual bankruptcy . . . of the bourgeois world . . . and of its authors." He is a bit distressed by the occasional tasteless "sexual coloring," such as Evelyn Nesbit's behavior. Nevertheless, he believes that the novel makes an important contribution by conveying the "music of history." Zasursky praises Doctorow as one of America's most skillful writers.

The Soviet literary scholar concludes his piece on *Ragtime* with the following remarks: "The title of the novel . . . expresses alarm about the contemporary development of American society, about that blind alley into which society has gotten itself, in its spiritual, ethical, political, and in recent years, economic crisis. Doctorow's historical narrative, *Ragtime,* retrospectively develops this thought: already at the beginning of the century, something was happening in America, and the country cannot to this day free itself. . . . There is one substantial difference, though, and that is that the make-up of America today, with its rock-opera and pop music, is even farther away from its ideal than was the ragtime epoch."

As can be seen from the Anastas'ev and Zasursky approaches to *Ragtime,* Soviet literary scholars have not spoken in one voice about the book. This phenomenon is typical of Soviet literary criticism of the recent past. One line, represented here by Zasursky, continues the tradition of viewing literature as a reflection of social and political realities. Literature is closely connected to ideological concerns. At the same time, another line, represented here by Anastas'ev, analyzes literature according to purely literary criteria. These two general approaches to literature coexist today in the Soviet Union. It is now possible, as Anastas'ev demonstrates, to talk about literature in exclusively aesthetic terms. This would have been unthinkable a few years ago. Thus, there is no monolithic system of literary criticism to which all critics must adhere. Although the ideological perspective is still very much in evidence in the Soviet Union, it is not the only show in town.

Notes

1. *Inostrannaia literatura,* –9, 1978, pp. 32-90; –10, 1978, pp. 119-181.

2. In a book on modern Soviet literature, American scholar Deming Brown has stated, "No contemporary Soviet writer . . . surpasses him [Aksenov] in terms of formal inventiveness and exploratory daring." *Soviet Literature Since Stalin* (Cambridge University Press: Cambridge, England, 1978), p. 197. For more on Aksenov, see Priscilla Meyer, "Aksenov and Soviet Literature of the 1960's," *Russian Literature Triquarterly,* No. 6, Spring, 1973, pp. 447-460; P. Dalgaard, *The Function of the Grotesque in Vasilij Aksenov,* n.p., 1981.

3. *Metropol,* facsim. ed. (Ardis Publishers: Ann Arbor, Michigan, 1979). An English translation of *Metropol* is scheduled for publication by W.W. Norton and Company in October, 1982. For more on the fate of *Metropol,* see Kevin Klose, "Moscow Journal Challenges Tight Control of Arts," *Washington Post,* January 24, 1979, pp. A1, A18; Craig R. Whitney, "Soviet Rebuffs Top Authors Seeking to Get Censored Works Printed," *New York Times,* January 28, 1979, p. 14; Kevin Close, "Moscow Harasses Top Writers Over Unofficial Journal," *Washington Post,* February 4, 1979, p. A25; "U.S. Authors Protest Suppression of Soviet Authors," *New York Times,* August 12, 1979, p. 5; Feliks Kuznetsov, "A Soviet Reply to 5 U.S. Authors," *New York Times,* September 8, 1979, p. 21; Feliks Kuznetsov, "O chem shum?" ("Why the Uproar?"), *Literaturnaia gazeta,* September 19, 1979, p. 9; Craig R. Whitney, "Writers Say Soviet Yields in a Dispute," *New York Times,* October 24, 1979, p. 9; and Anthony Austin, "Letter from Moscow: The Metropol Affair," *New York Times Book Review,* March 2, 1980, pp. 3, 19.

4. N.A. Anastas'ev, "Ot pervogo litsa (Zametki o zarubezhnoi proze 70-kh godov)," ("In the First Person (Remarks on Foreign Prose of the '70's)"), *Voprosy literatury,* No. 7, 1977, pp. 82-118. Especially relevant are pages 110-115.

5. "Sovremennaia khudozhestvennaia literatura za rubezhom," ("Contemporary Literature Abroad"), No. 3, 1976, p. 76, as quoted in Anastas'ev, *op. cit.,* p. 112.

6. *Ibid.,* p. 113.

7. *Ibid.,* p. 114.

8. Ia. Zasurskii, "Populiarnyi roman i muzyka istorii," ("A Popular Novel and the

Music of History"), *Inostrannaia literatura* (*Foreign Literature*), No. 10, 1978, pp. 182-185.

9. For a more extensive treatment of Zasursky's approach to Dos Passos, see Yasen Zasursky, "Dos Passos' Experimental Novel" in *Twentieth-Century American Literature: A Soviet View,* tr. Ronald Vroon (Moscow: Progress Publishers, 1976), pp. 331-350.

From *U.S.A.* to *Ragtime:*
Notes on the Forms of Historical
Consciousness in Modern Fiction
Barbara Foley

WHEN E. L. DOCTOROW's *Ragtime* recently soared to success among critics, academics, and the general public, a number of reviewers commented upon its marked resemblance to Dos Passos' *U.S.A.* trilogy. John Seelye, impressed by the structural and ideological connection between the two works, remarked that

> what Doctorow has done, in effect, is to take the materials of Dos Passos'
> *U.S.A.*—a sequential series of fictional, autobiographical and historical
> episodes—and place them in a compactor, reducing the bulk and hopelessly blurring the edges of definition. And yet the result is an artifact which
> retains the specific gravity of Dos Passos' classic, being a massively cynical
> indictment of capitalistic, racist, violent, crude, crass and impotently
> middle-class America.[1]

Calling attention to an important contrast between *U.S.A.* and *Ragtime,* another critic observed:

> . . . Logically, this is the kind of novel that should focus on the lives of
> its fictional characters, interrupting the narration only as Dos Passos did in
> the biographical sections of *U.S.A.*
> What Doctorow manages to do, however, is even more intriguing. In
> Dos Passos' great trilogy, the biographical is used as a counterweight to
> the fictional. In Doctorow, the stuff of J. P. Morgan is, indeed, the stuff
> of fictional life.[2]

Other reviewers as well noted the admixture of fact and fiction in Doctorow's novel and compared his achievement to that of Dos Passos.[3] While these scattered observations have been helpful in stimulating our awareness of the relation between these two authors, little effort has been made to ascertain the exact nature and extent of Dos Passos' influence upon Doctorow. One purpose of this essay will be to provide such an assessment, with the aim not only of illuminating Doctorow's sources for subject matter and technique but also of suggesting the continuing impact which Dos Passos' work is having in our time.

But such narrow ''influence'' studies have limited value at best. What emerges from an extended comparison of *U.S.A.* with *Ragtime* is an equally pronounced sense of the profound divergence between the two works—a divergence which comments significantly upon the changing strategies by which novelists of the twentieth century have chosen to depict historical materials in their fiction. For all its obvious similarity to the great trilogy of Dos Passos, *Ragtime* bears a closer relation in outlook to such diverse works as Gabriel García Márquez's *One Hundred Years of Solitude,* John Berger's *G.,* or even John Fowles's *The French Lieutenant's Woman.* My primary goal here is thus to locate both *U.S.A.* and *Ragtime* in the more general development of the historical novel and to touch upon the major tendencies which historically conscious fiction is exhibiting today.

I

Like *U.S.A., Ragtime* contains a satiric commentary upon the development of American society in the early years of the twentieth century. Its time-span is for the most part confined to the prewar years chronicled in *The Forty-Second Parallel,* although it skims briefly over the years covered in *Nineteen-Nineteen* and foreshadows the era of *The Big Money.* While Doctorow evinces a far keener awareness of the problems stemming from sexual and racial oppression in the prewar period, he and Dos Passos are similarly concerned with formulating a radical critique of capitalism. At the same time both authors infuse into their portraits a curious admixture of nostalgia: for all the brutality underlying its bravado, the era of Theodore Roosevelt is seen as the final age of innocence before the decisive molding of modern America.

In addition, despite some evident disparities in technique, *Ragtime* and *U.S.A.* have a number of crucial structural elements in common. The anonymous Boy who provides Doctorow's most important angle of fictional vision—and who might indeed be the narrator himself as a child—performs a function very like that of Dos Passos' Camera Eye: both respond with almost excruciating sensitivity to the callousness of their historical worlds and thus furnish a naive but clear-eyed standard of ethical judgment for the narratives in which they appear. Moreover, while he has eliminated the dramatic breaks in narrative that characterize the earlier trilogy, Doctorow often adopts the broadly ranging public stance of Dos Passos' newsreels and offers a streamlined version of the *simultanéisme* which his predecessor had learned from the Cubists, the Italian Futurists, and such experimenters with cinematic montage as Eisenstein. Indeed, the opening passage of *Ragtime* in some ways echoes the ironic dawn-of-the-century newsreel that begins *The Forty-Second Parallel:*

> Patriotism was a reliable sentiment in the early 1900's. Teddy Roosevelt was President. The population customarily gathered in great numbers either out of doors for parades, public concerts, fish fries, political picnics, social outings, or indoors in meeting halls, vaudeville theatres, operas, ballrooms. There seemed to be no entertainment that did not involve great swarms of people. Trains and steamers and trolleys moved them from one place to another. That was the style, that was the way people lived. Women were stouter then. They visited the fleet carrying white parasols. Everyone wore white in summer. Tennis racquets were hefty and the racquet faces elliptical. There was a lot of sexual fainting. There were no Negroes. There were no immigrants.

What is more, although many "real" historical figures enter into the plot of Doctorow's novel with an audacity undreamed in Dos Passos' more somber work, *Ragtime* also contains numerous sketches of historical personages— e.g., Theodore Dreiser and Sigmund Freud—who, in the characteristic Dos Passos manner, remain peripheral to the main action of the fiction. Finally, the spectrum of American society reflected in the stories of the nameless Anglo-Saxon and Jewish families and in the dramatic saga of the black Coalhouse Walker furnishes a broadly representative microcosm of society in many ways akin to the rich fictional world built up around Mac and J. Ward Moorehouse, Margo Dowling, and Charley Anderson. In short, the four-part structure of *U.S.A.* survives in *Ragtime,* although in compressed and integrated form.

Dos Passos' trilogy has influenced not only the shape but also, I believe, much of the specific content of Doctorow's novel. There appears throughout *Ragtime* a multitude of characters and incidents, both major and minor, which contain distinct echoes for those familiar with *U.S.A.* For instance, the portrait of the prewar radical movement so central to the rhetoric of *The Forty-Second Parallel* is also sketched in *Ragtime.* The Lawrence textile strike, which is chronicled in Camera Eye, reappears in the story of Tateh, the socialist immigrant. Big Bill Haywood, the Wobbly leader, enters Tateh's life in Lawrence much as he enters Mac's during the Goldfield strike. Emma Goldman's lover, Ben Reitman, participates in the same I.W.W.-led San Diego free speech fight which causes Mac to give up his settled married life and join the insurgent rebels in Mexico. Younger Brother, the revolutionary idealist, disappears in the thick of the Mexican Revolution at the end of *Ragtime,* just as the more politically wavering Mac does at the end of *The Forty-Second Parallel.* Even the colorful portrait of Emma Goldman is prefigured in the Camera Eye's description of the anarchist: "Afterwards we went to the Brevoort it was much nicer everybody who was anybody was there and there was Emma Goldman eating frankfurters and sauerkraut and everybody looked at Emma Goldman and at everybody else that was anybody and everybody was for peace and the cooperative commonwealth and the Russian revolution. . . ."[4]

Doctorow clearly shares Dos Passos' fondness for the Wobblies and Anarchists of the prewar era. He introduces in *Ragtime,* however, a much broader range of historical personalities and events that are, I suggest, also drawn from the pages of *U.S.A.* Edison, Steinmetz, and Burbank, all subjects of biographies in *The Forty-Second Parallel,* parade through the pages of *Ragtime,* and furnish a similarly skeptical perspective on science and technology in the prewar years. The monstrous details of Teddy Roosevelt's safaris are treated with delight by Dos Passos and Doctorow alike. Halley's Comet offers the same fascination for the Boy as it does for the young Camera Eye. Doctorow's Wilson, with his "prim renunciatory mouth of someone who had eaten fish with bones in it," calls to mind Dos Passos' hypocritical "public champion of right" with his "grey stony cold face" and "little smile around the mouth [that] looked as if it had been painted on afterwards."[5] And, finally, J. P. Morgan and Henry Ford, the respective villains of *Nineteen-Nineteen* and *The Big Money,* are immortalized in the discussion of reincarnation so central to the satiric political commentary of *Ragtime. U.S.A.* exercises not merely a peripheral influence upon *Ragtime:* it furnishes a crucial model for the blending of fact and fiction and supplies a mine of historical particulars that enrich the panorama of Doctorow's created world.

Doctorow's evident reliance upon Dos Passos' trilogy thus suggests that, contrary to the prevailing critical assessment, Dos Passos can perhaps more profitably be seen as a pioneer in contemporary treatments of fact in fiction than as a figure closing out the earlier naturalistic tradition in the American novel.[6] Doctorow's adaptation of Dos Passos' materials and form—as well as the influence of Dos Passos upon other contemporary authors, most notably Norman Mailer—suggests that the enduring power of Dos Passos' best work may lie not so much in his literary "collectivism" or even in his radical technical experimentation as in his construction of a fiction based upon the illusion that the central events depicted in his narrative "did," as Carlyle put it, "in very deed occur."

II

The very neatness of the parallelism between Dos Passos and Doctorow, however, makes all the more striking the important differences between the treatments of history in the two works. For history provides the frame of the "plot" in *U.S.A.* with a solidity and confidence wholly alien to the conception of *Ragtime*—or, indeed, I would suggest, to that of any historical novel written in the last forty years. As Alfred Kazin has commented, "The old faith that 'history' exists objectively, that it has an ascertainable order, that it is what the novelist most depends on and appeals to, that 'history' even supplies the *structure* of the novel—this is what distinguishes the extraordinary invention that is Dos Passos' *U.S.A.* from most novels published since 1940."[7] Determining the exact nature of this "structure" will be crucial if we wish to understand Dos Passos' significance in the development of historical fiction and to account for Doctorow's subsequent divergence from his model.

What does it mean to say that history provides the frame for *U.S.A.?* In part, it means that the lives of the characters coincide with what Henry Adams called the "lines of force" in any historical epoch; as Georg Lukács would propose, it requires that the "crises in the personal destinies of a number of human beings coincide and interweave within the determining context of an historical crisis."[8] In this sense the intersecting fates of the characters in Dos Passos' fictional cross-section of the United States recall works of classical historical fiction like *War and Peace* or *Henry Esmond,* in which the conflicts and dilemmas of fictional characters mirror the contending historical forces of the times. But, in the examples of Tolstoy and Thackeray—both of whom, incidentally, Dos Passos acknowledged as influences on *U.S.A.*—historical significance resides more in general cur-

rents than in specific figures and events: Kutuzov and Napoleon, Marlborough and the Pretender are peripheral elements in actions which find their
center of interest in the historically representative experiences of a group of
imagined characters. Indeed, remarks Lukács, in the classical historical
novel "it matters little whether individual . . . facts are historically correct
or not. . . . Detail . . . is only a means for achieving . . . historical faith-
fulness . . . , for making concretely clear the historical necessity of a
concrete situation."[9] The battle of Borodino and the fall of Moscow are,
accordingly, vital historical elements in *War and Peace* insofar as they
endow with epic significance the fates of the fictional characters; but the
reader is not led to question whether or not Tolstoy has described these
military operations with utmost historical accuracy, or whether his characterization of Kutuzov corresponds to the personality configuration of the "real
life" Russian general. Using Tolstoy's novel as a vehicle for distinguishing
historical from fictive discourse, Murray Krieger has argued, "Tolstoy's
Kutuzov . . . has a different 'material' status from that of history's Kutuzov," since *War and Peace* has a "different responsibility toward those
beings and events which it is . . . *presumably* about" than does a work of
historical narrative.[10] Similarly, in *Henry Esmond* the curve of the hero's
personal and political fortunes reflects and also illuminates the crucial shift
from absolute to constitutional monarchy which is encompassed by the span
of his life. Nonetheless, the reader's attention remains primarily fixed upon
Esmond himself, and in particular upon the rising and falling plot centering
upon the transfer of his affections from the Augustan Beatrice to the proto-
Victorian Rachel. Indeed, in such a historical novel as *Esmond*, as Herbert
Butterfield shrewdly observed, "sometimes a wrench has to be given to
history in order to subdue it to the demands of the novel."[11] At the end of
Esmond, such a "wrench" is in fact given: "And you might have been
king," remarks Esmond to the lascivious Pretender, "if you hadn't come
dangling after Trix."[12] The "real" reasons for the Pretender's failure to
attain the throne are audaciously distorted to accommodate the demands of
the story: fiction takes command of history. Borrowing the useful formulation of Warner Berthoff, we may say that both *War and Peace* and *Esmond*
are not primarily historical documents, in which the "problem is verification," but fictional documents, in which the "problem is veracity."[13]

In the strange medley of fact and fiction which is *U.S.A.*, however, history provides the frame for the novel in a far deeper sense. Not merely representative historical trends, but externally verifiable historical events, furnish the structure for the narrative, and the fictional lives which constitute the focus of interest in the classical historical novel are relegated to subordinate status. Where the fall of Moscow serves as a tragic backdrop for the death of Prince Andrei and the moral awakening of Pierre, the execution of Sacco and Vanzetti occupies the foreground of action in *The Big Money,* and Mary French's participation in the movement to stay the anarchists' deaths functions principally to flesh out and comment upon this historical event. Where Tolstoy's Kutuzov emerges as a semimythic figure embodying the spirit of an entire people, Dos Passos' Frederick Taylor, founder of the "American Plan," is inseparable from the actual person described in biography, history, and technological manuals.[14] And where the fate of Thackeray's Augustan hero furnishes a microcosmic fictional embodiment of historical change, even to the point of distorting historical particulars, the fate of Dos Passos' exemplar of the Wobblies, Mac, functions in quite a different way.

Indeed, to turn around Butterfield's helpful phrase, in Mac's case a wrench is given to fiction to subdue it to the demands of history. To begin with, the time sequence of Mac's story is cleverly juggled in order to highlight the rapid rise and fall of the I.W.W. during the first two decades of the century. Mac leaves Chicago when he is seventeen, and after a year of vagabondage he lands in San Francisco. Almost immediately he experiences the San Francisco earthquake of 1905 and then participates in the Goldfield, Nevada, strike of 1906-1907, the first significant strike led by the Wobblies. If we compute his age by dating forward from his childhood, then, he is about nineteen in 1906-1907. By the time he quits his wife during the San Diego free speech fight of 1912, however, he is depicted as being considerably older than twenty-five; and when he reflects back upon his life from the midst of the Mexican Revolution in 1915 or 1916, he reveals that he is "close to forty." Which is he—twenty-eight or twenty-nine, or ten years older? By telescoping two decades of fictional time into a single decade of historical time, Dos Passos has created the illusion that Mac's shift from militant class solidarity to petty bourgeois individualism encompasses not merely his youth but a significant span of his maturity. The "truth" of Mac's futile career is thus determined not by the internal coherence of fiction, but by the external coherence of history; he is less a character in his own right than a vehicle for exploring the weaknesses and contradictions of a broader historical phenomenon. Moreover, the thread of Mac's story is then abruptly dropped, without any kind of fictional resolution, in order to compound Dos Passos' historical critique: Mac's "dropping out" of *The Forty-Second Parallel* is a fictional analogy to the behavior of many "real life" Wobblies. Mac's career is, of course, being delineated in the picaresque mode, for which Dos Passos had a marked affinity. But in even the most episodic and open-ended of picaresque narratives, such as *Gil Blas,* which Dos Passos ardently admired, the reader is apprised of the hero's eventual fate. In *The Forty-Second Parallel,* however, the shaping power of the plot derives from history itself, and not from the principles of form inherent in any mode of fictional narrative. If we seek a "shaped" life which recapitulates *in parvo* the tensions of the I.W.W., we must look to the biographies of Big Bill Haywood or Wesley Everest: not because biography is *per se* a more structured species of narrative discourse than fiction, but because, for the imagination informing *U.S.A.,* history is more dynamic and coherent than fiction. Novelistic elements may enrich and broaden the scope of *U.S.A.,* but the principal thread of unity in the narrative is history itself. *U.S.A.* thus encompasses but also transcends the strategy of the classical historical novel, making historical actuality the focus of literary interest and perceiving in the flow of public events a plot with an inherently moving pattern of rise and fall. Indeed, in his overall conception Dos Passos approaches more closely the tragic historical imagination of Gibbon—whom Dos Passos on several occasions acknowledged as his most valued mentor in the writing of the trilogy.

Within the framework for discussing historical fiction which I have set forth above, *Ragtime* occupies a peculiar position. Doctorow's practice clearly diverges from that of Dos Passos insofar as the informing "plot" of his novel is patently fictional. For all his boldness in making "characters" of historical figures like Houdini and Emma Goldman, Doctorow treats history ultimately as motif—what one critic has called "post-Passos pastiche"[15]—and relies upon Coalhouse Walker's supremely fictional clash with the racist establishment to provide his novel with a sense of direction and a point of climax. It bears mention here that the story of Coalhouse Walker is, like the rest of *Ragtime,* cleverly derivative; but its source is not in historical fact but, rather, in fiction: in a little-known 1930's novel by George Milburn entitled *Catalogue*[16] and in Heinrich Kleist's *Michael Kohlhaas*. Milburn's novel climaxes with the lynching of a black owner of a Model T who has been viewed as "uppity" by a redneck neighbor; while Kleist's novella chronicles the resort to arson and outlawry on the part of a medieval horse-dealer who, after refusing to pay an unjust toll, has lost his horses and failed to obtain redress from the Elector of Saxony. There are many parallels with Kleist's tale in *Ragtime,* starting with Doctorow's daring pun on "Kohlhaas" in his own hero's name.[17] The significance of these sources lies, however, not so much in what they reveal about Doctorow's literary tastes as in what they indicate about the relative weights which he assigns to historical and fictional elements in his narrative. The first half of *Ragtime* may provide a highly entertaining survey of notorious historical figures of the day, but it is willfully chaotic in its sudden shifts of character and locale; only in the second half, with the mounting crisis of Coalhouse Walker's story, does the novel attain momentum. However amusing history may be, Doctorow seems to be saying, it does not provide a sufficiently coherent—or, perhaps, merely a sufficiently interesting—pattern around which to structure a causally related train of events. No Sacco and Vanzetti climaxes for Doctorow: fiction—albeit a borrowed one—must provide the model for his plot.

This subordination of the historical to the fictional calls to mind Thackeray's rather cavalier treatment of historical particulars in *Esmond.* Can *Ragtime* thus be seen as representing a return to the practice of the classical historical novel? Not quite. In the first place, historical figures like Kutuzov or the Pretender may be "wrenched" from strict historical fidelity in order to accommodate the demands of fiction, but such departures from the historical record must be confined to the realm of plausibility. Events so audaciously "invented" as Freud's and Jung's trip through the Tunnel of Love at Coney Island or Emma Goldman's massage of Evelyn Nesbit clearly violate this canon of historical decorum. Doctorow is doing something quite different here: he is utilizing the reader's encyclopedic knowledge that a historical Freud, Jung, Goldman, and Nesbit did in fact exist in order to pose an open challenge to the reader's preconceived notions about what historical "truth" actually is. Asked on one occasion whether Goldman and Nesbit ever really met, Doctorow has boldly replied, "They have now."[18]

In his satiric debunking of Swift, Addison, and Marlborough, Thackeray never approached such willful manipulation of the historical record: the venture of the two writers differs not in degree but in kind.

In the second place, Doctorow diverges from classical historical fiction in his treatment of the novel's main fictional personality. For fundamental to the strategy of a Thackeray or a Tolstoy is a necessary condition that the principal invented characters be, in the fullest sense, "typical" of the age which they inhabit and illuminate—as Esmond is "typical" of the wavering aristocrat witnessing the decline of absolute monarchy. Lukács argues, "typical" characters are those who "in their psychology and destiny always represent social trends and historical forces."[19] While the anonymous Anglo-Saxon and immigrant families in *Ragtime* are clearly representative of their age, it is significant that Coalhouse Walker, the novel's hero, is in no way "typical" of the prewar years; nor is the climactic event of the novel a plausible occurrence of the times. This is not to imply that significant struggles against racism did not take place during the Progressive period. These were, after all, the years of the Brownsville rebellion and of W. E. B. DuBois' vigorous ideological opposition to the concessionary politics of Booker T. Washington; during this period the seeds were sown for the Garveyite movement and for the massive antiracist upheavals in the nation's major cities immediately after the war. But Doctorow, it seems, has deliberately overlooked many of the fictional possibilities inherent in the historical materials at hand. The terrorist bombings of the "Coalhouse" gang, their designation of themselves as the "Provisional American Government," their takeover of the Morgan mansion as a symbolic political gesture—these are elements more distinctly reminiscent of the 1960's than of the ragtime era. Both the hero and the climactic event of the novel are, I think, outrageously and deliberately anachronistic. Doctorow is commenting upon the age of Wilson by importing a dramatic example from the age of Nixon, and his point is, quite clearly, that the forms of present-day racism have their roots in the past. While Doctorow's ethical strategy here is effective, it also carries the implication that historical change is itself chimerical. A primary goal of most nineteenth-century historical novelists was to recreate a bygone era in the fullness of its specificity: reacting against the eighteenth-century notion of "generic man"—epitomized by Fielding's lawyer who is not only alive, but has been so for four thousand years—they implicitly endorsed a progressive view of history and sought to uncover what was uniquely characteristic of a chosen epoch in the past. In *Ragtime,* however, Doctorow seems to be implying that accurate representation of the past is less crucial than revelation of the haunting continuity of the past in the present. Just as his Emma Goldman and Freud and Jung tease our epistemological assumptions about how we know historical fact, his proto-Black Panther hero teases our complacency about the supposed superiority of our own time over the age of Teddy Roosevelt. As a "typical" historical representative of the ragtime era Coalhouse Walker is a fraud; but as a means of commenting upon the racism continuing in our own time he projects an alarming degree of truth.

What I hope to have demonstrated thus far is that both *U.S.A.* and *Ragtime,* in different ways, represent a significant departure from the form and outlook of classical historical fiction. Although Dos Passos creates a typical and microcosmic fictional world, he subordinates the fates of his invented characters to the "plot" of history itself. Although Doctorow subordinates historical particulars to a structural pattern which is clearly fictional, he aims less at constructing a fully convincing representative picture of the Progressive era than at enhancing the historical self-consciousness of his readers. What the two writers share, in contradistinction to nineteenth-century historical novelists, is a reduced reliance upon the mimetic illusion and an increased tendency to intrude "documentary" particulars into the realm of fiction. Where they diverge is in the effect which they extract from these particulars: Dos Passos frames his narrative around facts which are ordinarily held to be "true," in the sense that they are externally verifiable; whereas Doctorow treats with equal aplomb facts that are "true" and those that are "created," thus calling into question our concept of factuality and, indeed, of history itself.

III

Before we investigate the important differences between *U.S.A.* and *Ragtime* as works of historical fiction, it is useful to establish their common derivation from an ancestry which predates the classical historical novel of the nineteenth century—namely, that grouping of factual and pseudofactual narratives popular in the seventeenth and eighteenth centuries, best typified in the work of Defoe.[20] Works like *A Journal of the Plague Year* and *Moll*

Flanders are "historical" not in the usual sense of the word—i.e., as evocations of past eras—but in the sense that they make an implicit, if at times false, claim to veracity. Their narrators assume the pose of real persons telling of real events, and much of the reader's pleasure in these narratives derives from this pronounced effect of historicity—even if at times it is, paradoxically enough, felt to be an illusion. The complexity of this grouping of narratives, however—and its important bearing upon the work of Dos Passos and Doctorow—stems from the variety of ends to which this illusion of factuality can be directed. In *Moll Flanders,* for example, the narrator claims to be a "real" person, but the historical plausibility of her tale collapses rapidly and the reader almost immediately recognizes her pseudo-factual ontology: Moll is, in the fullest sense, a fraud, though one that is to be openly acknowledged and enjoyed as such. The link between this narrative approach and what Doctorow is doing in *Ragtime* is evident. In *A Journal of the Plague Year,* on the other hand, Defoe utilizes a number of the tools of fiction, yet the ultimate goal of his work is to evoke by imaginative means a historically true picture of London at the time of the plague.[21] Here the reader willingly accepts numerous fictional accretions, such as the lengthy story of Thomas and John, as reinforcing elements in a work whose principal effect remains primarily factual. The kinship between this strategy and Dos Passos' achievement in *U.S.A.* should be equally apparent. In addition, there appeared at this time a number of falsified biographies and travel journals, of which Madame d'Aulnoy's *The Lady's Travels into Spain* furnishes a good example, that baldly lied about the historicity of their content and presented imagined incidents as externally verifiable fact. Dos Passos clearly has little relation to this tradition (although readers who dispute his political outlook might be led to challenge the "factuality" of such evidently partisan diatribes as his biography of Woodrow Wilson). The way in which Doctorow flirts with true and false "facts" in *Ragtime,* however, suggests a possible relation to these earlier "false true documents"—although Doctorow obviously does not share the fraudulent ends of a Madame d'Aulnoy.

In short, the peculiar richness in the varied factual and pseudofactual strategies of these prenovelistic "true histories" suggests a seminal relation between these earlier works and the works of Dos Passos and Doctorow—and perhaps, of a whole host of writers of the contemporary period.

Interestingly enough, both Dos Passos and Doctorow have been most willing to acknowledge their indebtedness to Defoe. Dos Passos praised Defoe's conception of the "novel as natural history" and admitted that he learned from the earlier writer's "behavioristic" method of "generating the insides of characters by external description."[22] More explicitly, Doctorow has described his approach in *Ragtime* as a resurrection of the method of Defoe:

> [Defoe] claimed to be the 'editor' of *Robinson Crusoe*. At the same time he relied on the public's knowledge of Alexander Selkirk [the real-life model for Crusoe]. Selkirk's whole life was justified by 'giving' Defoe his life story.
>
> From the beginning, novelists have used strategies, have mixed up fact and fiction. That's the region where *Ragtime* is located—halfway between fiction and history.
>
> Kenneth Rexroth said that *Moll Flanders* is a false document because Defoe wrote in a voice of a prostitute. My book is a false document. A true document would be the Gulf of Tonkin Resolution or the Watergate tapes.[23]

Norman Holland has speculated that, beginning in the late Renaissance, writers based their narratives upon balanced claims to historicity and fiction because they feared that their readers would distrust any work which admitted to be wholly a product of the creative imagination.[24] While the question has of course been of continuing interest since the time of Plato, critics and writers of this period were especially preoccupied with the issue of truth and falsehood in literature.[25] Sidney based much of his argument in the *Apology* on the contention that poetry projects a "truth" superior to that of history, while Bishop Pierre Daniel Huet, one of the earliest commentators on the emerging genres of fiction, decried the dishonesty of simulated histories "invented only for default of truth."[26] The historical world has obviously undergone vast alteration since the time of Sidney, Huet, and Defoe; yet it is possible that some of the ontological skepticism experienced by earlier writers and audiences pertains again today, though for very different reasons. Bernard Bergonzi has established such a link between contemporary writers of documentary fiction and eighteenth-century writers working in the pseudofactual mode. Both, he notes, share a "comparable uncertainty about the nature of the form and its power to convey reality"— the principal difference being that the uncertainty of the earlier writers "stem[med] not from extreme sophistication or critical self-consciousness, but from simple temerity [sic] about the enterprise of writing novels."[27] Have readers begun once again to question the value of fictions and to hunger for documents—false or true—more explicitly related to their own world? Have writers lost a degree of faith in the powers of the mimetic imagination, preferring instead to rely upon a concrete "sense of the real"?

The historian Barbara Tuchman has noted that particularly rich opportunities are opening up for the contemporary historian:

> Given the current decline of the novel and the parallel decline of poetry and the drama, public interest has turned toward the literature of actuality. It may be that in a time of widening uncertainty and chronic stress the historian's voice is the most needed, the more so as others seem inadequate, often absurd. While the reasons may be argued, the opportunity, I think, is plain for the historian to become the major interpreter in literary experience of man's role in society.[28]

We may not fully agree with Tuchman about the "decline of the novel": certainly large numbers of "novelistic" fictions appear every year, and, as Malcolm Bradbury reminds us, there is a continuing impetus toward "realism" in contemporary fiction.[29] The difference between the treatments of fact in *U.S.A.* and *Ragtime*, however, suggests that significant changes have indeed occurred in the strategy of the historical novel over the past forty years. In a sense, *U.S.A.* can be seen as occupying a watershed position in the development of the genre, insofar as it represents an amalgam of the microcosmic portrayal of the historical world embodied in the nineteenth-century historical novel with the felt sense of historical truth informing many works of the time of Defoe and before. And the trilogy achieves such a balance largely because it is posited upon an assumption that historical reality is knowable, coherent, significant, and inherently moving. It would appear, however, that since the time of Dos Passos there has occurred a curious polarization of these two strategies. Writers interested in retaining the specifically historical have tended to opt for a far narrower canvas, taking a small slice of historical reality and endowing it with "plot" and significance. Works such as Capote's *In Cold Blood,* Mailer's *The Armies of the Night,* Hunter Thompson's *Hell's Angels,* or Ernest Gaines's *The Autobiography of Miss Jane Pittman*[30] typify this "documentary" grouping: they bring to bear the techniques of fiction upon their reconstruction of history, but they take care to define and limit the particular segment of historical reality which is their concern and to shun any broader interpretation of historical change. On the other hand, writers committed to a full imaginative recreation of the past have moved in an increasingly "apocalyptic" direction, subordinating "fact" to a mythic or highly personal view of history. The writer working in this mode often relies upon his readers to supply necessary information—as Fowles does with his barely disguised intrusion of Christina Rossetti at the end of *The French Lieutenant's Woman*—but utilizes this sense of immediate historicity to create an effect of the bizarre. In the "apocalyptic" historical novel history is itself ultimately absurd, and whatever coherence the novelist extracts from it is a reflection not of any pattern immanent in his materials but of his own narrative control. Other examples of "apocalyptic" historical novels would include Pynchon's *V.*, Berger's *G.*,[31] Barth's *The Sot-Weed Factor,* García Márquez' *One Hundred Years of Solitude*—and Doctorow's *Ragtime.*[32]

Doctorow himself has been most explicit about his sense of alienation from the school of "documentary" writers (who have also been called "new journalists" and "nonfiction novelists"). His plan in *Ragtime,* he states, is to "deify" facts: "give 'em all sorts of facts—made up facts, distorted facts. It's the reverse of Truman Capote. I see all these new journalists as guys on the other side."[33] Pursuing the epistemological implications of this practice, he has remarked that he is currently testing the proposition that

> there's no more fiction or nonfiction now, there's only narrative. All the nonfiction means of communication employ narrative today. Television news is packaged using devices of drama and suspense and image. News-magazines package fact as fiction—in the sense of organizing and composing the material esthetically. There's something else: the reader of a novel usually thinks, well, these things really happened to the author, but for legal or other reasons he's changed everybody's name. In *Ragtime* I've just twisted that around and written about imaginary events in the lives of undisguised people.[34]

In fundamental outlook, however, Doctorow may not be as distant from Capote as he believes. Georg Lukács, discussing the writer's alienation from history in the modern period, has observed that, once the writer loses faith in the direction of history, it either becomes "a collection and reproduction of interesting facts about the past" or "a chaos to be ordered as one likes."[35]

David Lodge draws a similar conclusion from his analysis of contemporary fiction:

> *The Armies of the Night* and *Giles Goatboy* are equally products of the apocalyptic imagination. The assumption behind such experiments is that our 'reality' is so extraordinary, horrific or absurd that the methods of conventional realistic imitation are no longer adequate. . . . Art can no longer compete with life on equal terms, showing the universal in the particular. The alternatives are either to cleave to the particular—to 'tell it like it is'—or to abandon history altogether and construct pure fictions which reflect in an emotional or metaphorical way the discords of contemporary experience.[36]

The imagination which conceives Houdini as "the last of the great shameless mother-lovers" is, perhaps, subtly allied with that which insists that Robert Lowell was on the steps of the Lincoln Memorial in the fall of 1967: both, in Doctorow's words, "deify" facts—the principal difference being that Mailer displays the journalist's reverence for facts which are externally verifiable, while Doctorow pays equal homage to facts corroborated in the historical record and those which are the products of his own imagination.

It is, however, with the contemporary school of "apocalyptic" historical novelists—whom Mas'ud Zavarzadeh, in his recent *The Mythopoeic Reality*, would dub "transfictionists"[37]—that Doctorow has a closer affinity. To group under this single rubric such diverse writers as Barth, Fowles, Pynchon, Berger, García Márquez, and Doctorow is, of course, a problematic enterprise. First, as Martin Green has pointed out, Berger, Fowles, and Doctorow actually belong to a subgenre within this grouping, whose distinguishing characteristic is, in addition to elegance, taste, tact, and erudition, a penchant for "teas[ing] . . . the reader . . . to discover the imaginative status of [their] characters and events—the status and character of the imaginative experience he is being offered."[38] Second, it is questionable whether a writer like Pynchon can be said to be "apocalyptic" in *Gravity's Rainbow* in exactly the same way that he is in *V.*: in Pynchon and other contemporary novelists, the 1970's may be witnessing a somewhat different version of the "apocalyptic" outlook of the decade before. Nonetheless, what the various writers of this tendency have in common is a fundamental skepticism about the "objective" nature of historical reality—or, to put it another way, about the necessary subjectivity which any writer infuses into his attempt to reconstruct a picture of the past. Aware that distortions of "history" have often been legitimated in the name of objectivity, writers like Berger and García Márquez are openly challenging the positivist view of history: hence the patent mysticism of Melquiades' prophecy to the unchanged generations in *One Hundred Years of Solitude,* and the equally mystical process by which G. discovers a rationale for committed political action in the present through reversion to memories of senseless violence buried deep in his subconscious mind.

In one sense what such novelists are confronting is an epistemological problem which has been familiar to practicing historians and philosophers of history for some time: the crucial distinction between what Charles Beard called "history as past actuality" and "history as thought."[39] In another sense, however, the pronounced historical self-consciousness of a Fowles or a Barth significantly corresponds to the historicist tendency of much post-World War II historical writing, which projects a keen awareness of the historian's inbuilt bias and tends to shun the positivist application of general "covering laws" to a given series of historical particulars.[40] Doctorow's bold grafting of fictional invention onto the historical experience of a Houdini or a Goldman is curiously related to Collingwood's definition of history as a "web of imaginative construction":[41] implicit in both is an open acknowledgement of the process of selection—indeed, of creation—which is inherent in the task of the historical writer. Like Tom Stoppard in *Travesties* or Nicholas Meyer in *The Seven-Per-Cent Solution,* Doctorow wants not only to entertain his audience with audacious historical improbabilities but also deliberately to carry the process of historical "creation" to the threshold of fantasy. "One of the governing ideas of this book," he has declared, "is that facts are as much of an illusion as anything else."[42]

There is no denying that Doctorow's particular method of playing fast and loose with the materials of history has a definite appeal—as does that of a number of other contemporary historical novelists. In his extreme self-consciousness, however, there is also a certain mannered quality which we may occasionally find bothersome. It would not be quite accurate to say that *Ragtime* is decadent, since it is clearly radical in outlook and proposes an unillusioned confrontation with class, race, and sexual oppression in the nation's past—and present. But if Doctorow's mannerism is not itself decadent, it is, like all mannerism, associated with a period of decadence; if it does not suggest that history is meaningless, it does imply that the meanings we find in it are chimerical and at best highly subjective. What I ultimately find disturbing about *Ragtime*—and about many other works of contemporary historical fiction, whether "apocalyptic" or "documentary"—is its underlying postulate that whatever coherence emerges from the represented historical world is attributable to the writer's power as teller of his story, with the result that the process of historical reconstruction itself, rather than what is being represented, comes to the fore. "Once History inhabits a crazy house," writes Mailer, "egotism may be the last tool left to History."[43]

For all its cynicism about the possibilities of rescuing history from the grasp of POWER SUPERPOWER, I find *U.S.A.* a more inspiring work, insofar as it leaves one with the sense that the problems which Dos Passos confronts reside to a large extent in his materials themselves, and not just in the working of his own historical imagination. Like the Beard of *An Economic Interpretation of the Constitution of the United States,* Dos Passos boldly incorporates his selective bias into his depiction of past events and directs his skepticism not toward the integrity of his own enterprise, but toward the integrity of people and forces at work in his represented historical world. All readers may not share the view of class conflict which informs the best work of Beard or Dos Passos. Yet it would be difficult to gainsay the comprehensiveness and power of the materialist treatments of history in *An Economic Interpretation* or *U.S.A.,* or to suggest more than a handful of works of the postwar era which approach them in scope or rhetorical power. For the majority of novelists and historians writing today, history does indeed seem to inhabit a crazy house, and the ingenious strategies which they adopt to uncover a method in its madness bear testament to the fundamental alienation from history experienced by even the most resilient imaginations of our time.

NOTES

1. John Seelye, "Doctorow's Dissertation," *New Republic,* CLXXIV (April 10, 1976), 22.
2. Leonard Kriegel, "The Stuff of Fictional History," *Commonweal,* CII (Dec. 19, 1975), 632.

3. See Roger Sale, review of *Ragtime, New York Review of Books,* XXII (Aug. 7, 1975), 21; Walter Clemens, "Houdini, Meet Ferdinand," *Newsweek* (July 14, 1975), 73; Marcus Cunliffe, "Material for Every Appetite," *Manchester Guardian Weekly,* CXIV (Feb. 11, 1976), 22; and Emma Tenant, "Boneyard," *Listener,* XCV (Jan. 22, 1976), 92. The influence of Dos Passos is also noted by Kenneth L. Donelson in the recent "Teaching Guide to E.L. Doctorow's *Ragtime*" (New York, 1976).

4. John Dos Passos, *The Forty-Second Parallel, U.S.A.* (New York, 1937), p. 350.

5. A highly probable source for Dos Passos' cynical portrait of Wilson is John Maynard Keynes's *The Economic Consequences of the Peace* (New York, 1920), which Dos Passos has termed "historical vituperation in the grand manner" (*Mr. Wilson's War,* Garden City, New York, 1962, p. 501).

6. For such a critical assessment of Dos Passos, see Wilbur M. Frohock, *The Novel of Violence in America* (1950, rev. ed. 1957; rpt. Boston, 1964), pp. 3-51, and Andrew Hook's "Introduction" to the recent Twentieth-Century Views collection on Dos Passos (Englewood Cliffs, N.J., 1974).

7. Alfred Kazin, "Introduction," *The Forty-Second Parallel* (1930; rpt. New York, 1969), pp. v-vi.

8. Georg Lukács, *The Historical Novel,* trans. Hannah and Stanley Mitchell (1937; rpt. London, 1962), p. 41.

9. Lukács, p. 59.

10. Murray Krieger, "Fiction, History, and Reality," *Critical Inquiry,* 1 (Dec., 1974), 344.

11. Herbert Butterfield, *The Historical Novel: An Essay* (1924; rpt. Ann Arbor, Mich., 1974), p. 32.

12. William Makepeace Thackeray, *The History of Henry Esmond, Esq., The Works of William Makepeace Thackeray,* X (New York, 1910), p. 509.

13. Warner Berthoff, "Fiction, History, Myth," in *Fictions and Events: Essays in Criticism and Literary History* (New York, 1971), pp. 39-40.

14. Indeed, Dos Passos' account of Taylor's life adheres so closely to its source, Frank B. Copley's *Frederick W. Taylor: Father of Scientific Management,* that the biographer accused the novelist of plagiarism. See Charles Townsend Ludington's description of this episode in *The Fourteenth Chronicle: Letters and Diaries of John Dos Passos* (Boston, 1973), pp. 424, 490-491. Such strict adherence to biographical sources is characteristic of Dos Passos' practice in writing the biographies throughout *U.S.A.*

15. Tenant, p. 92.

16. For the discovery of this source, I am indebted to Seelye, p. 22.

17. The parallels between *Michael Kohlhaas* and *Ragtime* are close to the point of imitation. Just as Coalhouse Walker's name echoes that of Kleist's hero, Willie Conklin, Coalhouse's redneck adversary, calls to mind Wenzel Von Tronka, Kohlhaas's opponent. Kohlhaas's two black horses, the subject of his dispute with Von Tronka, are a medieval analogy to the Model T. Like Sarah, Kohlhaas's wife is crushed in the chest when attempting to plead with the powers-that-be on her husband's behalf, and shortly thereafter she dies. For more on the relation between the two tales, see John Ditsky, "The German Source of *Ragtime:* A Note," *Ontario*

Review, IV (Spring-Summer, 1976), 84-86. As Walter Clemens has commented, however, the "confounding of fact and fiction is particularly intricate here, since Kleist's novella was based on an actual revolutionary incident in medieval Germany" (Clemens, p. 76).

18. Quoted in Donelson, p. 22.

19. Lukács, p. 34.

20. For a stimulating assessment of Defoe's reliance upon factual illusion, see Ralph W. Rader, "Defoe, Richardson, Joyce, and the Concept of Form in the Novel," in *Autobiography, Biography, and the Novel: Papers Read at a Clark Library Seminar* (Los Angeles, 1973), pp. 31-72. Rader also discusses the formal qualities of nonfiction in his "Literary Form in Factual Narrative: The Example of Boswell's *Johnson,*" *passim.*

21. Michael Moore Boardman (Ph.D. dissertation, University of Chicago, 1975) offers an able comparison of Defoe's various factual and pseudofactual strategies, on which I have based some of my observations.

22. Ludington, pp. 452, 522.

23. Mel Gussow, "Novelist Syncopating History in *Ragtime,*" *New York Times* (July 11, 1975), p. 12.

24. Norman Holland, *The Dynamics of Literary Response* (New York, 1961), p. 70.

25. For a discussion of the ontological problems encountered by the Renaissance writer, see William Nelson, *Fact or Fiction: The Dilemma of the Renaissance Storyteller* (Cambridge, Mass., 1973).

26. Bishop Pierre Daniel Huet, *A Treatise of Romances and Their Original,* trans. anon. (London, 1672), p. 9.

27. Bernard Bergonzi, *The Situation of the Novel* (New York, 1979), p. 189.

28. Barbara Tuchman, "The Historian's Opportunity," *Saturday Review of Literature,* L (Feb. 28, 1967), 27-28.

29. Malcolm Bradbury, "The Postwar English Novel," in *Possibilities: Essays on the State of the Novel* (London, 1973), pp. 167-180.

30. Gaines's work is somewhat different from the other three cited in that its materials are largely fictional. Nonetheless, he assumes the stance of an "editor" of taped interviews, and the goal of *The Autobiography* is to convince the reader that such a person as Miss Jane Pittman did exist. *The Autobiography* is thus pseudofactual in the same way that *A Journal of the Plague Year* is: fictional material is used for a factual end.

31. The curious similarity between the anonymous titles and central figures of the two novels suggests, perhaps, a parallel concern with steering away from the depiction of the fleshed-out, "typical" hero or heroine so central to the traditional historical novel.

32. In recent months there have appeared two book-length studies which examine the phenomenon of the "nonfiction novel" in considerable depth. John Hollowell's *Fact and Fiction: The New Journalism and the Nonfiction Novel* (Chapel Hill, N.C., 1977) explores the social and political context of recent documentary fiction and provides some useful insights into the literary techniques employed by the New Journalists. Hollowell generally avoids, however, any discussion of the larger theoretical and literary-historical questions raised by the works he examines. Mas'ud Zavar-

zadeh's *The Mythopoeic Reality: The Postwar American Nonfiction Novel* (Urbana, Ill., 1977) is a considerably more ambitious enterprise. Zavarzadeh provides a thorough analysis of the epistemological underpinnings of the nonfiction novel, offers a cogent description of its generic identity, and gives illuminating readings of a wide range of texts. He coins a disturbing number of neologisms, however, and insists perhaps too strongly upon the novelty of the genre and upon the prevalence of absurdist philosophical premises among all writers of contemporary nonfiction novels. Zavarzadeh's book nonetheless makes a significant contribution to our understanding of the relationship between the documentary novel and contemporary fiction in general, and it boldly challenges a number of widely held beliefs about generic distinctions.

33. Gussow, p. 12.

34. Clemens, p. 76.

35. Lukács, pp. 176, 181.

36. David Lodge, "The Novelist at the Crossroads," in *The Novelist at the Crossroads and Other Essays on Fiction and Criticism* (Ithaca, N.Y., 1971), p. 33.

37. Zavarzadeh, pp. 38-41.

38. Martin Green, "Nostalgia Politics," *American Scholar,* XLV (Winter, 1975-1976), 841.

39. Charles Beard, "Written History as an Act of Faith," *American Historical Review,* XXXIX (Jan. 1934), 219; rpt. in Hans Meyerhoff, ed., *The Philosophy of History in Our Time: An Anthology* (Garden City, N.Y., 1959), p. 140.

40. For a stimulating account of the relationship between contemporary historicism and the "apocalyptic" novel—especially *V.*—see Mark A. Weinstein, "The Creative Imagination in Fiction and History," *Genre,* IX (Summer, 1976), 263-277.

41. R. G. Collingwood, *The Idea of History* (1946; rpt. London, 1967), p. 242.

42. Quoted in Donelson, p. 22.

43. Norman Mailer, *The Armies of the Night: History as a Novel, the Novel as History* (New York, 1968), p. 54.

The German Source of *Ragtime:*
A Note
John Ditsky

THE BRILLIANT "invented" style of E. L. Doctorow's *Ragtime* is in part the result of a straightfaced fusion, apparently undiscerning, of historical "fact," improbable history, and fictional invention. What may not be recognized amid a critical adulation for *Ragtime* that threatens to damage by overpraise, however, is the book's barely disguised reliance upon a basis in previous literature. *Ragtime* is, in fact, a modern American version of that classic 1808 German novella, Heinrich von Kleist's *Michael Kohlhaas.*

The unifying narrational thread in *Ragtime* is the story of one Coalhouse Walker Jr., a black pianist who comes to claim the unwed mother Sarah, who has been living at Mother and Father's house in New Rochelle. Having persuaded Sarah to marry him, Coalhouse—a man of impeccable elegance and grace—attempts to drive his splendid Model T Ford back to New York City, but is stopped (in a scene of Faulknerian outrageousness) by the members of a volunteer fire company under the direction of Fire Chief Willie Conklin. The Chief demands the payment of a toll for use of the highway in front of the firehouse, and in the ensuing argument over the need to pay a toll for a public highway to the obviously racist firemen, jealous that a black man should be the owner of such a magnificent automobile, Coalhouse Walker is made to go along to the police station. Upon his return, he finds his car quite destroyed, and his newfound enemies enjoying this joke at his expense. In the attempt to secure justice for Walker, Sarah is accidentally but brutally killed by the men guarding the Vice-President.

Whereupon Walker begins a careful campaign of guerilla violence directed against his tormentors, all in the cause of restitution of his property. When Walker and his followers take over the Morgan Library and all of its valuable art treasures, a siege of military proportions begins—ending only when the car, restored, is brought around to the Morgan Library in accordance with Walker's demands. His men use the car for their escape, and when Walker finally emerges from the Library building, he is cut down without mercy by the bullets of the uniformed authorities. Doctorow then draws the several other strands of the narrative together—accounting for not only the famous characters employed but also the family of Mother and

Father—and ends the book with the picture of the crazed murderer Harry K. Thaw marching yearly in the Armistice Day parade.

The parts of the novel I have sketched here are the ones which clearly parallel the characters and events in *Michael Kohlhaas*. In Kleist's masterpiece, the horse dealer Kohlhaas is on his way to Leipzig on business when he encounters another spurious toll booth, this one manned by a servant of the Junker Wenzel von Tronka. Unable to have his way by force of argument, Kohlhaas leaves his prize pair of black horses behind and continues his journey; on his return, he finds that the horses have been abused and allowed to deteriorate into a woeful state. Attempts at legal redress fail; and Lisbeth, the wife of the horse dealer, is given the same fatal chest wound by a guard of the Elector that Sarah suffered, and like Sarah during an attempt to deliver an appeal for justice.

After a funeral as elaborate as the one Coalhouse Walker gives his fiancée, Kohlhaas turns to violence to achieve his ends: he becomes the leader of a rebellious army that overturns the established order and burns cities. At last, Kohlhaas has his way; the horses are restored to him, but he must be executed for his crimes. He gives the horses to his sons and mounts the scaffold, where his head is struck off. And one opponent, the Elector of Saxony, returns to Dresden in a ''shattered'' state.

Kleist's narrative (most recently available in a Signet collection of Kleist's work called *The Marquise of O——— and Other Stories*) comes close to Doctorow's, quite obviously, in a number of striking ways. Not only are the names Michael Kohlhaas/Coalhouse Walker quite similar (as are Wenzel von Tronka/Willie Conklin), but the succession of events is essentially the same in both works. Kleist's narrative, moreover, involves the leading names of its time (Martin Luther appears, for example), though not to the elaborate extent of Doctorow's; yet it is the *spirit* of the two pieces that is the most stunningly parallel: in both, there is the offhand telling of an outrageous miscarriage of justice, with the result that the reader of each shares the wrath that impels the central character of each to a path of violent retribution. And in substituting the wonderful automobile for the pair of splendid blacks, Doctorow not ony updates the story in a fairly predictable way, but provides a literal vehicle for the expression of the racial injustice that underlay the placid historical exterior of turn-of-the-century America, an era we were once continually being asked to look back to with nostalgic regret.

Most importantly, what Doctorow achieves in spite of the frequently hilarious occurrences in *Ragtime* is something of Kleist's tone of dispassion-ate rendering of historical event: This happened in such-and-such a way, and justice was done. But what justice! As in *The Book of Daniel*, *Ragtime*'s immediate predecessor, the effect is a very bad taste in the reader's mouth where the workings of legal justice are concerned—a marked disquiet with the way things are, if not an anger.

There is at least one further appearance of the matter of *Michael Kohlhaas* in *Ragtime*; it comes at the point where District Attorney Whitman is attempting to communicate with the besieged Walker inside the Morgan Library by shouting his offers to talk over a megaphone:

> Then for a moment the small window adjacent to the front entrance opened. A cylindrical object came flying into the street. . . . only after several minutes did someone using binoculars make the object out as a silver tankard with a lid. . . . The curator asked to see it and advised that it was from the seventeenth century and had belonged to Frederick, the Elector of Saxony. I'm really pleased to hear that, Whitman said. . . .

Whitman doesn't understand the significance of the container of Walker's message nor, presumably, could Walker have. But though Michael Kohlhaas dealt with an Elector of Saxony from the previous century, not the seven-teenth, it is as though an object from Kleist's story had come crashing into *Ragtime*'s action. In a way, this tankard is a metaphor for what its "maker," Doctorow, has done: reused the leavings of the past to speak contempt for its glossed-over, all-too-frequently romanticized injustices.

The Conspiracy of History: E. L. Doctorow's *The Book of Daniel*

Paul Levine

IN E. L. DOCTOROW'S BEST-SELLING NOVEL, *Ragtime,* there is a wonderful description of Sigmund Freud's visit to the United States in 1909. As Doctorow recounts it, the visit is a fiasco. Freud's disciples take him to see the sights of New York but the great man is not impressed. "What oppressed him about the New World was its noise. The terrible clatter of horses and wagons, the clanking and screeching of streetcars, the horns of automobiles.'' They drive to the Lower East Side where Freud cannot find the toilet he so desperately needs: "They all had to enter a dairy restaurant and order sour cream with vegetables so that Freud could go to the bathroom.'' Finally, the party goes to Coney Island where Freud and Jung take a boat trip through the Tunnel of Love together. "The day came to a close only when Freud tired and had one of the fainting fits that had lately plagued him when in Jung's presence." But the worst is yet to come:

> A few days later the entire party journeyed to Worcester for Freud's lectures. When the lectures were completed Freud was persuaded to make an expedition to the great natural wonder of Niagara Falls. They arrived at the falls on an overcast day. Thousands of newly married couples stood, in pairs, watching the great cascades. Mist like an inverted rain rose from the falls. There was a high wire strung from one shore to the other and some maniac in ballet slippers and tights was walking the wire, keeping his balance with a parasol. Freud shook his head. Later the party went to the Cave of Winds. There, at an underground footbridge, a guide motioned the others back and took Freud's elbow. Let the old fellow go first, the guide said. The great doctor, age fifty-three, decided at this moment that he had had enough of America. With his disciples he sailed back to Germany on the *Kaiser Wilhelm der Grosse.* He had not really gotten used to the food or the scarcity of American public facilities. He believed the trip had ruined both his stomach and his bladder. The entire population seemed to him over-powered, brash and rude. The vulgar wholesale appropriation of European art and architecture regardless of period or country he found appalling. He had seen in our careless commingling of great wealth and great poverty the chaos of an entropic European civilization. He sat in his quiet cozy study in Vienna, glad to be back. He said to Ernst Jones, America is a mistake, a gigantic mistake.

This passage in *Ragtime* provides a convenient place to enter E. L. Doctorow's work because it contains three essential characteristics that we shall also find in *The Book of Daniel*. The first is Doctorow's concern with history. Each of his major novels deals with an important moment in American history: the settling of the West in *Welcome to Hard Times;* the transformation of American life at the turn of this century in *Ragtime;* the significance of the Depression in *Loon Lake;* and the legacy of radicalism and repression in post-war America in *The Book of Daniel*.

Each of these novels is not simply a faithful recreation of an historical event but rather an imaginative revisioning of an historical epoch. *Welcome to Hard Times* imagines the life and death of an archetypal Western town. *Ragtime* weaves real and imagined figures into a tapestry of modern American society. *The Book of Daniel* transforms a real event—the execution of Julius and Ethel Rosenberg—into a meditation on post-war American radicalism. In each case, Doctorow is more concerned with imaginative truth than with historical accuracy. That is, he is concerned with what *truly* happened rather than with what *really* happened. Thus it does not matter whether Freud and Jung did, in fact, take a boat through the Tunnel of Love at Coney Island in 1909. Doctorow's description reveals in a witty image a psychological truth about their relationship. In this connection, when Doctorow was asked whether some of the events in *Ragtime* had actually happened, he responded: They have now. In an interview, he observed:

> I'm under the illusion that all my inventions are quite true. As, for instance, in *Ragtime* I'm satisfied that everything I made up about Morgan, for instance, or Ford, is true, whether it happened or not. Perhaps truer because it didn't happen. And I don't make any distinction any more and can't even remember what of the events or circumstances in *Ragtime* are historically verifiable and what are not.[1]

Finally, each of Doctorow's novels addresses itself in some significant way to Freud's judgment that America was a "gigantic mistake." By this, I do not mean that Doctorow shares Freud's judgment but rather that he is describing the gap in American life between its ideals and its reality. Moreover, each novel describes the end of an era—the frontier, peacetime America, post-war radicalism—that symbolized the end of a certain kind of American innocence. At the conclusion of *Welcome to Hard Times,* after history has repeated itself tragically, the narrator writes:

I can forgive everyone but I cannot forgive myself. I told Molly we'd be
ready for the Bad Man but we can never be ready. Nothing is ever buried,
the earth rolls in its tracks, it never goes anywhere, it never changes, only
the hope changes like morning and night, only the expectations rise and
set. Why does there have to be promise before destruction?

In other words, Doctorow's novels are not analyses of American illusions
but rather meditations on American dreams. Thus it is important to see that
The Book of Daniel is not simply a history of the Rosenberg case but a
threnody for the victims of the radical movement. That is, the novel describes
what Doctorow has called "the sacrificial role that the Left plays in this
country" and dramatizes what the historian Christopher Lasch has named
"the agony of the American Left." In the final analysis, as Doctorow has
suggested, the book is not about the Rosenbergs but about the idea of the
Rosenbergs. Only by comprehending this can we come to terms with the
moving ending of *The Book of Daniel* and its Biblical quotation:

and there shall be a time of trouble such as never was since there was a
nation . . . and at that time the people shall be delivered, everyone that
shall be found written in the book. And many of them that sleep in the dust
of the earth shall awake, some to everlasting contempt. And they that be
wise shall shine as the brightness of the firmament; and they that turn many
to righteousness, as the stars for ever and ever. But thou, O Daniel, shut
up the words, and seal the book, even to the time of the end. . . . Go thy
way Daniel: for the words are closed up and sealed till the time of the end.

In an article entitled "Afterthoughts on the Rosenbergs," published in
1953, Leslie Fiedler observed that there were in fact two Rosenberg cases:
"The first Rosenberg case, which reached its climax with their trial in March
1951, involved certain questions of fact about the transmission of secrets to
the Soviet Union, culminating in the handing over of sketches for the
detonating device of the atom bomb."[2] According to Fiedler, this case,
which was "clear beyond doubt," created scarcely any stir in the press or
among the public either in the United States or in Europe. In fact, he notes
that the Communist Party maintained an official silence about the case for
more than a year after the Rosenbergs were indicted.

In Fiedler's view, "the second, or legendary, Rosenberg case was invented, along with the Committee to Secure Justice in the Rosenberg Case, at
the end of October 1951." As he sees it, "the revised Rosenbergs were no

longer spies, but 'political prisoners' in the European sense, victims of the class struggle and the Cold War, defenders of the peace, a persecuted minority . . . these very people, it must be remembered, who would not confess their political allegiance in court, and who for six years had been under instructions not even to appear 'progressive.' "[3] In Fiedler's judgment, the Rosenbergs were clearly guilty and their defenders were either agents or dupes of an even larger conspiracy.

Despite his expressed bias and his Cold War rhetoric, Fiedler did correctly note that there were indeed two Rosenberg cases which rarely touched. Now, nearly thirty years later, opinion is still as strongly divided. Recently, in *The New Republic,* Sol Stern and Ronald Radosh published an article based upon a reexamination of all the existing evidence which concluded that Julius Rosenberg was indeed a spy but that his wife Ethel was innocent. Needless to say, the article raised a·storm of protest from *both* sides.[4]

But there is a *third* Rosenberg case beyond the two that Fiedler described and this third case is the subject of Doctorow's novel. This third case involves more a social rite than a jury trial. As Doctorow has put it, "the specific dramatic interest I had was solely in terms of what happens when all the antagonistic force of society is brought to bear and focused on one or possibly two individuals, what kind of anthropological ritual is that?" (CBC Interview) Here it matters little that Doctorow has changed some of the facts of the case: that David Greenglass has become Selig Mindish; that the two Rosenberg boys have been transformed into a brother and sister; that the Isaacsons are poorer and more proletarian than the Rosenbergs were. Here it matters less whether the accused are guilty or innocent—in the novel Daniel never finds out—than that they have been selected as scapegoats in a ritual drama beyond their comprehension. As a knowledgeable reporter puts it in the novel, "Shit, between the FBI and the CP your folks never had a chance." The implications of this ritual suggest the themes of the novel. In describing the humanitarian protest against the execution of the Rosenbergs, Leslie Fiedler provides us with an insight into the plight of the Isaacsons:

> The final protest that existed behind all the others based on stupidity or malice or official dogma was the humane one. Under their legendary role, there were, after all, *real* Rosenbergs, unattractive and vindictive but human; fond of each other and of their two children; concerned with operations for tonsillitis and family wrangles; isolated from each other

during three years of not-quite-hope and deferred despair; at the end, prepared scientifically for the electrocution: Julius' mustache shaved off and the patch of hair from Ethel's dowdy head (and all this painfully documented by the morning papers in an America that can keep no secrets); finally capable of dying. This we had forgotten, thinking of the Rosenbergs as merely typical, seeing them in the context of a thousand other petty-bourgeois Stalinists we had known, each repeating the same shabby standard phrases. That they were individuals and would die they themselves had denied in every gesture—and we foolishly believed them. In the face of their own death, the Rosenbergs became, despite themselves and their official defenders, symbols of the conflict between the human and the political, the individual and the state, justice and mercy; and this symbolic conflict only those who knew they were guilty could fully appreciate.[5]

Here is Doctorow's theme: the Isaacsons are "symbols of the conflict between the human and the political, the individual and the state, justice and mercy." Moreover, they symbolize the legacy that one generation leaves another: the legacy of the Cold War and of the Old Left. Thus the subject of the novel is this legacy, Daniel's legacy, and that is why it is Daniel's book:

DANIEL'S BOOK: A Life Submitted in Partial Fulfillment of the Requirements for the Doctoral Degree in Social Biology, Gross Entomology, Women's Anatomy, Children's Cacophony, Arch Demonology, Eschatology, and Thermal Pollution.

In an interview Doctorow provided an insight into how the book was constructed and, not incidentally, what it means:

I started to write the book in the third person, more or less standard past tense, third person novel, very chronologically scrupulous, and after 150 pages I was terribly bored and I realized—in fact, that was a moment of great despair in my life because I thought if I could really destroy a momentous subject like this then I had no right to be a writer. That moment when I threw out those pages and hit bottom as it were I became reckless enough to find the voice of the book which was Daniel's. I sat down and put a piece of paper in the typewriter and started to write with a certain freedom and irresponsibility and it turned out Daniel was talking and he was sitting in the library at Columbia and then I had my book. (CBC Interview)

The finished novel is neither a standard third-person narrative nor very chronologically scrupulous. Rather its fractured sense of time and its vivid sense of language reflect the narrator's own sense of dislocation and outrage: this is very much Daniel's book and it contains his feelings of pain and hostility. Though he describes himself as looking "cool, deliberately cool" on the second page of the novel, it does not take the reader very long to find out that he is anything but cool. As he tells us later, his involvement with his sister Susan "has to do with rage" and, indeed, rage is his ruling emotion until the end of the novel when hostility gives way to compassion and alienation gives way to understanding. This movement is reflected in the chronological organization of the novel. We begin on Memorial Day 1967 and move through Halloween—the night of the witch hunt—to Christmas, the season of rebirth and fellowship. It is in this context, as we shall see, that we can understand the three endings offered to the novel.

There is another way of comprehending the chronological structure of the novel. It primarily oscillates between the early 1950's and the late 1960's: that is, between the high point of the Cold War and the low point of the Old Left, on the one hand, and the low point of the Vietnam War and the high point of the New Left, on the other. In other words, we are concerned with a double legacy: Vietnam as a legacy of the Cold War and the Old Left legacy to the New Left. Thus at the center of the novel stands the double inheritance of repression and radicalism during the Cold War period and after. Daniel puts it this way:

> The Berlin Wall is not a wall. It is a seam. It is a seam that binds the world. The entire globe is encased in lead, riveted bolted stripped wired lock tight and sprocketed with spikes, like a giant mace. Inside is hollow. Occasionally this hot lead and steel casing expands or cracks in the heat of the sun, and along the seams, one of which is called the Berlin Wall, a space or crevice appears temporarily that is just big enough for a person to fall through. In a world divided in two the radical is free to choose one side or the other. That's the radical choice. The halves of the world are like the spheres of Mengleburg. My mother and father fell through an open seam one day and the hemispheres pressed shut.[6]

If the radical choice is one part of the radical legacy, then it is understandable why Daniel feels ambivalent about this dubious gift. The seam that binds the world also divides it into two opposing halves that are mirror images of each other. The so-called Free World may not be free but the so-called Revolutionary World is certainly not revolutionary either. Daniel recalls E.H. Carr's analysis of Stalin's triumph as the victory of nationalist over revolutionary forces. As Daniel sees it:

> This insight of Carr's is useful in understanding such moments of agony to world-wide socialism as the Soviet refusal to support the Communist-left coalition in Germany that might have prevented Hitler's rise to power; the Soviet betrayal of the Republican cause in Spain (many of the purge victims were veterans of the Spanish campaign); the cynical use of the popular front and collective security as elements in Soviet diplomacy; and the non-aggression pact. Thus, to those critics who see in Stalin the "Genghis Khan" he was called by Bukharin, or the extreme paranoid he is sorrowfully admitted to have been by today's Soviet leadership, we must say: no revolution is betrayed, only fulfilled.

The radical who must choose between these two tainted positions is faced with a tragic choice. Necessarily, it seems, every commitment must involve betrayal. Daniel knows "that within twenty-four hours of my father's arrest, both he and my mother were written out of the Party. They were erased from the records. The Party did not want to be associated with anyone up on an espionage rap. Quickly and quietly erased out of existence." No wonder that he imagines his mother thinking, "Communists have no respect for people, only for positions."

But Daniel realizes that this betrayal also involves self-deception. If, as he is told, "a radical is no better than his analysis," then his parents were guilty of faulty analysis. His father "would never believe that America was not the cafeteria at City College; and as often as it was proved to him he forgot it."

> But with Paul you couldn't help feeling that the final connection was impossible for him to make between what he believed and how the world reacted. He couldn't quite make that violent connection. Rochelle was a realist. Her politics was the politics of want, the things she never got, the chances she never had. If my mother had been anything but poor, I don't think she would have been a Red.

Daniel's mother may have been a realist but her pessimism is merely the converse of her husband's dreamy optimism: both are signs of the inability to make connections.

> Her weaknesses were not as obvious to me as Paul's [Daniel observes]. If someone claims to deal with life so as to survive, you grant him soundness

of character. But she was as unstable as he was. In her grim expectations. In her refusal to have illusions. In her cold, dogmatic rage. As if there were some profound missed thing in her life which she could never forget. Some betrayal of promise.

Finally, both parents are guilty of self-deception and thus become accomplices in their own destruction. For this is one of Doctorow's themes: the compulsion of the Left in the United States to implicate itself in its own martyrdom. As Daniel sees it, "The world was arranging itself to suit my mother and father, like some mystical alignment of forces in the air; so that frictionless and in physical harmony, all bodies and objects were secreting the one sentiment that was their Passion, that would take them from me." So we may say that *The New York Times* reporter was right: "between the FBI and the CP your folks never had a chance." But there is another party to the conspiracy and that is the victims themselves.

It is this complex legacy that the children in the novel must confront. And the burden of this inheritance falls on all. Thus when, near the end of the novel, Daniel confronts Mindish's daughter Linda in order to find out the truth about the past, he recognizes the identity of their situations. "For one moment I experienced the truth of the situation as an equitability of evil," he says. "I saw her as locked in her family truths as we were locked into ours." In different ways the children are imprisoned in the past, burdened with the sins of the fathers, and the novel recounts their struggles to deal with this problem.

In the characters of Daniel, Susan and Artie Sternlicht, the New Left radical who sounds like Yippie leader Jerry Rubin, Doctorow depicts the problematical inheritance bequeathed by the Old Left. For Sternlicht, the problem is simply resolved. The Old Left heritage must be rejected. "You want to know what was wrong with the old American Communists?" he asks. "They were into the system. They wore ties. They held down jobs. They put people up for President. They thought politics is something you do at a meeting. When they got busted they called it tyranny. They were Russian tit suckers. Russia! Who's free in Russia? All the Russians want is steel up everyone's ass. Where's the Revolution in Russia?" In Sternlicht's view, the Old Left was simply part of the same system that must be destroyed. No wonder he concludes: "The American Communist Party set the Left back fifty years. I think they worked for the FBI. That's the only explanation. They were conspiratorial. They were invented by J. Edgar Hoover. They were his greatest invention.''

As Sternlicht sees it, revolution requires a total transformation of consciousness: you must turn your back on the past and act only in the present tense.

> "You've got to put down anything that's less than revolution. You put down theorizing about it, dreaming about it, waiting for it, preparing for it, demonstrating for it. All that is less than being it and therefore not it, and therefore never will be it. A revolution happens. It's a happening! It's a change on the earth. It's a new animal. A new consciousness! It's me! I am revolution!''

Sternlicht wishes to overthrow the past by an act of will. "We're going to overthrow the United States with images!'' he exclaims. This is a position of radical individualism which reveals two weaknesses. First, it underestimates the political power of the State and, second, it overestimates the revolutionary power of the individual. According to Sternlicht, "Society is a put-on so we put on the put-on. Authority is momentum. Break the momentum.'' Society may be a put-on but it still has the power to electrocute you as Daniel, an authority on "Thermal Pollution,'' knows. Moreover, Sternlicht's own power is exaggerated, as he himself admits. "I have no energy,'' he confesses. "I'm sick. I can't get off my ass.'' Finally, though he realizes that "the revolution has more martyrs than it needs,'' he is still willing to be martyred himself. He says:

> I mean someday they're gonna really off me. When the Federales wake up and see I'm not just some crazy acidhead, when they see that all the freaks are together and putting it together we will be set up for the big hit or the big bust or both, which is all right because I don't give a shit about dying, when you're into revolution you have to die, and you can't be a revolution unless you're willing to die. But man, if they ever put me on trial my action will be to show them up for the corrupt fuckers they really are. That trial will be my chance. I will turn that courtroom on, and what I say and do in that courtroom will go out on the wire, and the teletype, and kids all over the world will be at that trial and say, 'Man, who is that dude, dig the way he's got his shit together!'

Susan Isaacson stands in opposition to Sternlicht. She is imprisoned in the past, governed by the rage to preserve her parents' memory. This is her cause. "For Susan there are still issues,'' Daniel observes. "For Susan the

issues must be preserved. Everything about Daniel's recent life is irrelevant—except as it confirms his loss to the cause.'' Susan's obsession with
her parents' execution is the driving force of her radicalism; the Foundation
which she wishes to establish has as its first objective the commemoration
of their martyrdom. But as Sternlicht says, ''the revolution has more martyrs
than it needs.'' Thus Susan's obsession with history effectively cuts her off
from the other young radicals who wish to abolish history. Daniel realizes
this when he gets her note: ''they're still fucking us. She didn't mean Paul
and Rochelle. That's what I would have meant. What she meant was first
everyone else and now the Left. The Isaacsons are nothing to the New Left.
And if you can't make it with them who else is there? YOU GET THE PICTURE.
GOODBYE, DANIEL.''

Susan's obsession with the past and resentment of the present turns her
inward and becomes madness. Like the mythical starfish whose five points
''lead not outward as is commonly believed, but inward, toward the center,''
she aspires to a self-sufficiency that can only lead to her death. ''Today
Susan is a starfish,'' Daniel tells us. ''Today she practices the silence of the
starfish. There are few silences deeper than the silence of the starfish. There
are not many degrees of life lower before there is no life.'' Like her parents
before her, Susan has lost the ability to make the connections between what
she believes and how the world turns. ''My sister is dead,'' Daniel concludes. ''She died of a failure of analysis.''

Finally, we may say that Susan dies of heart failure: the failure of the
heart to keep itself intact in the face of the world's injustices. She is simply
too open-hearted to be self-protective. As Daniel puts it, ''nothing Susan did
lacked innocence: no matter how loud, how demanding, how foolish, how
self-destructive, nothing Susan did lacked innocence.'' Susan's heart failure
is the result of the generosity of her responses; she simply does everything
wholeheartedly. In this she resembles the other females in her family. Daniel
imagines them all in a medical textbook. ''This is a medical textbook. The
meaning of the picture is in the thin, diagrammatic arrow line, colored red,
that runs from Grandma's breast through your mama's and into your sister's.
The red line describes the progress of madness inherited through the heart.''

Susan's problem then is not that she keeps her feelings in but that she
cannot keep the world out. Daniel's problem is the opposite: not that he
cannot let his feelings out but that he refuses to let the world in. This is the

basis of his rejection of his parents, his foster parents, his wife and even his son. It seems that he too suffers from a heart condition. Musing on the difficulties that medical science encounters in perfecting the heart transplant, he observes that "Doctors still have a lot to learn about why we reject our hearts." This is Daniel's problem: his inability to accept the inclinations of the heart, his compulsion to reject both his past and his present. Daniel begins in a state of rage and alienation but his odyssey leads him to a condition of compassion and acceptance. In the end he is able to forgive his parents, his sister, his enemy Mindish, even himself. After such forgiveness he is again capable of action.

"In a world divided in two the radical is free to choose one side or the other. That's the radical choice." Throughout the novel Daniel is urged to choose; in the words of the song that Sternlicht sings to him: "WHICH SIDE ARE YOU ON?" Finally, Daniel makes the radical choice but he learns to do it without rejecting his heart. In two climactic scenes—first, in his encounter with the State on the steps of the Pentagon and, then, in his encounter with Mindish in the heart of Disneyland—Daniel is finally liberated from his past by confronting it and accepting it. "Listen," he tells his wife after he has been arrested, "It looks worse than it is. There was nothing to it. Is it a lot easier to be a revolutionary nowadays than it used to be."

This is where Daniel's acceptance of his radical legacy is more whole-hearted than either Sternlicht's or Susan's. For Sternlicht, the past must be repudiated before the future can be redeemed. As he says, "EVERYTHING THAT CAME BEFORE IS ALL THE SAME!" His refusal of history is a sign of his own weakness. For Susan, obsessed with the execution of her parents, the present must be repudiated until the past is redeemed. Her refusal of reality is a symptom of her insanity. Finally, it is left to Daniel to make the connection between the past and the present, to bury the past and bear witness to it in the present.

Perhaps we are ready now to make sense of the three endings that Doctorow has provided for his novel. In the first, Daniel returns to his parents' house only to discover that he is a stranger viewed with suspicion by the present poor black occupants. "I would like to turn and ask the woman if I can come in the house and look around," he says. "But the children gather up the cards and go inside and their mother shuts the door. I will do nothing. It's their house now." In the second, Daniel must bury his sister and, at the same time, relive the funeral of his parents. And he must accept his grief without rejecting his heart. In a moving scene, he has Kaddish, the Jewish prayer for the dead, said over the graves of both his sister and his parents:

> The funeral director waits impatiently beside his shiny hearse. But I encourage the prayermakers, and when one is through I tell him *again,* this time for my mother and father. Isaacson. Pinchas. Rachele. Susele. For all of them. I hold my wife's hand. And I think I am going to be able to cry.

Having buried the dead, Daniel must now turn to the present. "For my third ending," he writes, "I had hoped to discuss some of the questions posed by this narrative. However, just a moment ago, while I was sitting here writing the last page, someone came through announcing that the library is closed." It is 1968 and the students are closing down Columbia University in protest against the war in Vietnam. "Close the book, man," he is told, "what's the matter with you, don't you know you're liberated?" This is finally what Daniel must do: close the book and re-enter the world. "I have to smile," he concludes. "It has not been unexpected. I will walk out to the Sundial and see what's going down." Like Daniel, the reader is led back to the real world of social relations at the end of the novel.

In a sense, the novel's three endings suggest a lack of finality: only the continuation of the struggle for liberation and self-realization which is history. "I think the beginnings and ends and moments are artificial constructions," Doctorow has observed (CBC Interview). "It's possible to cut and slice history really any way you want to so that something is seen to be a beginning or ending. That's probably why history belongs more to the novelists and the poets than it does to the social scientists. At least we admit we lie. That's our innocence. That's why we're to be trusted because we're the only discipline that doesn't pretend to have a connection to objective empirical truth." For Doctorow, artists are the only honest liars and it is their independent honesty which makes them subversive. "In the largest, most philosophical sense," he has noted, "the writer has to be subversive, of course. If he exists simply to endorse the complacent vision or the lies of the society then there's no reason for him to exist" (CBC Interview). No wonder, then, that Daniel writes his book instead of his doctoral dissertation and that he names Edgar Allan Poe as our "archetype traitor" and "master subversive . . . who wore a hole into the parchment and let the darkness pour through.''

Finally, we may say that in Doctorow's view the subversive writer is always political in the best sense of the word: not in the sense that his work is programmatic and prescriptive but in the sense that it is speculative and descriptive. This means that the writer must be willing to move beyond the ''truth'' as defined by the prevailing ideologies. ''But surely the sense we have to have now of twentieth-century political alternatives is a kind of exhaustion of them all,'' Doctorow has said (CBC Interview). ''No system, whether it's religious or anti-religious or economic or materialistic, seems to be invulnerable to human venery and greed and insanity.'' *The Book of Daniel* is a political novel in the same special sense that it is a family novel. In reviewing his own work, Doctorow has suggested that ''there is some kind of disposition, and no more than that, to propose that all our radicals, and we've had an astonishing number of them . . . have really been intimate members of the family, black sheep, as it were, who no one likes to talk about. And I suppose one could make a case for my disposition to suggest that they are indeed related, they are part of the family and they've had an important effect on the rest of us'' (CBC Interview).

In my opinion, *The Book of Daniel* is the best and most important American novel of the 1970's. Not only does it reveal a piece of our recent history which has remained buried too long but it returns to our great literary tradition which has always been concerned with the dialectical relationship between self and society. In Doctorow's novel we not only re-enter the world of social relations but we experience the sense of identification and catharsis that is common to all great works of art. Like its Biblical counterpart, it is an intense and complex song of lamentation, full of pity and pathos, both passionate and prophetic.

NOTES

1. Paul Levine, Interview with E. L. Doctorow, Broadcast over the CBC on March 3, 1978. Subsequent references to this interview will be cited parenthetically in the text.

2. Leslie Fiedler, *A Fiedler Reader* (New York: 1977), p. 44.

3. *Ibid.,* pp. 45-6.

4. Sol Stern and Ronald Radosh, "The Hidden Rosenberg Case," *The New Republic* (June 23, 1979), pp. 13-25, and "The Rosenberg Letters," *The New*

Republic (August 4 and 11, 1979), pp. 24-29 and 47. Stern and Radosh conclude their rebuttal to the letters with this remark: "We are confident that the full picture emerging from any such impartial investigation will be the paradoxical one that so many people now find hard to digest: that a great miscarriage of justice occurred, but that there was also espionage" (p. 47).

5. Fiedler, pp. 51-2.
6. Clearly, Daniel means the *hemispheres* of Magdeburg.

Surviving McCarthyism:
E. L. Doctorow's
The Book of Daniel
Barbara L. Estrin

E. L. DOCTOROW'S NOVEL, *The Book of Daniel*, is a description of the hysteria of McCarthyism as it surfaced during the trials of Ethel and Julius Rosenberg. Moreover, it shows the devastating effect of the mentality of the period on the subsequent decades. Reviewed enthusiastically when it first appeared in 1971, Doctorow's novel has been given scant critical attention since. Yet, perhaps more deeply than any other contemporary novel, it reflects on the relationship between literature and politics in the nuclear era, providing an answer to William Faulkner's Nobel prize acceptance speech. In the 1950 speech, Faulkner warned that writers ought to evade the central political and moral fact of post World War II existence: the presence of the atomic and, soon to be proliferating, hydrogen bomb.[1] Most contemporary writers, either consciously or unconsciously, have taken heed. Modern fictional man may suffer from suffocating cities, dwindling countrysides and monotonous suburbs—all symptomatic of ancient diseases caused by what Faulkner called a prevailing subject: "the human heart in conflict with itself."[2] But rarely does a character face the possibility that, because of the bomb, nearly all hearts everywhere might one day suddenly stop beating.

This contingency exists throughout *The Book of Daniel* even though the novel is traditional in many ways.[3] Doctorow deals with mid-twentieth-century American children and childhood as an inexhaustible state, with contemporary affairs and eternal human conflict. This dualism lends the novel its compelling power. On the one hand lurks the spectre of the end of time, on the other what appears to its central persona as "most monstrous . . . sequence," life continuing as always despite the possibility of cata-clysm. *The Book of Daniel* centers on the discovery by its hero that sequence may be worse than death. A fictionalized child of the Rosenbergs,[4] Daniel Isaacson-Lewin, as he is called, is a product of the fifties grown up in the sixties. The novel juxtaposes the present, a few months in 1967, with the past, spanning the entire post-war era. Its writer-hero submits the work as his Ph.D. thesis in English at Columbia, finishing it just in time for the student revolution to render it obsolete. Opening with the hero's visit to his sister, Susan, at the Worcester State Hospital, where she has been confined after a suicide attempt, Daniel closes several months later with her funeral. His effort to save Susan by proving the innocence of their parents forms the quest of the novel, a quest doomed to failure both by the inherent ambiguity of the case and its seeming irrelevance to the New Left of the sixties.

The Book of Daniel cultivates an illusion of grandiose innocence and terminates with the reality of mundane and harsh experience. Thematically, its oppositions lie in the simultaneous movements towards life and death, fame and obscurity, warmth and chill, kindness and cruelty to which its hero submits. Structurally, these oppositions become a narrative method as Daniel emerges both writer and subject, victimizer and victim: the ultimate son and father. The disparity is sharpened by the distinction between the character who hides his past and assumes the name of his foster parents, becoming Daniel Lewin, and the author who confesses his history and acclaims, with a mixture of apology and pride, that he is Daniel Isaacson. Contradicting even the novel's dualism is its single-minded attempt to fulfill a traditional literary formula revolving around a theme which is as old as Greek mythology and the Bible: the myth of the lost child. Broadly speaking, mythical foundling plots involve an exposed child, usually a prince or princess, who is saved and raised by foster parents only to be discovered through some talisman or birthmark and returned, usually at the moment he is about to marry, to his real family so that he might thereby continue a royal line interrupted during his absence. The theme can be brought forward easily into the great novels of the eighteenth and nineteenth centuries simply by changing the prince into a wealthy man. Thus Tom Jones is really heir to Squire Allworthy, and Esther Summerson ends up decidedly not the pauper she was originally thought to have been. What determines worth is birth. Foundling novels depend upon a longing towards aristocracy, a belief in the value of heredity over environment, on the part of the audience to which they are directed. Insofar as he orders the experience of his childhood, Daniel Isaacson, the designer of *The Book of Daniel*, dwells on these proclivities in himself and in his reader, molding his reputability by affirming his genteel background and emphasizing his vulnerability by playing up his harsh abandonment.

Behind all the protestations towards equality, the arguments on behalf of the commoner in communism, which Daniel professes and with which his parents endowed him, hides an inherited aristocratic tinge. The novel constructs the image of the Isaacsons as traditional foundlings upon a strong sense of blood rights. Early on, Daniel and his sister feel themselves apart by virtue of their very abandonment:

> Without saying much of anything, without even caring if he was there, Susan could restore in him the old cloying sense of family, and suggest that his wife was not in the same class and his child a complete irrelevance. That it was their thing, this orphan state, and that it obliterated everything else and separated them from everyone else, and always would, no matter what he did to deny it.

Their sense of superiority becomes, as it does in orthodox foundling novels, an expression of genetic position. Daniel's wife is not in the "same class." The determining fact of his existence is the state of his orphanhood, a state which operates both retrospectively (governing his evaluation of his own past) and projectively (determining the future which is the present form of his evolving novel). Daniel describes the sudden notoriety achieved by the Isaacsons with their arrest as the logical extension of their illusions of grandeur: "the universe stood in proper relation at last to the family ego." When they sit alone in the first black limousine behind the hearse driving their parents to their graves the children feel their power in the one-word sentence Daniel uses to describe their estate: "Aristocracy." His mother's endurance during the trial illustrates what Daniel calls "a regality of suffering."

Daniel searches for and delineates his distinguished origins, setting himself up as the sympathetic gentleman *manqué* of the traditional novel he writes. And the sympathy seems deserved, for the Isaacsons and their children face the wrath of a society without remorse. They are victims on a colossal scale, singlehandedly bearing "the brunt" of every defeat in Korea. The novel dramatizes the isolation and loss endured by these lost children. Daniel describes his final view of his "blue-veined" mother:

> She was last seen in her black cloth coat with the hem let down and a black pillbox hat. My mother was last seen with her tiny watch on her wrist, a fine thin wrist with a prominent wristbone and lovely thin blue veins. She left behind a clean house, and in the icebox a peanut butter sandwich and

an apple for lunch. In the afternoon, I had my milk and cookies. And she
never came home.

Through his own characterization, Daniel emerges the ''poor orphan,'' the
wistful Oliver Twist, of a very conventional novel. His desperation is
emphasized by the irrevocability of his position, the plain truth that his
mother never comes home again. In this *Book of Daniel* there can be no
deus ex machina; its machines, the golden images worshipped in the Biblical
Book of Daniel, here destroy utterly.

Daniel's helplessness in the face of inexorable powers is made apparent
through a misunderstanding of his sister's cryptic—and only—message to
him after the suicide attempt which spurs the novel on. ''They're still
fucking us,'' she said. ''Goodbye, Daniel. You get the picture.'' Despite
the fact that he listened alertly, Daniel could not be sure whether she said
''goodbye'' or ''good boy.'' The dilemma becomes a motif in the book.
The women in his life are always saying good boy to him just before they
say goodbye, or perhaps as a way of parting from him. His grandmother
calls him that, giving him a penny to affirm his worth. To the old woman,
who was victim of what she called fascist-pig cruelty, Daniel seemed a
species apart, someone not subject to the cruelties of an unremitting fate.
But she died insane, victimized by those forces which constantly deprived
her of the ability to strike back. For his mother, he is the ''good boy'' as
sweet child who endures the difficulties of being the son of two people
committed to completing what his grandmother had been unable, except in
her moments of lunacy, to do: attacking the system of poverty and exploitation which was their mutual gloom. But all these praises are still only
preludes to the fact that the women die, are taken away shortly after uttering
them, by the very forces that lead them to recognize in Daniel some degree
of remoteness from the darkening powers. What Daniel discovers in the
course of the novel is that Susan was overcome by those same evils,
personified this time by the New Left instead of the Old Right. Finally she
blamed not her parents for having left them but the world for having taken
them away:

> THEY'RE STILL FUCKING US. She didn't mean Paul and Rochelle. That's
> what I would have meant. What she meant was first everyone else and
> now the Left. The Isaacsons are nothing to the New Left. And if they can't

make it with them who else is there? YOU GET THE PICTURE. GOODBYE,
daniel.

Daniel "gets" here, clearly, the picture he inherited. He understands that to
be a good boy, an innocent unknowing child, is to be told goodbye.

But if Daniel contemplates, at this point, the futility of innocence, it is a
lesson he acquired long ago. *The Book of Daniel* presents two opposing
responses to unspeakable adversity: the first is that chosen by Paul, Rochelle
and Susan: to submit with dignity to the death conferred by society, and the
second is that chosen by Daniel: to become a death giver, an executioner.
As a character in the novel, Daniel survives by ignoring his Isaacson past,
by becoming a Lewin. If, as an Isaacson, he was the innocent victim of
society, he emerges from that experience a victimizer—a hip, cruel, "terrible
low down" "criminal." Doctorow's first novel, *Welcome to Hard Times,*
has as a theme the same circularity of evil. The survivors in a town of the
brutality of a stranger literally called "The Bad Man" become in the end
just like the man who initially defeated them; their moral demise is an
inevitable, an expected, result of their early psychological wounds. In
Doctorow's fictional world, the metaphor for this process lies in the alternation between warmth and chill. The extremes of physical torment forge the
grotesque monsters who inhabit his novels.

Following a pattern similar to that established by Doctorow for the Bad
Man in *Welcome to Hard Times,* Daniel Lewin is at once sexually brutal
and a fire demon. His relationship with his wife is based on the master-slave
principle. She becomes for him a "sex martyr." He describes his wife as
"the kind of awkward girl with heavy thighs and heavy tits and slim lovely
face whose ancestral mothers must have been bred in harems." Daniel risks
his posterity by his cruelty, in one scene wantonly tossing his son higher and
higher in the air, terrifying the infant and his mother with the possibility that
the child might not be caught. And he relishes the "small face . . . locked
in absolute dumb dread of the breathtaking flight into the sky and the even
more terrifying fall toward earth."

Throughout the novel, the images of fire prepare for the Isaacsons'
execution and their son's subsequent emergence as an executioner. Daniel
dreams of his parents' arrest before it happens and the dream culminates in
a funeral pyre. The child is afraid to go to sleep at night for fear of two
parallel nightmares, either "the house would burn down or . . . his parents

would go away somewhere without telling him." At the same time the fire is preceded by encroaching coldness. In his relation of the dream, Daniel sees as a direct cause for its blaze "the dark skies and cold weather." On the morning of his father's arrest the chill transmogrifies him: "The cold hung like ice from his heart. His little balls were encased in ice. His knees shifted in ice. He shivered and ice fell from his spine." Like Artie Stern-licht's revolutionary, Daniel begins in coldness and ends in fire. Sternlicht, the New Left leader who disappoints Susan, analyzes the causes of social upheaval in the same terms used to describe Daniel's metamorphosis: "All revolution begins with tenants freezing their asses off in the winter." Here, the frozen child emerges the hot lover of the novel. The scene where he ignites his wife becomes his vengeance for the "frying" of his parents:

> The rain drummed down. The thunder was fierce. Cars were passing on the left. The sky was black. Daniel leaned forward and pressed the cigarette lighter. His hand remained poised. Do you believe it? Shall I continue? Do you want to know the effect of three concentric circles of heating element glowing orange in a black night of rain upon the tender white girlflesh of my wife's ass? Who are you anyway? Who told you you could read this? Is nothing sacred?

The ritualistic torture is in itself, like a tribal ceremony, another extension of the circle of evil to the "tender white girlflesh" of his wife. At the same time, the coolness of Daniel is emphasized by the calm of his preceding directions, his calculated insistence on forcing her to submit in the speeding car to his incendiary sex.

Daniel thrives on the cruelty which initially defeated him, lashing out in his description of his bizarre revenge even at the reader who is absorbed into the act by his own morbid curiosity. To see the crime is to participate in it, as Daniel declares when he compares himself to Linda Mindish, daughter of the dentist who conspired against his parents:

> For one moment I experienced the truth of the situation as an equitability of evils. This is what happens to us, to the children of trials; our hearts run to cunning, our minds are sharp as claws. Such shrewdness has to be burned into the eye's soul, it is only formed in fire. There is no way in the world either of us would not be willing to use our sad lives; no betrayal impossible of our pain; no use too cheap of our patrimony. . . . There was enough hard corruption in Linda Mindish and me, flawless forged criminals of perception to exhaust the fires of the sun.

In order to live, Daniel and Linda had to be cunning creatures of prey. They were cast, like iron, into the hardness of evil, shaped by the trial of their lives—both the literal judgment of their parents and the actual struggle of their individual survivals. The phrase "flawless forged criminal of perception" occurs elsewhere in the novel and seems both jarring and true. Why is it criminal to perceive? In the contradictions of the epigram are implied simultaneously the crouching voyeur, the child snooping on his parents' daily routines and here, the unyielding authority, the adult bearing knowledge inherently corrupt. Daniel and Linda understand the nature of the fires that burned them and their knowledge renders them in turn deadly. They become the objects of their perception, reciprocating the burden of the evil they inherited. In short, they survive without changing the world.

In this picture of himself, Doctorow's hero emerges, like Linda Mindish, anonymously small, cat-like or bird-like, with sharpened claws and quick wits. As Daniel Lewin he is different from Paul, Rochelle and Susan, lacking what he calls "that family talent . . . the capacity to do things in a big way—that gift for causing public commotion." But as Daniel Isaacson telling his story, he displays the talent in his novel, making their life-style his writing style. Thus, the reader can distinguish between the character, Lewin, whose object is to subsist, and the author, Isaacson, whose goal (like that of his parents and sister) is to end. Outraged at Susan's plans to use the money left and invested for them by the Isaacson Defense Fund for promoting New Left causes, Lewin objects to Susan's reference to her parents by their last names: "There it is, the fucking family gift for self-objectification. You hear that? She calls her own mother and father the Isaacsons!" But self-objectification is the technique of Daniel Isaacson whose novel begins in the third person and fluctuates back to the first. Isaacson's story, like the one in the Biblical Book of Daniel, testifies that, despite the holocaust, its teller lives to rework the plot. The original Daniel uses, as a device, the same change between persons of narration as the Doctorow novel. The abruptness of the alternation from objective to subjective lends to the fact told by the third person narrator an "I was there" ring and to the confession by the first person author an impartial verifiability.

In the Bible, the prophet, as resident of Babylon, continues to function despite what he sees: "And I Daniel fainted and was sick certain days;

afterwards I rose up and did the king's business.'' (Daniel 8.27) Daniel, the seer, may be ill but he knows how to recover; he conducts the affairs of state. What he does with his vision finally is to bury it. He follows the divine command to ''shut up the words and seal the book,'' as the concluding quote of the Doctorow novel demonstrates. He goes his own way and ends the story. The clue to personal survival is thus a literary suicide.

At the opening of the novel, Daniel Isaacson mocks a passage from the Bible which he had quoted earlier. The quotation is: ''I Daniel was grieved in my spirit in the midst of my body and the vision of my head troubled me . . . My cogitations much troubled me, and my countenance changed in me but I kept the matter in my heart.'' Shortly thereafter, Isaacson outlines the topics to be taken up in his book and ends up with topic number 7: ''The Isaacson Foundation. IS IT SO TERRIBLE NOT TO KEEP THE MATTER IN MY HEART, TO GET THE MATTER OUT OF MY HEART, TO EMPTY MY HEART OF THIS MATTER? WHAT IS THE MATTER WITH MY HEART?'' By the end of the syllogism the substance of the vision (matter as subject of the novel) becomes evidence of an inward trouble (matter as illness). The need to confess, to get the matter out, appears as the inspiration for the book. But the exposure of the symptom cannot cure the disease, so that as the story proceeds, its teller seeks another alternative: a conclusion. The mere fact of unburdening becomes itself a torture:

> What is most monstrous is sequence. When we are there why do we withdraw only in order to return? Is there nothing good enough to transfix us? If she is truly worth fucking why do I have to fuck her again? If the flower is beautiful why does my baby son not look at it forever? Paul plucks the flower and runs on, the flower dangling from his shoelace. Paul begins to hold, holds ends of the flower against the sky, against his eye to the sky. I engorge with my mushroom head the mouth of the womb of Paul's mother. When we come why do we not come forever? The monstrous reader who goes on from one word to the next. The monstrous writer who places one word after another. The monstrous musician.

The possibility of quick death is not as dreadful as the necessity of prolonged life. Sexual climax is followed only by sexual hunger; the generations keep perpetuating themselves. The reader craves more; the writer gives it to him. Daniel Lewin survives and becomes the grotesque hero of the novel. But

Daniel Isaacson wants to destroy the monster he created. His object is to return to a state of innocence prior to the "matter" of his book, to eliminate all sequence simply by stopping his story.

In taking their parents away, the state robbed the Isaacson children of their heritage, speaking in the crudest psychological terms, of their home and origins. As a result of this deprivation, the lost children embark on a search for their proper, if primitive, beginnings. They are on a quest for the outlined Isaacson Foundation. Susan finds it by retreating to what Isaacson calls the silence of a starfish, a state where "there are not many degrees of life lower before there is no life." If death is the elimination of possibilities, then renewed life is the elimination of hindrances, perfect simplicity and silence. Susan may be dying but her death is in itself an act of defiance, a tearing away of the barriers to life:

> We understand that when St. Joan led them into battle none of the soldiers watched the way her ass moved. We understand that Churchill found it of immense value to have played with toy soldiers as a child. Every line of every novel of Henry James has been paid for. James knew this and was willing to accept the moral burden. We can accept our moral burdens if our underlinen is clean. That is why we have toy soldiers. Susan digs all this. A starfish is not outraged. We must preserve our diminishing energies insofar as we direct them to the true objectives. A certain portion of the energy must be used for the regeneration of energy. That way you don't just die on a parabolic curve. You die in the course of attack. Susan knows this. To be a revolutionary you need only hold out your arms and dive. It is something like the sound barrier, there's a boom when you break through, a concussion of space, a compression of the content of space. An echo ricochets through the red pacific twilight all the way over the ocean.

The passage unites the oppositions in the book by bringing together Isaacson, the child, and Lewin, the man, by affirming their common, if cruel, humanity and their mutual possibility for limited nobility. But it is not a passionate plea for self-destruction in the name of a red pacific twilight. The image of the phoenix rising out of the ash, though beautiful, is honed finally not by an outside disaster but by a willed restitution of an innate brutality. To return to one's origins is to return to a rather Hobbesian beginning. Churchill played with toy soldiers. If the surface of a James novel is one of polished politesse and societal laughter, underneath it (as James saw when he visited the family grave at Mount Auburn cemetery) lies "the ineffable . . . the cold Medusa face of life, of all the life lived, on every side."[5]

In order to ricochet back, Daniel Isaacson needs to end his novel, to stop feeding the monstrous reader with his continuing prose. Finally, he completes on his own terms what, in the cigarette lighter scene, he used a Buñuel film to finish: the *auto-da-fé*. He provokes the reader now: "I suppose you think I can't do the electrocution. I know there is a you. There always has been a you. *you*: I will show you that I can do the electrocution." And he does the execution, making it the logical climax of all the flashbacks in the book, connecting his parents' funeral to Susan's funeral via the procession that affirms their aristocracy. Logically and systematically three endings are provided, entitled: THE HOUSE, THE FUNERAL, and THE LIBRARY. The triad enforces the sealing of the book partially because each section is somewhat flimsy and anti-climactic. After the final countdown, Isaacson provides no big bangs, only an insignificant birthplace, an impersonal and paid shamas chanting words for a Susan he does not know, and an unimportant revolution representing an effete sacrifice. "Close the book," commands the young radical who turns out the library lights. Daniel obeys. The retreat he makes is one of accidental, though inevitable, silence brought on, finally, like that of the starfish, without rage and without the expected struggle—very much in the family tradition. *The Book of Daniel* reconciles the split personality of its author-hero through its somewhat cynical admission that Lewin's future lies in the burial of Isaacson's confession. To survive in the sixties is to drown out the fifties. The completion of the work becomes, like the Ph.D. thesis it mocks, merely a meal ticket purchased towards a minimal subsistence.

NOTES

1. William Faulkner, *Essays, Speeches and Public Letters,* ed. James B. Meriwether (New York: Random House, 1965), pp. 119–121.
2. *Ibid.,* p. 119.
3. Armageddon is more visibly present in Doctorow's second novel, *Big as Life* (New York: Simon and Schuster, 1966), a science-fiction satire in which two Brobdingnagian monsters hover over, and terrorize, New York City, forcing the inhabitants to come to terms with the possibility of imminent extinction.
4. In the reader's mind are the events of the Rosenberg case, the probability that the truth, in this particular instance, may be even uglier than fiction. Doctorow has

changed all the names of the cast of characters and certain details of its drama. The Rosenberg children are depicted as a boy and girl instead of as two boys. The charges of conspiracy are corroborated not by Ethel Rosenberg's brother and sister-in-law (the Greenglasses) but by the fictional couple's friend (the dentist, Selig Mindish).

5. Henry James, *Notebooks,* ed. F. O. Matthiessen and Kenneth B. Murdock (New York: Oxford University Press, 1961), p. 321.

History as Fate in E. L. Doctorow's Tale of a Western Town

Marilyn Arnold

◆────────────────────────────

HUMAN HISTORY IS IN SOME SENSE the story of human confrontation with the wilderness, both exterior and interior, with the unknown, the unexplained, the untamed. But the story of that confrontation may take more meaning from the interpreting intelligence of the recorder than from any actual occurrences. We are all living what will one day be history, but what finally will be said and taken for fact about our era will be the interpretive work of persons who draw conclusions from their own memories and from recorded observations of participants (themselves interpreters), after the fact. In *Welcome to Hard Times,* E. L. Doctorow looks at historical processes through the consciousness of an observer-recorder, and suggests that such processes tend to create the future in the image of the past, producing an inevitable cycling of history. Doctorow uses the settling, the destruction, the resettling, and the redestruction of a Western frontier town, Hard Times, for his metaphor. And an appropriate metaphor it is, for with it he is able to compress into a few years the rising and falling cycles that sometimes stretch through centuries in other cultures. At the same time, he can represent structurally and thematically the conflict between civilization and wilderness.

Doctorow's recorder, a man in his late forties named Blue, writes an interpretive history of Hard Times after the town is destroyed a second time and he himself is near death. Blue gives ample attention to himself as recorder, to his role as historian, and frets over whether or not, given his limitations, the truth will be told:

> And now I've put down what happened, everything that happened from one end to the other. And it scares me more than death scares me that it may show the truth. But how can it if I've written as if I knew as I lived them which minutes were important and which were not; and spoken as if I knew the exact words everyone spoke? Does the truth come out in such scrawls, so bound by my limits?

The events Blue describes take on new and complex meanings as he draws toward the end of his account, where, finally, he succumbs to spiritual fatigue. The first two-thirds of the book is largely an account of events as they occurred, interpreted primarily by feelings Blue recalls having had at the time. But in the last third of the book, and especially in the concluding pages, the very act of recording events has set Blue's mind astir and changed the shape of his memory. What Blue has observed determines what he writes, but what he writes also affects his memory and his interpretation of what he thinks he has observed. The book grows highly interpretive toward the end, and Blue derives more and more meanings out of his own labored words. And he grows increasingly fatalistic. Earlier, Blue had naively assumed that fate, or the wilderness, could be overcome; but by the time he completes his story, Blue concedes that civilization is doomed: "Of course now I put it down I can see that we were finished before we ever got started, our end was in our beginning."

Doctorow is at least suggesting the possibility that our surest fate may well be history, the past. Since it is what we know, it is what we make happen again. The novel appears to be, among other things, a study of the historian as unconscious prophet. By seeing history as a pattern that has repeated itself and will continue to repeat itself, he ensures the repetition of that pattern. Every move to the frontier, every attempt to force the wilderness into retreat, every effort to establish a new town, every hope for a new start, challenges an historical imperative which militates against the notion of a new start. Such an imperative assumes that the birth and death of a frontier town is only a replay of an old cycle in a different locale, with a different cast of characters, and that the wilderness, like the past, is just another face of fate. Blue tries to resist that kind of historical necessity, but he also becomes an historian, and thus an accessory to the force he is fighting. He becomes an enemy of his own will and a destroyer of his own hope.

Since Blue is, by nature, one who hopes, it is ironic that he must record the story and become a fatalist by the persuasion of his own narrative. The story opens with the arrival of Clay Turner, the Bad Man from Bodie—the town's fate personified—in Hard Times. He takes over the town, brutally slaughtering the only two men who dare to stand up to him. He also kills Flo, one of the town's two bar-girls, and leaves Molly, the other, half dead. In the aftermath of Turner's rampage, another townsman dies of a stroke. After setting fire to the town the Bad Man departs, and the disheartened inhabitants scatter with their salvage across the treeless prairie, looking for a new home. Only Blue, designated mayor by virtue of his penchant for record-keeping; Jimmy, son of the slain carpenter, Fee; Molly; and John

Bear, a stoical old Indian, remain. Aided by John Bear's natural doctoring, Molly's burns scar over and she recovers, rising like a phoenix from the ashes of Hard Times. Blue assumes care of Molly and Jimmy, and after surviving a terrible winter, the three become, for a time, almost like a family. Even Molly warms briefly toward Blue, seeming to forgive, for the moment, his cowardice before the Bad Man from Bodie. As others arrive and stay, largely at Blue's urging, his hopes rise and feed his longing for civilization and community. The reborn town's first arrivals are the Russian, Zar, with his wagon of delights—mainly liquor and women. Finding a ready clientele in the miners who come down from the hills on Saturday nights, Zar decides to stay. Eventually the town is humming again and optimism runs high. But the mine plays out, the expected road is never built, and Hard Times collapses with the weight of its own fraudulent speculation. The time is ripe for the Bad Man, and he appears, bringing a second whirlwind of destruction. A ruined Hard Times is deserted once again, by all but the dead, wounded, or crazy. This time the Bad Man too is destroyed, but that does not save the town. Seriously wounded, Blue grimly writes the town's story on his old ledger sheets.

For a substantial part of the story, as Blue records events of the rebirth and growth of Hard Times, he describes himself as a man of hope, a man whose very expectations infuse life and optimism into the town. He earnestly believes that no Bad Man from Bodie, no black destiny, can overtake Hard Times if people settle there and make a home, a community. Blue's first act of restoration, after burying the dead, is to begin work on a cave shelter. When Jimmy asks what he is doing, he answers, "I'm making a place to live." It is clear that Blue will not leave, that he wants a home, that he will cling to hope in Hard Times. When he assures the skeptical stage driver that Hard Times has a future, the driver answers with a revealing jest: "Well now Blue I always liked you, yessir. If you was hanging by your fingers from a cliff you'd call it climbin' a mountain." Blue wants to make a home, to find a stay against isolation and the wilderness, and he admits that "it wasn't the site but the settling of it that mattered." For him, hope lies in community, in the ascendancy of civilization. Even during that first terrible winter when the few straggling inhabitants of the town gather together for a few moments on Christmas Day, his heart surges with hope. He is glad just for "the fact that all of us are here. And I asked myself whether these weren't already better times: here was some people and we had a root in the land where there was nothing but graves a few months before.''

In the town's rebirth Blue looks anxiously for every hopeful sign and celebrates it, though hindsight too readily undercuts his optimism. In Molly's early acceptance of his help and Jimmy's apparent willingness to work beside him Blue sees reason for hope: ''A person cannot live without looking for good signs, you just cannot do it, and I thought these signs were good.'' Then he realizes that Molly and Jimmy scarcely had another choice and sighs, ''Therefore where were my good signs?'' Nevertheless, he continues, ''if I felt like believing we were growing into a true family that was alright: if a good sign is so important you can just as soon make one up and fool yourself that way.'' Even Molly carries remembrances of civilizations in her heart, and shares them one rare night, pushing the wilderness back just a little. When the cold of their first long winter breaks, Blue himself feels a sudden, irresistible surge of hope and rejoices like a babe in a new world. As if in answer to the call of the season, people begin arriving and making plans to settle. For Blue it is ''a bloom in the heart, a springing of hope.'' And ''even when I pressed myself with doubts, the hope squeezed out like a nectar.'' He and Molly talk together for the first time, like ''two new people sprung from our old pains.'' So full of new hope is he that Blue begins keeping books again, establishing order in the resurrected town. Even as time goes by and the expected road still is not built and the settlers grow restless, Blue refuses to read the signs of fate. He stubbornly insists, ''Once there was work, once there was money . . . everything would be alright. It was the promise of a year, a settlement growing towards its perfection.''

But the more he writes, the more Blue comes to see how foolish he has been, the more he acquiesces to the power of fate. He begins to see his early optimism as blindness and his desire for community as an idle dream. His moment of family feeling with Molly and Jimmy is simply an episode snatched out of time, ''silently come and gone, a moment long, just an instant in the shadow of one day, and any fool who was still waiting for it . . . didn't know what life is.'' With painful eloquence he recalls, ''Sometime between that heady evening she relented and that day we danced— there must have been a moment when we reached what perfection was left to our lives. . . . When was the moment, I don't know when, with all my remembrances I can't find it. . . . Really how life gets on is a secret, you only know your memory, and it makes its own time. The real time leads you along and you never know when it happens, the best that can be is come and gone."

Relentlessly working against Blue's hope is Molly's terrible conviction that the Bad Man from Bodie will return. He is her fate. He is her past, and he will be her future. She begs Blue to take her away, but Blue insists that fate cannot be defeated by running from it. "You don't think it's different anywhere else do you? You don't think there's only one Turner riding this land!" Molly knows, indeed, that there are "hundreds," even "thousands. And they're going to get me—they're all coming for me!" Still Blue argues that the Bad Man can be resisted, admitting that, yes, we will "draw our Man from Bodie," but "this time we'll be too good for him. Listen to what I say: I don't mean I'll stand up to his gun, I mean I won't have to. When he came last time, the minute Flo walked over to him we were lost. Before Fee went in Avery's place with his stick of wood we were lost. You fight them, you just look at them, and they have you." Blue maintains that only civilization, community, can defeat the Bad Men, the forces of fate and the wilderness and the past: "a settled town drives them away. When the business is good and the life is working they can't do a thing, they're destroyed." Blue tries to convince Molly that they had brought the Bad Man the first time by expecting him, by wanting him: "Listen to me, you know why he came that time? *We wanted him.* Our tongues were just hanging out for him. Even poor old Fee, he built a street but he couldn't make a proper town. He must have knowed when he picked up that board the hope was already dead." But Blue believes he can build a "proper town" in which hope lives and defeats the Bad Man. He pleads with Molly to "believe what I am saying, and that Turner will never get to us." Molly, of course, believes entirely in the Bad Man and not at all in Blue.

Perhaps the most tragic fallout of the Bad Man's visit is what happens to Jimmy. He has been reared on Molly's fear of the Bad Man, so he too expects him, he too will force a repetition of the past by that expectation. Blue tries to talk with him, but language, words, hold little sway in the wilderness. Blue urges, "Listen to me I said the day is coming when no Man from Bodie will ride in but he'll wither and dry up to dust. You hear me. I'm going to see you grow up with your own mind. I'm going to see you settled just like this town. . . . and I talked on and on as if words could do something." Blue's hopes for making a civilized man of Jimmy have no chance, for not only has Molly trained Jimmy to expect the Bad Man, she has trained him to become the Bad Man. She has designed his fate, and he is helpless before it. It is not until Blue writes the story that he realizes this: "She was training him for the Bad Man, she was breaking him into a proper mount for her own ride to Hell, and I hadn't seen it till now, I hadn't ever understood it was not me who suffered her, it was Jimmy."

For Blue, it is the Bad Man who "fixes" him in Hard Times, who molds his fate. Turner's "grinning face" haunts him, and his rage returns with the recollection that he let the Bad Man have Molly, that he picked up a drink with Turner instead of a gun. Turner represented "something that was too strong for me, something I could not cope with." In the earlier part of his narrative, Blue recalls representing Molly as his wife to newcomers, believing in some sense "that we had been wedded by the Bad Man from Bodie." But by the time he writes the concluding pages of his narrative, he realizes that Molly has never been his "wife" in any sense. It is only the Man from Bodie who matters to her and for whom she has been waiting, "a proper faithful wife"; and a fiendish Jimmy is the offspring of that unholy alliance. Even Blue, in the end, allows himself to become "Molly's final fool." In an act that is "a giving in to them all," he goes against Turner with force. Cagier than the foolhardy Jenks, who succumbs to Molly's pleas and promises and marches in the front door of the saloon with guns and mouth blazing, Blue strings a mesh of barbed wire in front of the saloon and calls to Turner. The Bad Man falls for the trick, and Blue has him. Blue does not finish Turner off, however, but hauls him to his cabin and dumps him on the eating table before Molly. She pounces on him with her stiletto and takes her revenge. Jimmy, horrified at the sight, claims Molly as his own in the only way he knows how, with a gun: "He spoke as she had taught him, manfully, with the proper instrument, booming of birth." At the instant Jimmy shoots Molly and Turner, at "the moment Turner's arms had closed around Molly as if in embrace," Jimmy is born as the figurative offspring of their union. There is even an afterbirth. Rioters outside just then tip over the water tank and Blue hears "the spread of water, an indecent gush." Later, wounded, for his hand was over the muzzle when Jimmy fired, Blue thinks about Jimmy. He realizes that Jimmy is gone, "riding hard, that mule and rig will take him places, another Bad Man from Bodie, who used to be Fee's boy."

The more Blue writes the story of Hard Times, the more he feels the weight of the past and the hopeless inescapability of fate—and the more he succumbs to Molly's pessimism just by writing about it. He remembers her scorn for his record-keeping and his efforts at civilizing the West: "Nothing fixes in this damned country, people blow around at the whiff of the wind. You can't bring the law to a bunch of rocks, you can't settle the coyotes, you can't make a society out of sand." Although Blue has been earnestly resisting Molly's fatalism, she had brought a shudder to his spine when she cried out, "if this town stretched four ways as far as the eye could see, it would still be a wilderness!" He was able to recover and smile then, thinking "how like a woman it was to scare in the good times." But later, writing the story, his hopes in shambles, he remarks, "That was only last winter but it seems like ancient days in my mind." As the story progresses, we become increasingly aware of Blue as a recorder. He begins backing up, questioning his original perceptions of events ("No, maybe I'm not telling it right"), distrusting his recollections and the meanings of those recollections. We sense his distending agony as he tries to sort out what has happened:

> I have been trying to write what happened but it is hard, wishful work. Time is beginning to run out on me, and the form remembrance puts on things is making its own time and guiding my pen in ways I don't trust. In my mind's eyes is an arch of suns multiplying the sky—or a long flickering night of one moon turning over and over into its shadows. I know this is trickery but I can't blot it out. I think Molly, Molly, Molly and she is the time, turning in her phases like that moon, smiling and frowning while the boy grows big. . . .
>
> Molly, could you really know what was coming? Or did it come because you knew it? Were you smarter than the life, or did the life depend on you?

Suspecting that the wilderness, symbolized by the Bad Man, returned because Molly knew it would, Blue views the past with increasing pessimism as he writes. He sees the mine's playing out as an analogy of his own folly and doom: "Like the West, like my life: The color dazzles us, but when it's too late we see what a fraud it is, what a poor pinched-out claim." Pondering the closing of the mine, Blue concludes: "There is no fool like a fool in the

West, why you can fool him so bad he won't even know his possibilities are dead, his hopes only ghosts." As he approaches the end of his record, he imagines a reader, safe in the comforts of civilization ("and isn't that a final curse on me, that I still have hope?"). He speaks to that reader about freedom and fate, about the weight of history: "Do you think, mister, with all that settlement around you that you're freer than me to make your fate? Do you click your tongue at my story? Well I wish I knew yours. Your father's doing is in you, like his father's was in him, and we can never start new, we take on all the burden. . . ." He goes on to scorn himself for keeping records as if such record-keeping could jerk the endless cycling of time from its established grooves, "as if notations in a ledger can fix life, as if some marks in a book can control things." The repetitious cycle of history is represented for Blue in the very record he writes, for he writes it in the ledgers, over the marks and lines that describe the transactions of a town that has ceased to exist. Blue observes wryly, "There is only one record to keep and that's the one I'm writing now, across the red lines, over the old marks."

Blue remembers the time when he thought the past could be buried ("I felt anyone new helped bury the past"), and in those days he demonstrated his belief figuratively by burying the casualties of the Bad Man's first rampage. Now he has no heart or strength for such an enterprise. The bodies of the Bad Man's latest victims, like the town itself, are consigned to the buzzards and bugs. Just as the past is always with us, so Blue comes to believe that the Bad Man had never left. Seeing Turner's reflection in the bar mirror, Blue thinks, "Two Bad Men, the Man multiplied. . . . He never left the town, it was waiting only for the proper light to see him where he's been all the time." In despair Blue speaks of life as a "Trick," a "mockery that puts us back in our own steps." Time goes on, but only to repeat itself: "Here the earth turns and we turn with it, around it spins and we go mad with it." (Interestingly, in that image of earth's fateful turning is an echo of the Bad Man's name, Clay Turner.) Later, Blue has an even more painful revelation. As he writes of carrying the half-dead Turner through the rioting, plunderous street of Hard Times, the thought strikes him: "And none of it had to do with Turner. He was just a man, my God! I felt his weight, I felt the weight of him over my shoulder, I smelled the sweat of him and the whiskey, it was blood that ran from his head and matted his hair." And then, most terrible of all, he realizes that he too has been the town's fate, he too has "farmed the crop of this country," bodies planted and bodies harvested, "the land's good yield along with Men from Bodie." His early optimism ironically contributed to the disaster by luring the Bad Man's next victims into Hard Times. He had forgotten that even if the external wilderness can be held off for a moment, the internal wilderness remains. In the end he summarizes:

> I can forgive everyone but I cannot forgive myself. I told Molly we'd be ready for the Bad Man but we can never be ready. Nothing is ever buried, the earth rolls in its tracks, it never goes anywhere, it never changes, only the hope changes like morning and night, only the expectations rise and set. Why does there have to be promise before destruction? What more could I have done—if I hadn't believed, they'd be alive today.

But here, after building to a monstrous climax of despair, Doctorow cannot resist a touch of comic relief. In the final lines of the novel, Blue contemplates setting fire to the town to scatter the buzzards and cremate the dead. He is, however, too tired for the labor, and besides, he allows (in the book's final sentence), "I keep thinking someone will come by sometime who will want to use the wood." Significantly, in the West, new towns are built with the wood from old.

What happens inside Blue as he probes his memory and records events becomes a chart of the novel's course from hope to despair—and then to a final flicker of hope. As has been suggested, the novel's dominant concern is the force of the past and the role of the historian in recording it. It centers around what the recording of events does to Blue, how the act of recording shapes his views of subsequent events, and hence his record of them. The more he records, the more he becomes aware of the power of fate, and hence the more he becomes an agent of fate. Blue's confession is vital to an understanding of the book:

> I'm trying to put down what happened but the closer I've come in time the less clear I am in mind. . . . I have the cold feeling everything I've written doesn't tell how it was, no matter how careful I've been to get it all down it still escapes me: like what happened is far below my understanding beyond my sight. In my limits, taking a day for a day, a night for a night, have I showed the sand shifting under our feet, the terrible arrangement of our lives?

Welcome to Hard Times is a testimony to human stories that keep repeating themselves, stories of greed, exploitation, hope, courage, cowardice, recklessness, love, need, revenge, death. This is human history, this is what keeps the earth turning back in its tracks. The struggle between wilderness and community will never cease, so long as there are human beings to struggle and human beings to record the struggle.